Pro WPF and Silverlight MVVM

Effective Application Development with Model-View-ViewModel

D1596052

Gary McLean Hall

Apress®

Pro WPF and Silverlight MVVM: Effective Application Development with Model-View-ViewModel

ISBN-13 (pbk): 978-1-4302-3162-2

ISBN-13 (electronic): 978-1-4302-3163-9

Printed and bound in the United States of America 9 8 7 6 5 4 3 2 1

President and Publisher: Paul Manning
Lead Editor: Jonathan Hassell
Technical Reviewer: Nathan Kannan
Editorial Board: Steve Anglin, Mark Beckner, Ewan Buckingham, Gary Cornell, Jonathan Gennick, Jonathan Hassell, Michelle Lowman, Matthew Moodie, Duncan Parkes, Jeffrey Pepper, Frank Pohlmann, Douglas Pundick, Ben Renow-Clarke, Dominic Shakeshaft, Matt Wade, Tom Welsh
Coordinating Editor: Debra Kelly
Copy Editors: Mary Behr and Sharon Terdeman
Compositor: MacPS, LLC
Indexer: BIM Indexing & Proofreading Services
Artist: April Milne
Cover Designer: Anna Ishchenko

Distributed to the book trade worldwide by Springer Science+Business Media, LLC., 233 Spring Street, 6th Floor, New York, NY 10013. Phone 1-800-SPRINGER, fax (201) 348-4505, e-mail orders-ny@springer-sbm.com, or visit www.springeronline.com.

For information on translations, please e-mail rights@apress.com, or visit www.apress.com.

Apress and friends of ED books may be purchased in bulk for academic, corporate, or promotional use. eBook versions and licenses are also available for most titles. For more information, reference our Special Bulk Sales–eBook Licensing web page at www.apress.com/info/bulksales.

The source code for this book is available to readers at www.apress.com.

For my wife, Victoria

Contents at a Glance

Contents

About the Author

 **Gary McLean Hall** lives in Leeds, England, with his wife, Victoria, and their dog, Isabella. He is the director of Four Minute Mile Ltd, a software development consultancy specializing in Microsoft technologies.

About the Technical Reviewer

■ **Nathan Kannan** serves as Director of GIS (Geographic Information System) at Sentinel USA, a company that specializes in providing GIS services and consulting to the utility industry. Mr. Kannan provides a wealth of talent and expertise to Sentinel USA and has contributed to the success of several high-profile development projects in the GIS technology arena. Mr. Kannan holds both a master's degree in Geographic Information Systems and Mapping (MS GIS) from The Ohio State University and a bachelor's degree in Civil Engineering (BE) from PSG College of Technology, India. His professional skills and contributions are in the fields of GIS Software and Custom Application Development, Advanced Spatial Database and Data Structure, Computational Cartography, GPS, and Photogrammetry. He is the inventor and one of the authors of the patent "Distance Correction for Utility Damage Prevention System, Publication No: WO/2007/067898, Publication Date: 14.06.2007."

Acknowledgments

Thanks to my wife, Victoria, for being perfect in every way.

Thanks to my parents, Pam and Les, for funding such an expensive hobby and underwriting the dial-up Internet bills of the late-90s.

Thanks to my brother, Darryn, for being a constant best friend, his wife, Jo, and their beautiful daughter, Eleanor.

Thanks to my Granda George for his selfless generosity.

Thanks to my editor, Debra Kelly, whose patience knows no bounds!

Thanks to my dog, Isabella, for her unconditional loyalty.

Thanks to everyone who has taught me, whether they knew it or not.

Introduction

This book was conceived from a need to explain the MVVM pattern and how it helps structure WPF and Silverlight applications. I had worked on a number of projects where these technologies were used but general best practices were ignored because no one had formally explained the MVVM pattern and how it compared to other patterns such MVP and MVC.

In **Chapter 1**, WPF and Silverlight will be explored in some detail and their respective features highlighted.

Chapter 2 introduces the foundation of the MVVM pattern: the databinding model that eclipses the equivalent functionality of Windows Forms or ASP.NET.

Chapter 3 explains why the model and the view must be separated in an application and provides various tips and tricks that can help achieve a strict separation of concerns.

Chapter 4 introduces the ViewModel that sits between the model and view layers and mediates between the two.

Chapter 5 discusses commands and events, weighing up the pros and cons of each.

Chapter 6 examines various options for implementing validation into an application.

Chapter 7 explores the best side effects of the separation of concerns achieved through MVVM: testability and unit testing.

Chapter 8 outlines how to implement a Data Access Layer into a Silverlight or WPF application and how the ViewModel can interact with this layer.

Chapter 9 explains how to serialize an object graph using WPF and MVVM, as well as exploring how WPF and Silverlight applications can be extended.

Chapter 10 ends the book with a sample application that ties together many of the features covered along the way.

CHAPTER 1

■ ■ ■

Overview of WPF and Silverlight

WPF and Silverlight

WPF and Silverlight are Microsoft technologies that facilitate the development of rich user interfaces. They are analogous to Windows Forms and Adobe Flash, respectively.

What Is WPF?

Windows Presentation Foundation (WPF) could be termed the next generation of Windows user interfaces. It *could* be, but there are too many companies that will be wedded to Windows Forms for many years to come. It may be more accurate to call WPF an *alternative* to Windows Forms. Although the two technologies differ in many ways, they both aim to achieve the same end: providing a user interface on the Windows desktop for applications written using the .NET Framework.

Architecture

Figure 1–1 shows the general architecture of WPF and its constituent parts.

The three subsystems that are the newly added ingredients that form WPF are highlighted with a dark background and drop-shadow. They are: Presentation Framework, Presentation Core, and MIL Core. Of the three, MIL Core is unmanaged, which enables it to wrap DirectX much more closely.

> *MIL Core* stands for Media Integration Layer. It is an unmanaged wrapper around DirectX and allows the Common Language Runtime (CLR) to interface with DirectX.

> *Presentation Core* contains all of the classes and interfaces that form the groundwork for WPF. It does not contain any user interface controls—it is more like the foundations that the controls are built on.

> *Presentation Framework* is the subsystem that contains all of the user interface components. It has a rich library of controls that can be used by WPF applications. You can think of your WPF application as sitting on top of all of this architecture, leveraging the functionality of the .NET Framework and WPF to produce something usable and, ideally, profitable.

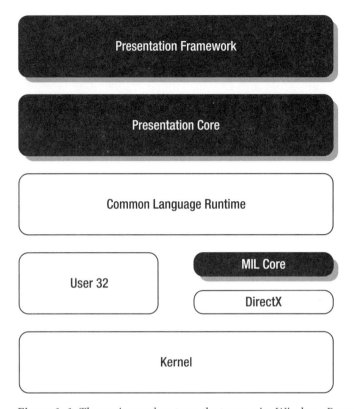

Figure 1–1. *The various subsystems that comprise Windows Presentation Foundation*

The other components in the diagram are no less important, but are not specifically related to WPF. The Kernel provides low-level operating system services such as primitive input and output (I/O), memory management, and process/thread creation and synchronization functions. User32 provides applications with the means to create graphical user interfaces (GUIs) by using the message queue, creating and managing windows, and so forth. DirectX provides an Application Programming Interface (API) for creating 3D graphics, either using software rendering or via 3D graphics accelerator cards. The Common Language Runtime (CLR) is Microsoft's implementation of the Common Language Infrastructure (CLI) standard: C# and Visual Basic .NET code are actually compiled into Common Intermediate Language (CIL) bytecode, which is compiled again by the CLR at runtime before being executed. All .NET languages operate this way and sit on top of the CLR.

DirectX, Not GDI+

As Figure 1–1 shows, WPF is built on DirectX, not GDI+. The Graphics Device Interface (GDI) API is contained within the GDI32.dll that ships with the Windows operating system, and has been deprecated since Windows XP. It provides facilities for low-level drawing of lines and curves, font rendering, and other menial graphical tasks that are expanded upon in other APIs, such as User32. Since Windows XP, GDI has been superseded by GDI+, which is a C++ implementation of a similar primitive graphics layer but adds support for extra features such as gradient shading and for JPEG and PNG graphics files. Much of the System.Drawing namespace and its container, the System.Drawing.dll assembly, is a managed code wrapper around GDI+. Windows Forms, in particular, makes extensive use of this wrapper and this is one of the key features that differentiates Windows Forms from WPF.

DirectX is an API built for graphically intensive applications, such as Computer Aided Design (CAD) applications or video games. It provides an interface for rendering graphical scenes represented in three dimensions onto a two-dimensional projection, such as your computer monitor. Along with OpenGL, it is the industry standard for developing such applications, and the X in DirectX is itself the inspiration for the X in XBox, so intrinsically linked are the two.

As managed .NET code can't use unmanaged APIs directly, WPF uses a wrapper around DirectX as an intermediary. MIL Core provides a low-level interface to the DirectX API, and WPF builds on top of this to perform all of its graphical rendering. There are two consequences that arise from all of this: WPF applications are graphically superior to Windows Forms applications; and WPF applications have a higher minimum hardware—and, in fact, software—requirement than Windows Forms applications. *Graphically superior* means that 3D is supported, cutting-edge graphical rendering techniques can be employed, and any hardware acceleration present in the machine that is running the application will be leveraged. The price paid for this is that WPF applications will run only on a minimum of Windows XP Service Pack 2 because this is, in turn, the minimum requirement for .NET Framework 3.0. Similarly, if you produce an application that makes use of advanced 3D rendering techniques, such as pixel shaders and the like, you will require that your end users have sufficient hardware to run such an application. If you *must* target operating systems such as Windows 98 or 2000, you may wish to use Windows Forms instead.

Media

WPF has native support not only for displaying images but also for the playback of audio and video multimedia.

As well as supporting established images formats—such as bitmap (BMP), Joint Photographics Expert Group (JPEG), Graphics Interchange Format (GIF), and Portable Network Graphics (PNG) — there is also an extensibility model for adding support for new image formats as they occur. This is built on a new API that eliminates some of the limitations of GDI and GDI+, like high fidelity image support.

The System.Windows.Media.Imaging namespace contains much of the functionality for working with images in WPF, while the System.Windows.Controls.Image class is the WPF control used for displaying an image. The Image class's Source property is used to set the location of the image file to display, as shown in the example in Listing 1–1.

Listing 1–1. *Displaying an Image Using the WPF Image Control*

```
<Image Source=" C:\Users\Public\Pictures\Sample Pictures\Desert.jpg"/>
```

WPF supports the Windows Media Video (WMV), Moving Picture Experts Group (MPEG), and Audio Video Interleave (AVI) file formats.

However, as the media component for WPF has Windows Media Player running behind the scenes, WPF can use any other codecs that the Media Player has installed. For the playback of audio and video files, the System.Windows.Controls.MediaElement control is used, again specifying a Source location of the file to use, as in Listing 1–2.

Listing 1–2. *Playback of a Multimedia File Using the MediaElement Control*

```
<MediaElement Source="C:\Users\Public\Videos\Sample Videos\Wildlife.wmv" />
```

Layout

While there are controls such as `Image` and `MediaElement` available to enable the creation of rich, modern user interfaces, controls that provide general layout are no less important. WPF's layout system contains a number of controls that allow the user interface designer to arrange content in distinct ways.

To lay out controls, the layout system must calculate a variety of measurements in order to position them before they are drawn. This is a recursive process because some controls can contain any number of child controls, and this nesting can be very deep in some user interfaces. It is clear that arranging a sufficiently complex layout may be an intensive process.

All controls possess a bounding box that invisibly demarcates its borders, and this can be tweaked on a per-control basis using the `Margin` property, which is inherited by all `FrameworkElement` subclasses. (See Listing 1–3.)

Listing 1–3. Using the Margin Property to Increase the Size of a Control's Bounding Box

```
<Button Text="Click Me!" Margin="5" />
```

In a similar vein, the *internal* space within a control can be altered using the `Padding` property, which is part of the `Control` class. (See Listing 1–4.)

Listing 1–4. Using the Padding Property to Alter the Internal Padding of a Control

```
<Button Text="Click Me!" Padding="5" />
```

Aside from altering layout-related properties on individual controls, there are controls dedicated to the placement of their children. These controls inherit from the `System.Windows.Controls.Panel` class and each has its own method of laying out the `UIElements` that form its `Children`.

As an example, the `Canvas` control allows its children to be positioned absolutely, using coordinates that are relative to the `Canvas`'s area. The `StackPanel`, on the other hand, will position its children serially, either vertically or horizontally.

Styling and Templating

WPF user interfaces often look more compelling than their Windows Forms counterparts. This is due, in no small part, to the styling and templating system within WPF. Styles allow you to define a common look and feel for multiple elements in a user interface. Templates, which come in different flavors, facilitate more powerful changes to the underlying structure of controls.

Styles contain lists of property names and associated values, which allow you to change the appearance of any controls that use the style. Listing 1–5 shows a button that is using an associated style.

Listing 1–5. Using Styling to Change the Appearance of Controls

```
<Style TargetType="Button">
    <Setter Property="FontSize" Value="14" />
    <Setter Property="Padding" Value="5" />
    <Setter Property="Foreground">
    <Setter.Value>
       <SolidColorBrush Color="LightGray">
    </Setter.Value>
    </Setter>
</Style>
```

The `TargetType` property is what links this style to the controls that will use it. In this example, this style will be used by all of the `Button` controls that are within the current scope. It is possible for styles to be used by single controls, referencing the style by key name. Styles can also be inherited and extended so that minor changes can be made for slight deviations from a theme.

Whereas styles can change only properties on controls, control templates can change the structure of a control, as in Listing 1–6.

Listing 1–6. *Changing the Structure of a Button Control using a Control Template*

```
<ControlTemplate TargetType="Button">
    <Border BorderThickness="1">
        <ContentPresenter Margin="2" HorizontalAlignment="Center" VerticalAlignment="2" />
    </Border>
</ControlTemplate>
```

This control template also applies to all `Buttons` in the current scope. However, rather than changing a couple of properties on the existing `Button` control, it entirely redefines the controls that constitute a `Button` control. The `Border` is a decorator around other controls that apply a visible border around its child control. The `ContentPresenter` control is a special type of control that takes the `Content` property of the original control—in this instance, the `Button`—and outputs it into the new control template. If you set the `Button`'s `Content` to some text, this text would be output within the border, with a `Margin` of 2, and centrally aligned, both horizontally and vertically. This is an example of how powerful the templating system is—you will not need to create your own control if its functionality is already provided in an existing control. Instead, simply edit the user interface that is supplied by default.

Data templates are similar to control templates in that they allow you to define an underlying structure. However, they relate to types that are not otherwise associated with any kind of user interface. For example, you can define a `Customer` class and indirectly assign it a look and feel using a data template. An example of this is shown in Listing 1–7. This brief explanation is enough for now as data templates are given more prominence in Chapter 4, which concentrates on data binding.

Listing 1–7. *Assigning a User Interface to a Plain CLR Class*

```
<DataTemplate DataType="{x:Type local:Customer}">
    <Label Content="Customer Name:" />
    <TextBlock Text="{Binding FullName}" />
</DataTemplate>
```

Themes are logical packages of styles, control templates, and data templates that define the look and feel of an application. All WPF applications will have a default theme, but you can create and associate additional themes that the user may select from at runtime. This need not be just a visual gimmick—the Windows desktop has multiple themes and some of them are aids for the visually impaired: large-text themes, high-contrast themes, and so forth. This kind of usability is an important concern in modern software, and WPF can ably cater to this.

What Is Silverlight?

Silverlight is a web application platform that Microsoft hopes will rival Adobe Flash. Like Flash, Silverlight runs in a plug-in sandbox inside the user's web browser.

Architecture

As Figure 1–2 shows, Silverlight runs inside the user's web browser. Silverlight supports the current most popular web browsers, each of which requires that the user download a plug-in to enable Silverlight application support.

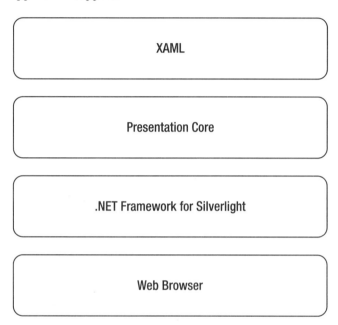

Figure 1–2. *The layered architecture of Silverlight*

.NET for Silverlight

Microsoft can't rely on end users having the .NET Framework installed because Silverlight runs within the user's browser. Instead, the company decided to create a stripped-down version of the .NET Framework specifically for Silverlight, much like the Compact .NET Framework for Windows CE machines. This reduced runtime is called *.NET for Silverlight* and is installed separately from other CLR runtimes that may be installed, once per Silverlight-enabled browser. Thus, if you have Internet Explorer, Mozilla Firefox, and Google Chrome all running on a machine, each requires its own plug-in to run Silverlight. This is exactly how Adobe Flash player works.

Silverlight 4

Silverlight 4 is the current version at the time of writing and it introduced a number of new features, including:

- Support for Google's Chrome web browser
- Access to the user's web cam and microphone, if present

- Mousewheel input

- Enhancements to existing controls, such as the `DataGrid`

- New controls, such as the `RichTextBox`

- Enhanced data binding support

- Managed Extensibility Framework support (see chapter 10 "Application Support")

- Bi-directional text support

- WCF RIA services

This list is by no means exhaustive, but it indicates some of the more prominent additions to Silverlight's feature set.

Differences Between WPF and Silverlight

Although WPF and Silverlight have a lot in common (a lot more now with the advent of Silverlight 4), there are still some key features that must be kept in mind when deciding their respective applicability to a product. A few of the more prominent differences are outlined here.

WPF Has 3D Graphics

WPF's rendering engine is built upon DirectX, so it has the capability to display real-time 3D graphics. Silverlight, on the other hand, typically runs inside a web browser and can't make use of the client's 3D capabilities.

If you wish to make extensive use of the more advanced 3D graphics available to WPF, such as pixel shaders, you will not be able to target Silverlight with the same application. At least, not without redesigning the interface you provide to your users.

WPF Targets Desktop

As mentioned earlier, WPF can be thought of as an *alternative* to Windows Forms, because it targets the Windows desktop application market. It is designed to be run like other desktop applications, with a standalone user interface, and to be operable both on- and offline. Silverlight, which is more analogous to Adobe Flash, is intended to be run inside a browser plug-in, which ties the browser dependency to all of your Silverlight applications.

This is a choice of deployment type more than anything. With Silverlight, you can deploy—and update—the application in one place and all subsequent users will run this one version. Deployment schemes such as ClickOnce can replicate this behavior with a WPF desktop application but, unless you disallow running the application while the user is offline, you *still* can't be entirely sure that users have a completely up-to-date version of the software.

Silverlight Targets More Browsers

WPF is not limited to running on the Windows desktop and can run inside web browsers, much like Silverlight, via XBAP (XAML Browser Applications) deployment. WPF XBAPs are supported by Internet Explorer and FireFox, whereas Silverlight has additional runtime plug-ins for Google Chrome and Apple Safari.

If you wish to target your application to the full gamut of common web browsers, Silverlight is your more likely choice. If, however, a Windows desktop client is sufficient, WPF is the more natural choice.

Silverlight Has Rich Online Media

As Silverlight is designed to be run inside a web browser, it is equipped with the streaming media capabilities you'd expect from such an online application platform. OK, so WPF has this, too, but there are two features Silverlight provides exclusively: timeline markers and Deep Zoom.

Timeline markers allow access to various parts of a video or audio stream without serially accessing the whole stream. Deep Zoom is used to load very high-resolution images progressively, while retaining a high frame rate. Deep Zoom is used by Microsoft's Bing Maps, so it is certainly mature enough for line-of-business applications.

These features are more useful for comparing Silverlight with Adobe Flash, which are more like rival technologies than Silverlight and WPF.

Silverlight can also leverage IIS' Smooth Streaming which provides streaming of media that adapts the streaming bit rate – and, therefore, quality – to handle changing network and processor contention.

WPF Has Full .NET Framework

Silverlight's implementation of the Common Language Runtime is necessarily smaller than that of WPF, which can leverage all of the functionality of the .NET Framework. The .NET Framework for Silverlight is a subset of the full .NET Framework, so there may be key features missing that you require, which may sway your decision toward WPF.

Some of the reduced functionality makes perfect sense and will not directly impact how you code your application. An example of this is the stripped down `System.Security` namespace—because Silverlight does not support Code Access Security (CAS). Other functionality *will* impact your daily development: the `String.Split()` method has six overloads in WPF, whereas there are only three available in Silverlight. If you are writing code that intends to target both WPF and Silverlight, you'll be limited to the methods that are common to both the full and reduced framework.

Silverlight Runs on Macs and Linux

WPF applications run only on Windows operating systems. The cross-platform, open source .NET implementation called Mono currently has no plans to support WPF. Conversely, Silverlight is supported within browsers that run on Windows, Mac, and Linux machines. Mono even supports Silverlight using the Moonlight SDK.

If your end users are likely to use operating systems other than Microsoft Windows, Silverlight is not limited to this platform and can run inside browsers on the most popular Windows alternatives.

WPF or Silverlight?

As with all questions in the format *X or Y?*, the answer is the same: *it depends*. We have discussed here some of the differences between the two options, and which you choose will very much depend on what sort of trade-offs you are willing to make. If you absolutely *must* have access to some .NET Framework capabilities that are missing in .NET for Silverlight, then perhaps WPF is the way forward.

If you wish to target Macs and Linux end users, you'd choose Silverlight over WPF. The choice may be dictated more by the skills of the developers on the team: if no one has any prior Silverlight experience, but a few key personnel are familiar with WPF, this might just clinch the decision in favor of WPF. It is important to focus on the problem at hand that is to be solved and choose a platform that will meet all necessary criteria to develop a working solution. For some applications, WPF will be a good fit whereas some applications will be more suited to Silverlight.

Multi-Target Platforms

The choice between WPF and Silverlight need not be mutually exclusive. It is possible to target both platforms without writing two entirely different applications. If you do share code between the two applications, be advised that you will have to use the restricted .NET Framework for Silverlight—even for the WPF application. Following are some of the tricks of the trade for targeting both Silverlight and WPF within the same codebase.

Separate Assemblies

By creating a separate assembly, you can deploy code that targets either Silverlight or WPF independently. For example, you could have an assembly that leverages the full .NET Framework functionality and targets only the WPF application. This code will not be shared with the Silverlight application and any classes it contains will not be visible by the Silverlight application, but at least you will not have to artificially dumb-down your WPF application.

In a similar respect, you can create an assembly that will be used only by the Silverlight application. There are a few features that Silverlight has that WPF does not. Deep Zoom is one example; it allows an extremely high-resolution image—in the range of *gigapixels*, let alone megapixels—to be loaded in manageable chunks on the fly over HTTP. This is optimized for Silverlight, and it is used by Microsoft's Bing Maps, so it (along with the rest of Silverlight and WPF) is definitely ready for line-of-business use.

Partial Classes

This is similar to using separate assemblies, but relevant to individual classes. .NET Framework 2.0 introduced the concept of partial classes, which are simply class definitions split over multiple files. Two or three such files would combine, one containing the code shared between Silverlight and WPF and the others expanding the class definition to target either technology more specifically. The WPF application would use both the shared code and the WPF-specific code, with the Silverlight application similarly using the shared code but also the Silverlight-specific code.

If you required that the class implement a specific interface, which was fulfilled by the WPF or Silverlight partial class definition, you could ensure that the rest of the code was able to use either version regardless of the current target platform, as Figure 1–3 shows.

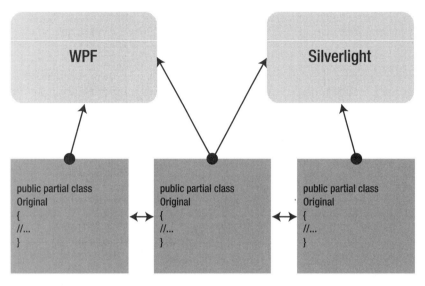

Figure 1–3. Targeting Silverlight and WPF separately by using partial classes

Extension Methods

.NET Framework 3.0 introduced extension methods—static methods with a certain signature that add functionality to an existing type. If a class required a specific Silverlight or WPF implementation, you could add this functionality via extension methods. You would add two static classes to the project: one for the Silverlight extensions and one for the WPF extensions, as shown in Figure 1–4.

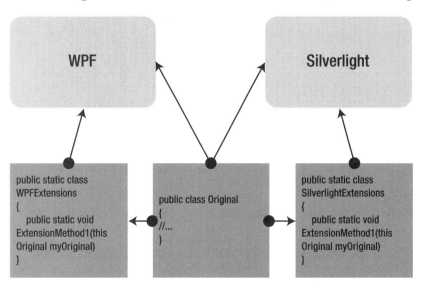

Figure 1–4. Targeting Silverlight and WPF separately by using extension methods

This is much less intrusive than partial classes as the original class definition is the only one. However, the price you pay is that extension methods can't access non-public members of the objects they are extending. This is often desirable as it maintains encapsulation (we cover encapsulation and its benefits in Chapter 2).

Compiler Directives

In the C and C++ languages, a compiler directive is a special hint supplied to the compiler's pre-processor. While .NET retains the concept and syntax for compiler directives, there is no separate pre-processor: these directives are processed as part of the lexical analysis phase.

Compiler directives can branch just like normal code and we can test a number of values, omitting or including different code depending on these values. The most common pre-processor test is checking whether we are compiling a Debug build and, if so, adding extra debugging in the code, as in Listing 1–8.

Listing 1–8. Testing Whether We Are Debugging

```
static class Program
{
    /// <summary>
    /// The main entry point for the application.
    /// </summary>
    [STAThread]
    static void Main()
    {
        Application.EnableVisualStyles();
        Application.SetCompatibleTextRenderingDefault(false);
        Application.Run(new Form1());

        Application.ThreadException += new System.Threading.↵
ThreadExceptionEventHandler(Application_ThreadException);
    }

    static void Application_ThreadException(object sender, System.Threading.↵
ThreadExceptionEventArgs e)
    {
#if DEBUG
        System.Diagnostics.Debug.Write(e.Exception.Message);
#else
        MessageBox.Show(e.Exception.Message);
#endif
    }
}
```

Here, we add an event handler to the application so that we are alerted whenever an exception is thrown on the main thread. How we handle the thrown exception differs, depending on whether we are running a Debug build or a Release build. In Debug mode, we merely log the exception's message to the Debug output window in Visual Studio. However, in Release mode, we alert the user directly by showing a MessageBox.

In a similar way, we can detect whether we are running in a Silverlight application by testing the SILVERLIGHT compiler variable, as in Listing 1–9.

Listing 1–9. Targeting Silverlight or WPF by Using Compiler Directives

```
public void MyMethod()
{
#if SILVERLIGHT
    // Silverlight-specific code goes here
#else
    // WPF-specific code goes here
#endif
}
```

As you can imagine, this method of targeting each technology individually is useful only on a small scale, mostly within single methods that require only a couple of lines of different code. Its main benefit is that it is the quickest and simplest way of targeting either WPF or Silverlight. See Figure 1–5.

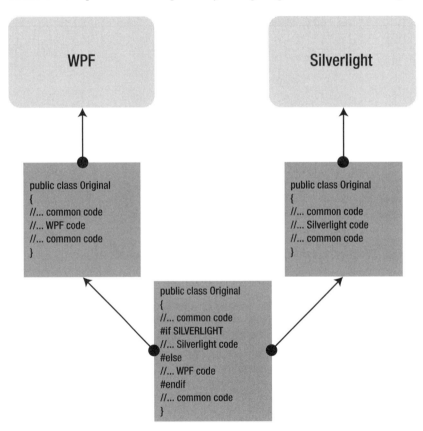

Figure 1–5. Targeting WPF or Silverlight using pre-processor directives

XAML

Extensible Application Markup Language (XAML) is an implementation of XML that is used for the specification of user interfaces. It follows all of the normal grammar rules of other XML-based markup languages, but also includes other, more specialized grammar that aims to squeeze in more data by using less markup. We will outline this and other elements of the XML grammar in order to give a more complete picture of XAML and how it is used.

Declarative User Interfaces

Object-oriented programming languages, like C# and Visual Basic, combine data with methods that operate on that data in order to solve a particular problem. This paradigm allows programmers to model their software on objects that map to both tangible and intangible real-world equivalents as defined by the problem domain. The result is an orchestration of objects composed of, and utilizing, other objects that, together, solve a particular problem.

Windows Forms makes use of this paradigm, building the user interface on top of object-oriented code. Whenever you use the Windows Forms designer, the underlying functionality is still provided by object-oriented code that instantiates control classes and sets their properties to reflect your design.

XAML provides an alternative to this that brings with it a number of benefits. XAML uses a declarative programming paradigm, which allows developers to lay out their user interface without any references to control flow. First, this means that XAML is more intuitive than Windows Forms code, because it is specialized for the purpose of describing a user interface. Second, it separates the user interface declaration from its code counterpart.

XAML Code-Behind

Windows Forms and ASP.NET WebForms have two distinct parts to them: the designed user interface and an associated source-code file called the code-behind. In the code-behind file, there is often interaction logic that relates to the form or control and typically includes things like event handlers and user input validation.

There is a school of thought that recommends against using the code-behind file. In fact, this book is geared around how to *avoid* using the code-behind file. It is not that the code-behind is considered evil, more that it can generate some unintended—and undesirable—consequences. Software engineering as a discipline is plagued with near-religious wars based around this sort of decision. While this book would not deign to force someone into a particular way of working, it is nonetheless partisan and will present some strong arguments as to why the code-behind file should be avoided *when possible* —that caveat is very important!

Almost Codeless

The quest to create a codeless XAML application is not merely a pointless pilgrimage for the software puritan. If you work on a team that is split into designers and developers, both types of personnel will need access to the XAML. The developers will create the elements that are required for the application to function, while the designers will concentrate on the look and feel of the application. It is impossible to put inline code into the XAML files and this is a very good thing.

XAML Elements

Much of the syntactic details that follow aim to expedite the process of writing XAML. Although Visual Studio provides a graphical editor for the design of XAML user interfaces, it is often necessary to get into the generated XAML and tinker with it so that it accomplishes exactly what we expect or desire. It is quite likely that you'll find writing the XAML by hand is actually *quicker* than using the designer—much like writing HTML by hand can be more productive than using a purportedly WYSIWYG designer.

■ **Note** Microsoft's Expression Blend is a WYSIWYG designer which generates XAML. It may be preferential to have user interface designers generate the XAML using this. Part of the attraction of the Model View ViewModel (MVVM) pattern explained in this book is that it allows designers to work on the user interface without impacting the work of programmers who integrate the functionality.

Furthermore, these elements are not exclusively used by the internals of the Presentation Framework: you can create your own markup extensions, type converters, attached properties, and the like.

XAML Objects

Each element within XAML code implicitly instantiates an object that is backed by a .NET class. Typically, the classes are part of the `PresentationFramework` assembly, which exposes a lot of user interface components that can be combined to form a working WPF or Silverlight application. Of course, you can create your own user interface classes, or use controls that have been developed by third-party developers.

Listing 1–10. A Trivial—if Not Useless—XAML Object Declaration

```
<Button />
```

The example in Listing 1–10 declares a `Button` that, intuitively, creates a clickable button user interface component. On its own, this is currently quite useless: not only does the button do nothing, it does not display any useful content.

XAML Attributes

Just as classes have properties that you can edit to change the class's behavior, XAML objects can have attributes that map (albeit indirectly) to these properties (see Listing 1–11).

Listing 1–11. A More Useful Button

```
<Button Name="myButton" Content="Click Me!" />
```

This button has its `Name` and `Content` properties explicitly set. The `Name` will allow this specific button to be referenced in code, using the `myButton` field name. The `Content` attribute dictates what is shown within the button in the application's user interface, as in Figure 1–6.

Figure 1–6. The Button as displayed at runtime

XAML Property Elements

The two properties of the button that we have set so far are fairly trivial string values. Some properties are significantly more complex than this and can't be set using the attribute name/value pair syntax. For these properties, we use the property element syntax as in Listing 1–12.

Listing 1–12. The Property Element Syntax Used on the Button's Background

```
<Button Name="myButton" Content="Click Me!">
    <Button.Foreground>
        <SolidColorBrush Color="Blue" />
    </Button.Foreground>
</Button>
```

The Button has a Foreground property, but its type is a Brush. By using the `<Button.Foreground>` syntax, we can set this property to a Brush by instantiating such an object as its direct child. A slight complication is that the System.Windows.Media.Brush class is declared abstract, meaning we can't instantiate the abstract Brush class in XAML, just as we can't instantiate it in code. What we can do, however, is instantiate one of Brush's subclasses—here, we have settled on the SolidColorBrush. This hints at the power of XAML: we have employed polymorphism (the ability of one type to be used as if it were a different type) *declaratively*.

XAML Collections

What if the property we are setting is a list of objects? Well, XAML can handle that scenario, too. See Listing 1–13.

Listing 1–13. Declaring Properties that Are Lists of Objects

```
<StackPanel>
    <StackPanel.Children>
        <Button Content="Button 1" />
        <Button Content="Button 2" />
    </StackPanel.Children>
</StackPanel>
```

The Children property of the StackPanel class is of type UIElementCollection. Notice that we have not declared such an object manually, instead adding the buttons directly to the property. XAML is clever enough to recognize that we need a container for these children and implicitly creates a UIElementCollection for us.

XAML Content

The previous example may appear to some to be overly verbose: surely all StackPanels, which are containers that exist solely to facilitate the layout of other controls, will have their Children property set? Indeed, this is true, and the prior code listing can be written more succinctly thanks to default content properties. Which property is used as the content property is determined on a per-class basis. For the StackPanel, the default content property *is* the Children property, as in Listing 1–14.

Listing 1–14. *XAML Default Content Properties Provide a Handy Shortcut*

```
<StackPanel>
    <Button Content="Button 1" />
    <Button Content="Button 2" />
</StackPanel>
```

Because XML can be naturally very verbose, this sort of timesaver can be invaluable and its use will yield cleaner markup, which can only be a good thing. It might also be worth noting, and hopefully not at all confusing, that the Button's content property is its Content property!

■ **Note** Not only have we used the content property shortcut here in Listing 1–14, we have also used the collection property shortcut. Imagine how confusing the markup would be without both of these features!

XAML Features

Markup Extensions

Sometimes, the XML syntax rules are too restrictive to specify data without being overly verbose, but the data declaration is too inherently complex to use a simple content or collection shortcut. In these cases, XAML provides markup extensions, which are strings that fit a specific pattern that can be parsed to provide much more detailed data without unnecessarily bloating the code. These extensions are used for a number of purposes, but the most common is for data binding and referencing resources. As we cover data binding in significant detail in Chapter 4, a brief overview of the resource referencing syntax will suffice here.

Listing 1–15. *The Markup Extension Syntax for Data Binding*

```
<Button Style="{StaticResource myButtonStyle}"/>
```

In Listing 1–15, rather than explicitly setting a value for this button's Style property, we have asked the XAML processor to parse this value as a resource reference. In this instance, we are referencing a StaticResource—a resource that is found at load time—called myButtonStyle. This resource, as with most, will be declared elsewhere in the XAML and this syntax allows us to reference a single resource in multiple locations. The alternative, for a one-off Style declaration, would be to define the Style using the aforementioned property element syntax. All markup extensions use the curly braces { } to demarcate that this is a special value to be parsed separately.

Type Converters

Type converters allow a property to have a certain value that *can* be represented by a string value but is, in fact, *not* a string value. An implied example of this is if a property receives a numeric value, but the utility of type converters stretches even further. Most controls can specify a Margin value, which is the thickness of whitespace to leave as an invisible border around the control. This Margin property, inherited from `FrameworkElement` and thus available to almost all controls, is of `Thickness` type. You could set a button's `Margin` using the property element syntax, as shown in Listing 1–16.

Listing 1–16. Setting the Margin Property Explicitly

```
<Button Content="Click Me!">
    <Button.Margin>
        <Thickness Left="25" Top="5" Right="10" Bottom="15" />
    </Button.Margin>
</Button>
```

However, in the continuing spirit of saving precious keystrokes, there is a type converter available that will parse a comma-delimited list of integers, as Listing 1–17 shows.

Listing 1–17. Setting the Margin Property Using the Type Converter

```
<Button Content="Click Me!" Margin="25,5,10,15">
```

As you may suspect, the order of the values is important: Left, Top, Right, Bottom; or, *clockwise from left.*

Attached Properties

Imagine that you have a control or other element that almost exactly fits your requirements but is missing a property that would otherwise make it perfect. Well, XAML allows you to extend controls unobtrusively with attached properties. The most common usage scenario for attached properties is for the children of container controls to inform their parent of a certain value. As ever, an example will enlighten (see Listing 1–18).

Listing 1–18. An Attached Property Reports the Location that Each Child Should Dock within a DockPanel

```
<DockPanel>
    <Button DockPanel.Dock="Left"/>
    <Button DockPanel.Dock="Right" />
</DockPanel>
```

The syntax for an attached property follows the same pattern as `OwnerType.AttachedProperty`. Buttons do not, by default, have a `Dock` property—nor should they; layout and positioning is not their remit. Instead, this behavior is attached to them by their `DockPanel` parent. *Any* controls that are added to the `DockPanel` container are able to specify where within the `DockPanel` they will dock by using the `DockPanel.Dock` attached property.

Namespaces

XML supports the concept of namespaces and so does XAML. It would be no use creating your own controls if you couldn't import them into other applications for use! Just like XML, XAML requires a single root-element and this is where your namespace declarations will reside, as shown in Listing 1–19.

Listing 1–19. Namespace Declarations in the Root XAML Element

```
<Window x:Class="XAMLTest.MainWindow"
    xmlns="http://schemas.microsoft.com/winfx/2006/xaml/presentation"
    xmlns:x="http://schemas.microsoft.com/winfx/2006/xaml"
    Title="Main Window">

</Window>
```

This `Window` declaration is the first element within this particular XAML file. It has two namespace declarations (`xmlns`); one is the default namespace and the other is imported into the x prefix. The `Window` element itself does not have a prefix, thus it comes from the presentation namespace. You can add your own namespace declarations and attach to them whatever prefix you desire. However, rather than the URL syntax, you will use a `clr-namespace` syntax, which imports the contents of a .NET assembly, as in Listing 1–20.

Listing 1–20. *A clr-namespace Import*

```
xmlns:myCode="clr-namespace:MyNamespace;assembly=MyAssembly"
```

Let's break this syntax down a little. First of all, we specify `myCode` as the prefix that will be used to reference the classes we have supplied. Next, the `clr-namespace` indicates to the XAML parser that we are importing a .NET namespace from code. Finally, the assembly is the name of the assembly that contains the namespace that we are importing.

Assuming that we have a `CustomControl` class within this namespace, we can instantiate it just the same as any other XAML element. All we have to do is include the namespace prefix, as in Listing 1–21.

Listing 1–21. *Using a Custom Control Imported from a Namespace*

```
<myCode:CustomControl />
```

User Experience vs. User Interface

All software applications that are to be used by people require a user interface. Even if all that is provided is merely a primitive command line with switches and options, it is still termed a user interface. A user interface allows a person, or people, to interact with the functionality that the software provides. Accounting software will calculate the taxes that are owed at the end of the financial year, but you must first enter all of the relevant data, such as income and expenditure entries. So, data input is a large function of a user interface. The flip side of this is how the calculated data is presented back to the user, once calculated.

User interfaces can be broadly categorized into good and bad. It's likely that no software product's user interface is ever considered good by all users at all times. However, there are plenty of heuristics that can be followed to coerce a user interface into the good category.

The human-computer interface in software development has shifted focus from merely providing a user interface as a method of data input and data reporting toward evaluating and improving upon the quality of the interaction between user and application.

The term User eXperience, or UX, refers more broadly to how a person feels about using a system. This need not refer solely to software systems: the process of paying a bill over the phone, from picking up the receiver until replacing it, is an example of a real-world user experience. Once you put down the phone, you could have any number of emotions arising from the interaction. Perhaps you were initially routed through some automated menus before being patched through to someone who could take your payment details. For some, this is a valuable timesaver while for others it is frustrating not to be talking to a fellow person from the outset. Perhaps the person's telephone manner was unsatisfactory and may prompt you to complain. In software development, the user experience is gaining more prominence, with interfaces being designed around user expectations and desires, rather than being only a thin veneer around software intended to collect data in a prescribed format.

Summary

So far, we have outlined the features that WPF and Silverlight share, as well as some important differences. This can help to exclude or include the two technologies as potential candidates for your user interface implementation. This book would advocate neither WPF nor Silverlight in *all* situations—far from it.

We also looked at XAML, the XML-based markup language that allows developers to create user interfaces declaratively, rather than programmatically. This chapter's subsection on XAML is the sum total of our introduction to the language that will be used throughout this book, so a certain level of proficiency is assumed.

User interfaces (UIs) are no longer considered sufficient when designing applications. Instead, user-centric design focuses on the user experience (UX) that an application conveys. What users expect from interfaces is always held to be paramount, and deviating from these expectations is considered very bad form. Thinking of the users and keeping their experiences positive when using your software can help to temper the lure of the enhanced visual effects that WPF, in particular, provides.

Hopefully, this chapter has piqued your desire to see what can be achieved with WPF and Silverlight. The rest of this book will focus on how to organize applications most effectively to use WPF and/or Silverlight to provide a rich user experience.

CHAPTER 2

■■■

DataBinding

The view provides two services to the user: presenting data and interacting with data. The former involves reading data and displaying it in a certain format, whereas the latter implies editing existing or adding new data.

This chapter will focus on the methods available to developers for displaying data in WPF or Silverlight controls. We will attempt to remain entirely declarative, binding the controls to data via XAML.

The Power of DataBinding with XAML

In order to facilitate this new paradigm in databinding, the very lowest-level objects have to be enhanced. The functionality of System.Object subclasses, and the vanilla property system afforded to them, was not enough to support the databinding that WPF's developers had in mind. This resulted in the addition of System.Windows.DependencyObject and System.Windows.DependencyProperty, to handle to extra functionality required of objects and properties, respectively, that participated in the new databinding system.

Dependency Objects

Dependency objects differ from Plain Old CLR Objects (POCOs) in the services that are provided to them, which are otherwise absent from System.Object instances. To facilitate the supporting features that are required by declarative XAML markup, Microsoft added the DependencyObject base class, which unifies access to these services.

■ **Note** The acronym POCO denotes a class that does not necessarily inherit from a base class, implement a certain interface, or have any specific attributes attached to it. It indicates that no services or functionality are explicitly present in the class. As it stands, POCOs can't participate in the dependency property system, which has the requirement that an object inherit from DependencyObject. This is limiting to developers—because the CLR does not support multiple inheritance, the DependencyObject inheritance requirement rules out any further inheritance on the class.

Dependency Property Hosting

Dependency properties, covered in the next section, are the most significant *raison d'être* for DependencyObjects. When a DependencyProperty is registered, the result is stored in a field on a DependencyObject that is marked both public and static.

Only DependencyObjects can host a DependencyProperty, because it offers a number of methods that allow interaction with its hosted dependency properties, as shown in Table 2–1.

Table 2–1. DependencyObject Methods for Interacting with Dependency Properties

Method	Purpose
ClearValue	Clears the local value of the supplied DependencyProperty
CoerceValue	Invokes the CoerceValueCallback on the supplied DependencyProperty.
GetValue	Returns the current value of the supplied DependencyProperty as an object instance.
InvalidateProperty	Requests a re-evaluation of the supplied DependencyProperty.
ReadLocalValue	Reads the local value of the supplied DependencyProperty. If there is no local value, DependencyProperty.UnsetValue is returned.
SetValue	Sets the value of the supplied DependencyProperty.

Attached Property Hosting

Back in Chapter 1, we briefly introduced the concept of attached properties and saw how they allow existing controls to have new properties attached to them by new controls. Well, the reason this works is because all of the WPF and Silverlight controls have an ancestor of DependencyObject.

Once a DependencyProperty is registered as an attached property using the DependencyProperty.RegisterAttached method, that property can be set on *any* DependencyObject subclass.

■ **Caution** The targets of attached properties *must* inherit from DependencyObject, because the dependency property hosting services mentioned in the previous section are required for the attached property to work.

Dependency Property Metadata

Each DependencyProperty, in combination with one of its DependencyObject types, has metadata associated with it. DependencyProperty.GetMetadata requires a DependencyObject instance as an argument, but it only uses this to determine the DependencyObject's type. The resulting PropertyMetaData has a number of properties that apply to this specific use of the DependencyProperty (see Table 2–2).

Table 2–2. PropertyMetadata Properties

Property	Purpose
CoerceValueCallback	Used to inspect and/or change the value of a DependencyProperty whose value is dependent on other property values. Dependency properties are set in an undefined order.
DefaultValue	The default value of the DependencyProperty, or DependencyProperty.UnsetValue if no DefaultValue is present.
IsSealed	Returns the immutable status of the PropertyMetadata object: true means immutable, false means mutable.
PropertyChangedCallback	Returns the delegate that is called when the DependencyProperty's value changes.

The PropertyMetadata object may have been constructed implicitly or specified explicitly when the DependencyProperty was registered. It could also have been set after registration with the OverrideMetadata method.

DispatcherObject

DependencyObject does not derive directly from System.Object. There is yet another level of abstraction between DependencyObjects and POCOs: DependencyObjects derive from System.Threading.DispatcherObject.

DispatcherObject associates each instance with a Dispatcher object, which manages a queue of work items associated with a single thread. A DispatcherObject can't be directly accessed by any thread other than the one that created it. This enforces single-threaded interaction with a DispatcherObject, neatly circumventing all of the problems that concurrency presents.

In WPF and Silverlight, all of the interaction with the user interface happens on one thread, while a second thread takes care of rendering the controls. The UI thread owns all of the controls and, because they derive from DispatcherObject, they can't be accessed directly from other threads. If you wish to implement a threaded application using WPF, you must use the Dispatcher object as a mediator. This is covered in more detail in Chapter 4.

Dependency Properties

DependencyProperties automatically enable a number of services that are not available to plain properties. They are created very differently from plain properties and *must* be hosted inside a DependencyObject (see Listing 2–1).

Listing 2–1. How to Register a DependencyProperty

```
public class MyDependencyObject : DependencyObject
{
    public static MyDependencyObject()
    {
        MyDependencyProperty = DependencyProperty.Register("MyProperty", typeof(string),↩
```

```
    typeof(MyDependencyObject));
    }

    public static readonly DependencyProperty MyDependencyProperty;
    public string MyProperty
    {
        get { (string)GetValue(MyDependencyProperty); }
        set { SetValue(MyDependencyProperty, value); }
    }
}
```

There are a number of notable differences here that set dependency properties apart from plain properties.

- Dependency properties are declared public, static, and readonly.

- Dependency properties are registered via the static DependencyProperty.Register method, inside the static constructor.

- The Register method requires the string name and type of an instance property for the dependency property.

- The Register method requires the type of the host dependency object.

- There is an instance property that provides a façade for accessing the dependency property as if it were a plain property.

These parts, perhaps with slight variations, are common to all dependency property declarations. Dependency properties are an *alternative backing* to normal properties, which are backed by private fields (sometimes implicitly, using automatic properties). We will look at the services that are available to dependency properties that warrant such a verbose and awkward feature.

When discussing dependency properties, the term "dependency property" is commonly associated with the instance property that is *backed* by a DependencyProperty, as opposed to a DependencyProperty itself—and this is the terminology used in this book.

XAML Integration

Dependency properties can be accessed from code—just like any other property—but they can also be set from XAML markup, as Listing 2–2 shows.

Listing 2–2. Setting a Property Value from within XAML Markup

```
<MyDependencyObject MyProperty="Test!" />
```

Listing 2–2 shows the dependency object from Listing 2–1 declared in XAML. The dependency property MyDependencyProperty is also set to the value "Test!". Because this is a string property, the XAML parser is able to place this value directly into the dependency property. Even if the value was changed in the XAML to be an integer or floating point number, the result would still be a string in the dependency property. However, if the type of the dependency property was changed to be a System.Int32, the current value of Test! would be erroneous: it can't be automatically parsed into an integer value.

Bear in mind that dependency objects and dependency properties are not prerequisites for XAML integration: POCOs and vanilla properties exhibit this same level of XAML integration.

Databinding

Dependency properties can be set indirectly via databinding. This can use the binding object notation but, most commonly, the binding expression extension is used, as shown in Listing 2–3.

Listing 2–3. Binding a Button's Content Property Using the Binding Expression Syntax

```
<Button Content="{Binding Source=myBindingSource, Path=myContent}" />
```

This syntax is a shorthand way of hooking up databinding to a dependency property and will be used throughout this book. The bindings themselves have a lot of options that we'll explore—each one intended to customize the binding's behavior in some way.

Once the binding expression is set, the value of the Path is retrieved from the binding Source and the dependency property receives that value. Under certain circumstances, if the dependency property is updated, it will, in turn, update the binding Source value.

Property Value Inheritance

Dependency objects are organized in a tree structure, either directly via XAML markup or indirectly via the Visual Studio designer. Whenever a child is assigned to a parent, attached properties that are marked as inheritable are automatically assigned from the parent to the child.

Note that this is not inheritance as it is defined in object-oriented programming: between base classes and their subclasses. This is "containment inheritance," whereby an object merely has to be a contained child in order to inherit the parents' properties and their values.

This works using attached properties that are implicitly added to contained objects dynamically. An example of an inheriting property is shown in Listings 2–4 and 2–5.

Listing 2–4. The XAML Markup of an Inherited Property

```
<MyDependencyObject MyProperty="Hello!">
    <Button />
</MyDependencyObject>
```

Listing 2–5. The Code Behind that Makes MyDependencyProperty Inheritable

```
public class MyDependencyObject : DependencyObject
{
    public static MyDependencyObject()
    {
        MyDependencyProperty = DependencyProperty.RegisterAttached("MyProperty",↵
 typeof(string), typeof(MyDependencyObject), new FrameworkPropertyMetadata↵
(string.Empty, FrameworkPropertyMetadataOptions.Inherits));
    }

    public static readonly DependencyProperty MyDependencyProperty;
    public string MyProperty
    {
        get { (string)GetValue(MyDependencyProperty); }
        set { SetValue(MyDependencyProperty, value); }
    }
}
```

Here, the dependency property is registered as an attached property and given a default value of the empty string. `FrameworkPropertyMetadataOptions` are also added to the dependency property, indicating that this property should be inherited by child elements. The `Button` added to `MyDependencyObject` in the XAML markup will automatically inherit the value "Hello!" for the `MyProperty` dependency property. It can, of course, override this by explicitly assigning a value.

Styling

Similar to databinding, in that the value is retrieved from elsewhere, dependency properties are often used for visual styling properties like `Background`, `Color`, and `Foreground`, as shown in Listing 2–6. For each control there's a split between functionality and visual representation, and this separation allows the look and feel of controls to alter independently.

Listing 2–6. *Styling a Button Control*

```
<Style x:Key="myButtonStyle">
    <Setter Property="Control.Background" Value="Blue" />
</Style>
...
<Button Style="{StaticResource myButtonStyle}" />
```

Here, the `Button`'s `Style` value is set with a `StaticResource` reference. The `Style` example used is merely a collection of setters: property/value pairs that act on the target control. More dynamic user interfaces make use of triggers and animation so that, for example, a `Button` might appear to shimmer when the user hovers her mouse over it.

Binding Sources

We've discussed the infrastructure required for the targets of databinding: they must be `DependencyProperties` hosted by `DependencyObjects`. However, we haven't looked at the other side of the databinding coin: what types of objects can we bind *from*?

POCOs

Plain Old CLR Objects, and their vanilla properties, are perfectly acceptable binding sources. Although added functionality will be required of our POCOs—to support features like change notification— POCOs are used for ViewModel implementation throughout this book.

Databinding is acceptable on the properties, subproperties, and indexers of objects. You can even supply the object itself as the binding source, which, as we will see, is much more useful than it first appears.

Dynamic Objects

Dynamic objects and the `IDynamicMetaObjectProvider` interface are new in .NET 4.0. Integral to this new feature is the `dynamic` keyword. C# and Visual Basic .NET are both *statically typed* languages, meaning that they required method calls to be visible on the callee object at compile time. If the compiler can't find a method at compile time, it will output an error and compilation will fail.

Dynamic typing reverses this concept: the compiler will happily ignore the lack of method definition but, if the method is not subsequently found at runtime, the method call will fail. In .NET, the failure is characterized by a `RuntimeBinderException`.

There are a number of situations where dynamic typing is preferred, the most common example being the dynamic construction of XML objects. At compile time, the structure of the XML is defined in a schema document (XSD) or implied by the XML itself. The .NET Framework XSD.EXE application can be used to parse an XML document, output a compatible XSD file that can then be imported into Visual Studio to create a strongly typed dataset that has compile-time checking. This toolchain is a viable option but, with dynamic typing, the XML file could eliminate this requirement, allowing the developer to explore an XML document and defer type checking until runtime.

ADO.NET Objects

Databinding in Windows Forms and ASP.NET makes heavy use of ADO.NET objects such as the DataTable. This follows the Table Data Gateway—*Patterns of Enterprise Application Architecture* by Martin Fowler (Addison-Wesley, 2002), hereby referred to as PoEAA—pattern, whereby each DataTable provides an interface for interacting with the contents of a single database table or view.

This pattern, and the consequent use of ADO.NET DataTables, is somewhat anathema to the MVVM pattern. We are not binding our user interface controls to ADO.NET objects but to ViewModel classes, which subsequently may use a Domain Model, Transaction Scripts, Table Module, or Service Layer.

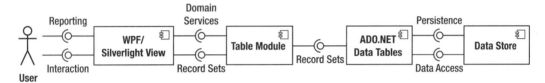

***Figure 2–1.** UML2 component diagram showing WPF/Silverlight architecture around ADO.NET for data mapping*

Figure 2–1 shows an architecture that uses ADO.NET for data mapping as well as binding: you can imagine that this is fairly quick to set up. However, it suffers from the same problem as other alternatives to MVVM: scalability. Once the ADO.NET data access layer returns a DataTable record set, the Table Module must provide the required Domain Services on this data model before passing the result—also as a DataTable record set—out to the View. This obviates the common requirement for a domain model that is rich in object-oriented design; polymorphism, inheritance, composition and the like are all unavailable.

XML Objects

Bypassing even a data-mapping layer and binding directly to the data source is possible when using XML. This creates a two-tier architecture, as shown in Figure 2–2.

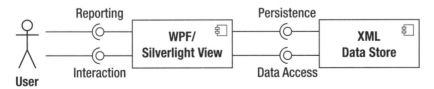

***Figure 2–2.** UML2 component diagram showing a two-tier architecture of WPF/Silverlight and XML*

27

This architecture has little scope of business logic outside of the functionality provided by XML transforms. The view writes directly to the XML structure, which is persisted on disk, and the XML data is presented to the user with typical user-interface controls.

Dependency Objects and Dependency Properties

As well as being the *target* of databinding, dependency objects and dependency properties can be the source of databinding. The choice of whether to use `DependencyObject` and `DependencyProperty` when implementing the ViewModel is discussed later in this chapter.

Binding Modes

There are three different binding modes: one-way, two-way, and one-way-to-source. Applications are likely to use a combination of all three of these modes in certain situations.

One-Way (Readonly) Binding

If you wish to present read-only data to the user via databinding, you can set the `BindingMode` to `OneWay` (see Figure 2–3). This is the default binding mode when the source of the binding has no applicable setter and is thus programmatically enforced as `readonly`. Listing 2–7 shows an example of one-way binding in XAML.

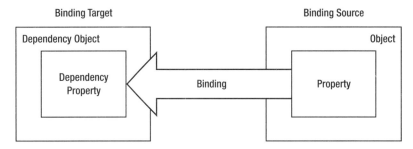

Figure 2–3. How two objects' properties interact in a one-way binding scenario

Listing 2–7. Declaring a One-Way Binding in XAML

```
<Button Content="{Binding Path=myProperty, BindingMode=OneWay}" />
```

Two-Way (Read/Write) Binding

Two-way binding is full databinding whereby editing one side of the binding concomitantly updates the other side (see Figure 2–4). This is the default binding mode when using editable controls such as the `TextBox` and `CheckBox`, assuming that the source property of the binding has an applicable setter. Listing 2–8 is an example of two-way binding in XAML.

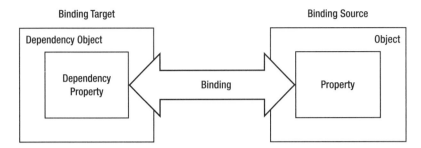

Figure 2–4. *How two objects' properties interact in a two-way binding scenario.*

Listing 2–8. *Declaring a Two-Way Binding in XAML*

```
<Button Content="{Binding Path=myProperty, BindingMode=TwoWay}" />
```

One-Way-To-Source Binding

In one-way-to-source binding, the relationship is inverted and the target control of the binding updates the source property, but the source property does not provide a databound value for the control (see Figure 2–5). At face value, this option appears to be of limited use, but look back for a moment at the respective requirements for sources and targets of databinding. This binding allows the automatic update of properties that *are not necessarily* dependency properties. However, this binding is restricted to readonly mode; there is not a related two-way-to-source binding. Listing 2–9 shows an example of one-way-to-source binding in XAML.

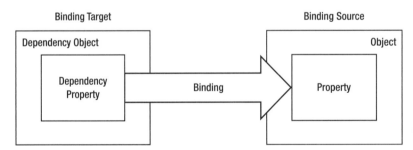

Figure 2–5. *How two objects' properties interact in a one-way-to-source binding scenario*

Listing 2–9. *Declaring a One-Way-to-Source Binding in XAML*

```
<Button Content="{Binding Path=myProperty, BindingMode=OneWayToSource}" />
```

One-Time Binding

One-time binding is similar to one-way (see Figure 2–6), except that the target value is only updated the first time that the view is shown and whenever the DataContext (see the next section, named "The DataContext") is changed. Listing 2–10 shows an example of one-time binding in XAML.

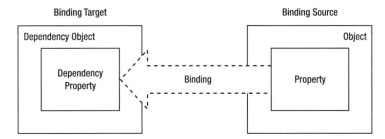

Figure 2–6. How two objects' properties interact in a one-time binding scenario

Listing 2–10. Declaring a One-Time Binding in XAML

```
<Button Content="{Binding Path=myProperty, BindingMode=OneTime}" />
```

The DataContext

All controls provided in the `System.Windows.Controls` namespace inherit from the `FrameworkElement` class. This class has a property called `DataContext`, of type `Object`, which specifies the default binding element for each control. Whenever controls are nested as children of other controls, they inherit the `DataContext` value from their parent, as shown in Listing 2–11.

Listing 2–11. Inheriting DataContext Values from Parent Controls

```
<Window x:Class="MvvmWpfApp.Window1"
        xmlns="http://schemas.microsoft.com/winfx/2006/xaml/presentation"
        xmlns:x="http://schemas.microsoft.com/winfx/2006/xaml"
        xmlns:viewModel="clr-namespace:MvvmWpfApp.ViewModel;assembly=MvvmWpfApp.ViewModel"
        Title="Window1" Height="300" Width="300">
    <Window.Resources>
        <viewModel:SampleViewModel x:Key="sampleViewModel1" />
        <viewModel:SampleViewModel x:Key="sampleViewModel2" />
    </Window.Resources>

    <Grid DataContext="{StaticResource sampleViewModel1}">

        <StackPanel Orientation="Vertical">

            <StackPanel Orientation="Horizontal">
                <Button Name="button1" />
                <Button Name="button2" />
            </StackPanel>

            <StackPanel Orientation="Horizontal" DataContext="{StaticResource↵
sampleViewModel2}">
                <Button Name="button3" />
                <Button Name="button4" />
            </StackPanel>

        </StackPanel>
    </Grid>
</Window>
```

In Listing 2–11, `button1` and `button2` will inherit their `DataContext` from their parent `StackPanel`. In turn, that `StackPanel` inherits its `DataContext` from further up the logical tree, specifically from the `Grid` control, whose `DataContext` has been explicitly set to `sampleViewModel1` (via a `StaticResource` binding). However, the `DataContext` of `button3`'s and `button4`'s parent has been overridden to reference `sampleViewModel2`, so these two controls will also have a similar `DataContext`.

Advanced DataBinding

So far, we have reviewed some simplistic databinding scenarios, laying the groundwork for more advanced situations. Databinding is not just intended for single-value properties—it can also read and write to collections of data. There are also a number of parameters available on a per-binding basis that allow customization of the minutiae of certain binding requirements. Finally, you can insert specialized value converters that can circumvent type impedence on either side of the binding. With these converters, you can transform the source data type into the target data type, decoupling both types.

Binding Parameters

The binding expression value has few required parameters, and an abundance of optional ones. Each parameter customizes the binding in some way, and they can be used in conjunction with each other to generate the specific binding behavior required in almost all scenarios. I'll briefly explain each parameter and follow with a short code example of the parameter in use in isolation.

BindingGroupName

You can group bindings together and encapsulate the access of a number of different, but related, bindings. Applications of this parameter are typically related to validation, which is covered in Chapter 6.

```
<TextBox Text="{Binding Path=myTextProperty, BindingGroupName=myBindingGroup}" />
```

BindsDirectlyToSource

When using a derivative of `DataSourceProvider`, such as `ObjectDataProvider` (which is covered later in this chapter), you are binding to the underlying data via a provider. If you wish to bind to the provider itself, you can set `BindsDirectlyToSource` to true, to override the default behavior.

```
<TextBox Text="{Binding Path=myDataSourceProvider, BindsDirectlyToSource=true}" />
```

Converter and ConverterParameter

The next section covers value converters in more detail. A common scenario for using a value converter is when binding a `Boolean` source property to a `UIElement`'s `Visibility` target property: the former is a true/false value, while the latter is an incompatible enumeration of the values `Visible`, `Hidden` and `Collapsed`.

```
<TextBox Text="{Binding myTextProperty}" Visibility="{Binding Path=isTextVisible,↵
 Converter={StaticResource myBooleanToVisibilityConverter}}" />
```

ElementName

The source of bindings can be dependency properties, as we have seen. The corollary to this is that a control may bind one of its properties to that of another control. In order to do this, the `ElementName` parameter is specified to reference a specific control that is currently in scope.

```
<TextBox Text="Hello!" Name="textBox1" />
<TextBox Text="{Binding ElementName=textBox1, Path=Text}" />
```

FallbackValue

There are situations where a binding will succeed at compile time, but fail at runtime. Failure should always be considered part of an application, and such circumstances need to be handled gracefully in order to maintain a positive user experience. Users don't expect software to be perfect, but they view uncontained failure negatively and will treat your application very differently if messy failures are endemic. Use the `FallbackValue` option to present your users with a friendly error message. If no `FallbackValue` is specified, binding failure results in the default value for the type which, in the case of string values, is the empty string.

```
<TextBox Text="{Binding Path=myTextProperty, FallbackValue='No value found'}" />
```

■ **Tip** Wrapping your `FallbackValue` in single quotes (' ') allows you to insert otherwise restricted characters, such as commas (,) and spaces.

IsAsync

Setting `IsAsync` to true fetches the binding value asynchronously, allowing a long-running process to proceed without blocking the rest of the view from binding. While the binding is retrieving the value, the `FallbackValue` is displayed, so use this to present users with a suitable message asking for their patience.

```
<TextBox Text="{Binding Path=myTextProperty, IsAsync=true, FallbackValue='Please wait…'}" />
```

NotifyOnSourceUpdated and NotifyOnTargetUpdated

You may wish to be informed whenever the source or target values are updated by the databinding mechanism. There are two steps to doing so: first, register an event handler for `SourceUpdated`, `TargetUpdated`, or both; then, set the `NotifyOnSourceUpdated` or `NotifyOnTargetUpdated` (or both) binding property to true.

```
<TextBox Text="{Binding Path=myTextProperty, NotifyOnSourceUpdated=true}"↵
 SourceUpdated="OnSourceUpdated" />
```

```
<TextBox Text="{Binding Path=myTextProperty, NotifyOnTargetUpdated=true}"↵
 TargetUpdated="OnTargetUpdated" />
```

Your event handlers should reside in the code-behind file and look similar to this:

```
private void OnSourceUpdated(object sender, DataTransferEventArgs args)
{
…
}
```

NotifyOnValidationError

Validation is covered in Chapter 6, and the `NotifyOnValidationError` binding property is one method of handling validation in WPF/Silverlight using the MVVM architecture.

```
<TextBox Text="{Binding Path=myTextProperty, NotifyOnValidationError=true}"↵
 Validation.Error="OnValidationError" />

private void OnValidationError(object sender, ValidationErrorEventArgs args)
{
…
}
```

Path

We have used the `Path` parameter extensively so far; its use is no secret. It is not strictly a required parameter: with the `DataContext` set, either explicitly or by being passed down to the contained children, you can bind to the `DataContext` by not specifying a path at all:

```
<StackPanel DataContext="{StaticResource myStringValue}">
    <TextBox Text="{Binding}" />
</StackPanel>
```

Similarly, the `Path` parameter doesn't need to be named if no other parameters are used in the binding expression:

```
<TextBox Text="{Binding myTextProperty}" />
```

You can also use the dot notation (.) to drill down into subproperties on the bound object:

```
<TextBox Text="{Binding Path=myObject.MySubObject.MyBoundProperty}" />
```

If you have an indexed property, you can specify the index value as part of the `Path`:

```
<TextBox Text="{Binding Path=myIndexedProperty[2]}" />
```

Collection views, which expose the concept of a current item, can be bound using the slash notation (/):

```
<TextBox Text="{Binding Path=myCollectionView/}" />
```

Source and RelativeSource

The `DataContext` supplies the bindings with the default `Source`, but it is common to bind to a separate object entirely. This can be specified with the `Source` parameter:

```
<Window xmlns:viewModel="clr-namespace:BusinessModel;assembly=MyBusinessModel"
...>
    <Window.Resources>
        <viewModel:BusinessObject x:Key="myObject" />
    </Window.Resources>
    <TextBox Text="{Binding Path=MyTextProperty, Source={StaticResource myObject}}" />
</Window>
```

Source, however, references an object absolutely, whereas it can be useful to reference an object relative to the binding target. The most common use is to bind to a property to another property on the same object:

```
<TextBox Text="{Binding Path=Foreground, RelativeSource={x:Static RelativeSource.Self}}" />
```

This example binds the Text property to the Foreground property of the TextBox. The resulting text will be the name of the color of the text written in that same color.

StringFormat

Just like the String.Format method, StringFormat applies a string formatting expression to the binding value before rendering the whole string to the view.

```
<TextBlock Text="{Binding Path=CurrentPrice, StringFormat='{0:c}'}" />
```

This example will output the CurrentPrice property (a decimal value) as the currently specified culture's currency value.

If a Converter is specified on the binding, in addition to the StringFormat, the Converter is applied first.

TargetNullValue

Whereas FallbackValue is used when the binding *fails*, TargetNullValue is used when the source of the binding is *null*. It is useful for specifying default display values for null inputs.

```
<TextBox Text="{Binding Path=FirstName, TargetNullValue='Please enter your first name…'}" />
```

UpdateSourceExceptionFilter

As with NotifyOnValidationError, UpdateSourceExceptionFilter is used in data validation scenarios as covered in Chapter 6.

```
<TextBox>
    <TextBox.Text>
        <Binding Path="FirstName" UpdateSourceExceptionFilter="ExceptionHandler">
            <Binding.ValidationRules>
                <ExceptionValidationRule />
            </Binding.ValidationRules>
        </Binding>
    </TextBox.Text>
</TextBox>
```

```
private object ExceptionHandler(object bindingExpression,  Exception exception)
{
…
}
```

UpdateSourceTrigger

There are three possible values—besides default—for the `UpdateSourceTrigger` enumeration. `PropertyChanged` updates the binding source as soon as the target property's value has changed. `LostFocus` updates the binding source when the target control loses focus. `Explicit` doesn't automatically update the binding source; instead, it manually calls the `UpdateSource` method on the `BindingExpression`. By default, the `TextBox`'s `Text` property has an `UpdateSourceTrigger` of `LostFocus`, while most other controls default to `PropertyChanged`. Sometimes, you will want to override the `TextBox`'s default to update the source as soon as the property is changed: that is, whenever the user types a new value into the textbox.

```
<TextBox Text="{Binding Path=FirstName, UpdateSourceTrigger=PropertyChanged}" />
```

Validation

As indicated, validation is such an important area of user interface programming that a whole chapter is devoted to it: Chapter 6. The `ValidationRules`, `ValidateOnDataErrors` and `ValidateOnExceptions` options are all covered there.

XPath

If you are binding directly to XML data rather than object data, the `Path` property is replaced by the `XPath` property. XPath is the XML Path language and is used to query XML data. You can construct XPath queries and set them to the `XPath` parameter to bind to that data. XML databinding is outside of the scope of this book.

```
<TextBox Text="{Binding XPath=/Author[@FirstName='Gary' and @LastName='Hall']}" />
```

Data Conversion

There are times where the data you are binding from differs by type from the data you are binding to. Unless you explicitly deal with this type mismatch, you will need to implement a value converter. Value converters handle the conversion process in both directions.

IValueConverter Interface

The `IValueConverter` specifies two methods that must be implemented:

```
object Convert(object value, Type targetType, object parameter, CultureInfo culture);
object ConvertBack(object value, Type targetType, object parameter, CultureInfo culture);
```

The direction of conversion naturally flows from source to target. Thus, `Convert` handles the conversion from the binding source to the binding target, while `ConvertBack` handles the opposite case: conversion from the binding target to the binding source. In each case, the parameters have the same meaning:

- `object value`: The value that the binding source or target produces. It is an object because the `IValueConverter` interface does not know what type you will be using, so it will have to be cast to the object that's applicable.

- `Type targetType`: This is the type the binding target (or binding source in `ConvertBack`) requires. It allows you to target a number of different binding targets with a single `IValueConverter` implementation.

- `object parameter`: `ConverterParameter` is a binding expression parameter. You can specify this parameter on a per-binding basis to further customize the outcome of your converter.

- `CultureInfo culture`: Many different types require culture-specific formatting. Currencies are a prime example of this, and have myriad variations depending on locale. The euro, for instance, is represented with at least three different notations.

Let's take the example from earlier in this section and implement a converter that will accept a Boolean value and output a `System.Windows.Visiblity` value. We will only implement converting the Boolean value to a `Visibility`, and not the `ConvertBack` scenario. Thus, for both brevity and clarity, this value converter will be applicable solely to one-way (readonly) bindings. An extra feature of this converter will be the ability to specify, as the `ConverterParameter`, what value to use when "false" is encountered on the binding source. `Visibility` has two applicable values: `Collapsed`, which removes all trace of the control, and `Hidden`, which reserves space for the element in the layout but does not show the element.

■ **Caution** There is a built in `System.Windows.Controls.BooleanToVisibilityConverter` that provides two-way conversion. It does not accept the desired `Visibility` value as the `ConverterParameter`, but it should be preferred to rolling your own solution, wherever applicable.

Listing 2–12. The Domain Object Provided to the Boolean Binding Source

```
public class DomainObject
{
    public DomainObject()
    {
        ShowText = false;
    }

    public bool ShowText
    {
        get;
        private set;
    }
}
```

Listing 2–12 shows the domain object we will be binding to in our example. It exposes a single, read-only Boolean property that will serve as our binding source. By default, the property is set to false in the constructor. Feel free to set this to true so you can see the effect on the `Visibility` property.

Listing 2–13. *The XAML Markup for the Value Converter Example*

```
<Window x:Class="BooleanToValueConverterExample.MainWindow"
        xmlns="http://schemas.microsoft.com/winfx/2006/xaml/presentation"
        xmlns:x="http://schemas.microsoft.com/winfx/2006/xaml"
        xmlns:system="clr-namespace:System;assembly=mscorlib"
        xmlns:local="clr-namespace:BooleanToValueConverterExample;assembly="
        xmlns:windows="clr-namespace:System.Windows;assembly=PresentationCore"
        Title="MainWindow" Height="350" Width="525">
    <Window.Resources>
        <local:DomainObject x:Key="myDomainObject" />
        <local:MyBooleanToVisibilityValueConverter x:Key="myBooleanToVisibilityConverter" />
    </Window.Resources>
    <StackPanel Orientation="Vertical">
        <TextBlock Text="Text above" />
        <TextBlock Text="This is some sample text..."
                    Visibility="{Binding
                        Source={StaticResource myDomainObject},
                        Path=ShowText,
                        FallbackValue={x:Static windows:Visibility.Visible},
                        Converter={StaticResource myBooleanToVisibilityConverter},
                        ConverterParameter={x:Static windows:Visibility.Collapsed}}" />
        <TextBlock Text="Text below" />
    </StackPanel>
</Window>
```

Listing 2–13 shows the Window that will host our example. We have a number of different XML namespace references, each of which imports something we will use in this example. The first use is in the Window.Resources section, where we declare two objects: the DomainObject (which is given a key of myDomainObject) and a MyBooleanToVisibilityValueConverter (the code for which is in Listing 2–14). The StackPanel is given an orientation of Vertical and there are three TextBlock controls declared, with the middle one the target of our example. This is because of the behavior of the Visibility.Hidden enumeration value: the control will not be shown, but there will be a blank space for it between the two other TextBlocks. With Visibility.Collapsed, this space is removed and the two remaining TextBlocks will appear on consecutive lines.

The Visibility binding itself has been split over a number of lines for clarity; sometimes bindings can become complex, but only proportionate to the features you are using. The Source is set to the DomainObject instance declared in the Window.Resources section: note that it is referenced with StaticResource, indicating that we are loading a predefined resource, the lookup should be done at load time, and it will not change over the lifetime of this view. The Path is simply the name of the property we are binding to. Next, we have used FallbackValue, just in case the binding fails for any reason (this is advisable almost all the time). The Converter is set using the same StaticResource syntax as the Source of the binding. Finally, we provide a ConverterParameter that, as we will see in Listing 2–14, is used to determine the value for Visibility when the binding source yields false.

Before we look at the implementation of the IValueConverter that this example uses, a quick note on the x:Static syntax used by the FallbackValue and the ConverterParameter. The general syntax looks like this:

```
{x:Static prefix:typeName.staticMemberName}
```

Our prefix is the Windows XML namespace, which references the System.Windows CLR namespace. The typeName is Visibility, which is the enumeration we are using, and staticMemberName is the enumeration value we wish to use. For the FallbackValue, we want to have the control Visible by default. And, if the binding source returns false, we wish to Collapse the control.

This x:Static syntax can be used to reference constants, static properties, and fields, as well as enumeration values.

Listing 2–14. Implementing an IValueConverter for Boolean to Visibility Conversion

```
public class MyBooleanToVisibilityValueConverter : IValueConverter
{
    public object Convert(object value, Type targetType, object parameter, CultureInfo↵
 culture)
    {
        object convertedValue = null;
        if(targetType == typeof(System.Windows.Visibility))
        {
            Visibility invisibleValue = Visibility.Hidden;
            try
            {
                invisibleValue = (Visibility)parameter;
            }
            catch
            {
                invisibleValue = Visibility.Hidden;
            }

            try
            {
                bool sourceBoolean = (bool)value;
                convertedValue = sourceBoolean ? Visibility.Visible : invisibleValue;
            }
            catch
            {
                convertedValue = Visibility.Visible;
            }
        }
        return convertedValue;
    }

    public object ConvertBack(object value, Type targetType, object parameter, CultureInfo↵
 culture)
    {
        throw new NotImplementedException();
    }
}
```

The first things to note about Listing 2–14 are that the IValueConverter has been implemented, but calls to ConvertBack result in a NotImplementedException being thrown. Thus, if we attached this converter to a two-way binding, *setting* a value back to the source would be erroneous.

The implementation of Convert has a couple of distinct parts. First, we ensure that our binding target is looking for a System.Window.Visibility enumeration value. If it is not, we simply escape early, returning null; this conversion is obviously not what we were built for, so we quietly walk away. Next, we try to retrieve the ConverterParameter value, which has been boiled down to a basic object. There is every chance that the user has neglected to supply such a parameter, or that it is of the wrong type, which is why it is wrapped in a try/catch block. The default value used whenever the binding source returns null is Hidden.

We then start a new try/catch block, this time to attempt to convert the binding source from an object to a Boolean. If it works we eventually test the Boolean and set the output value to Visible or to the invisibleValue previously configured. If the cast fails, we merely show the target control.

This is the crux of the IValueConverter and briefly demonstrates how to handle a type disparity between a binding source and target. Next, we will look at how to handle multiple binding source values and distill them to a single target value.

IMultiValueConverter Interface

The IMultiValueConverter is very similar to its single-valued sibling, with a couple of obvious differences:

```
object Convert(object[] values, Type targetType, object parameter, CultureInfo culture);
object[] CovertBack(object value, Type[] targetTypes, object parameter, CultureInfo↵
 culture);
```

With the Convert method, we have pluralized the value parameter, taking an array of objects instead of a single one. This is because we have a number of source values but we are still outputting to one single target value.

Conversely, the ConvertBack method is taking a single value and must return x converted values—hence the object array return value. Not only that, but these values may all be of disparate types, so we receive an array of Types. We can use this array of Types to determine how many values we are to return and what type to use for each indexed value.

The example presented in Listing 2–17 takes a month name and a decimal balance as input, and outputs a color that relates to these two values. A positive balance will always yield green, a zero balance will always yield black. However, a negative balance will yield a color between yellow and red (through orange), depending on which quarter we are in: Q1 through Q4. The idea is that the closer to the end of the year we get, the more urgent a negative balance becomes. As you may have guessed, this conversion process is lossy—we can't extrapolate the exact balance from the resultant color—so this converter will also be readonly.

■ **Tip** It is not advisable to handle monetary values as a simple decimal. Instead, consider implementing an encapsulated Money value type, as described by Martin Fowler in PoEAA, pp488.

Listing 2–15. *The Domain Object for Our Two Binding Sources*

```
public class DomainObject
{
    public DomainObject()
    {
        Month = "April";
        Balance = -1.00M;
    }

    public string Month
    {
        get;
        private set;
```

```
    }

    public decimal Balance
    {
        get;
        private set;
    }
}
```

In Listing 2–15, the domain object is almost as simple as before because it merely exposes the two properties that our converter requires: a string Month property and a decimal Balance property. The two values are hardcoded to April (representing Quarter 2) and -1.00. We will see in the next section how the ObjectDataProvider lets us specify constructor parameters in XAML.

Listing 2–16. *The window's XAML markup that will host our multibinding and multivalue converter*

```
<Window x:Class="MultiValueConverterExample.MainWindow"
        xmlns="http://schemas.microsoft.com/winfx/2006/xaml/presentation"
        xmlns:system="clr-namespace:System;assembly=mscorlib"
        xmlns:x="http://schemas.microsoft.com/winfx/2006/xaml"
        xmlns:local="clr-namespace:MultiValueConverterExample"
        Title="MainWindow" Height="350" Width="525">
    <Window.Resources>
        <local:DomainObject x:Key="myDomainObject" />
        <local:BalanceQuarterColorConverter x:Key="myBalanceQuarterColorConverter" />
    </Window.Resources>
    <StackPanel>
        <TextBlock DataContext="{StaticResource myDomainObject}" Text="{Binding Balance}">
            <TextBlock.Foreground>
                <SolidColorBrush>
                    <SolidColorBrush.Color>
                        <MultiBinding Converter="{StaticResource↵
myBalanceQuarterColorConverter}">
                            <Binding Path="Month" />
                            <Binding Path="Balance" />
                        </MultiBinding>
                    </SolidColorBrush.Color>
                </SolidColorBrush>
            </TextBlock.Foreground>
        </TextBlock>
    </StackPanel>
</Window>
```

As Listing 2–16 shows, the difference in this example from the single-valued converter example is that the TextBlock's Foreground uses a MultiBinding, whereby more than one binding is bound to the SolidColorBrush's Color property. As you can imagine, unless the target requires more than one value, you *must* provide a converter so that only one binding value is output.

Listing 2–17. *The IMultiValueConverter Implementation*

```
public class BalanceQuarterColorConverter : IMultiValueConverter
{
    public object Convert(object[] values, Type targetType, object parameter, CultureInfo↵
culture)
    {
```

```
        object convertedValue = null;
        if (values.Count() == 2)
        {
            string month = null;
            decimal balance = decimal.MinValue;
            foreach (object value in values)
            {
                if (value is string)
                {
                    month = value as string;
                }
                else if (value is decimal)
                {
                    balance = (decimal)value;
                }
            }

            DateTime monthDateTime = DateTime.MinValue;
            if (DateTime.TryParseExact(month, "MMMM", culture.DateTimeFormat,↵
DateTimeStyles.AssumeUniversal, out monthDateTime))
            {
                int quarter = (monthDateTime.Month + 2) / 3;
                convertedValue = ConvertQuarterAndBalanceToColor(quarter, balance);
            }
        }
      return convertedValue;
    }

    private Color ConvertQuarterAndBalanceToColor(int quarter, decimal balance)
    {
        Color outputColor = Colors.Magenta;
        if (balance == decimal.Zero)
        {
            outputColor = Colors.Black;
        }
        else if (balance > decimal.Zero)
        {
            outputColor = Colors.Green;
        }
        else
        {
            switch (quarter)
            {
                case 1:
                    outputColor = Colors.Yellow;
                    break;
                case 2:
                    outputColor = Colors.DarkOrange;
                    break;
                case 3:
                    outputColor = Colors.OrangeRed;
                    break;
                case 4:
                    outputColor = Colors.Red;
```

```
                    break;
                default:
                    outputColor = Colors.Magenta;
                    break;
            }
        }
        return outputColor;
    }

    public object[] ConvertBack(object value, Type[] targetTypes, object parameter,↵
CultureInfo culture)
    {
        throw new NotImplementedException();
    }
}
```

The conversion process is split into two parts: retrieving the data into the format we require, then the algorithm that will convert a month index (1-12, January to December) and balance to a `System.Windows.Media.Color` value. Notice that we do not presume to know which binding will be first, instead iterating over the list of source values and attempting to convert each one in turn.

What if our requirements change at some point in the future and negative balances in Quarter 1 are only considered problematic (and therefore should be colored yellow) if the balance is below 1,000? Currently, we would have to change this binding converter, which is quite closely wedded to the view. As we will see, this sort of business logic is more commonly placed in the model, so that its implementation can alter without impacting the view at all.

An alternative would be to factor out the `ConvertQuarterAndBalanceToColor` method into its own interface and utilize the Strategy Pattern—*Design Patterns: Elements of Reusable Object-Oriented Software* by Erich Gamma, et al, (Pearson Education, 1994), also referred to as the Gang of Four (GoF) book. This `IMultiValueConverter` interface would then have to accept our hypothetical `IQuarterAndBalanceToColorConverter` as a constructor parameter, so that we could use dependency injection to supply one of many algorithms. The problem we would then encounter is constructing our new converter in the XAML—we would no longer have access to the default parameterless constructor, which is a requirement for declaring objects in XAML. The next section explores how to supply construction parameters to objects, as well as how to bind to methods instead of just properties, so we can parameterize our bindings.

ObjectDataProvider

The previous examples declaratively instantiated domain objects as local resources, allowing their properties to be used as binding sources. However, there are a couple of key restrictions to this approach that can jeopardize its viability.

- The objects must be default constructible: they must have a parameterless constructor.

- You can only bind to public properties, methods can't be bound.

- Long-running processes will block the rest of the view's bindings.

We can overcome all three of these limitations by introducing a level of indirection between the binding source and target: the `ObjectDataProvider`.

As ever, there is no such thing as a free lunch. The `ObjectDataProvider` has a permissions requirement: the underlying domain object that is being wrapped must be accessible via reflection. If this is not the case, the `ObjectDataProvider` will not be able to find the constructors, methods, or properties you specify in your XAML markup.

Object Construction

Let's refactor our `DomainObject` from the multivalue data converter example (see Listing 2–18). Instead of hardcoding default values, we will accept values on construction. After that, however, the properties will remain immutable.

Listing 2–18. The Edited Domain Object That Will Accept Values on Construction

```
public class DomainObject
{
    public DomainObject(string month, decimal balance)
    {
        Month = month;
        Balance = balance;
    }

    public string Month
    {
        get;
        private set;
    }

    public decimal Balance
    {
        get;
        private set;
    }
}
```

If we try to compile the example as is, we will receive the following error message from the compiler:

```
Type 'DomainObject' is not usable as an object element because it is not public or does ↵
not define a public parameterless constructor or a type converter.
```

We need to indicate to the XAML how to construct this object, as shown in Listing 2–19.

Listing 2–19. Wrapping the Domain Object in an `ObjectDataProvider` for Construction

```
<Window.Resources>
    <ObjectDataProvider x:Key="myDomainObject" ObjectType="{x:Type local:DomainObject}">
        <ObjectDataProvider.ConstructorParameters>
            <system:String>September</system:String>
            <system:Decimal>-100.00</system:Decimal>
        </ObjectDataProvider.ConstructorParameters>
    </ObjectDataProvider>
    <local:BalanceQuarterColorConverter x:Key="myBalanceQuarterColorConverter" />
</Window.Resources>
```

Due to how expressive (or, if you prefer, verbose) declarative markup is, this code is fairly self-explanatory. We have keyed our `ObjectDataProvider` with the same value as before so that the binding need not be changed at all. The `ObjectType` parameter indicates which CLR class we want to instantiate. We then have a list of `ContructorParameters`: note how we are declaring a `string` instance with the value "September" and a `decimal` instance with the value "-100.00". The `system:` prefix is necessary because both types are built-in and reside in the `System` namespace, within the `mscorlib` assembly.

Once constructed, we can transparently reference the properties of the wrapped DomainObject because the ObjectDataProvider delegates any requests straight through to it.

Method Binding

Suppose that the architect in charge of our hypothetical project has decided he dislikes the use of `IMultiValueConverter` and wishes to place the business logic it represents directly on our domain object. The refactoring required will replace the two instance properties with a single method call that will accept the month string and balance decimal as parameters, as shown in Listing 2–20.

Listing 2–20. The Refactored DomainObject Class

```
public class DomainObject
    {
        public Color ConvertQuarterAndBalanceToColor(string month, decimal balance)
        {
            int quarter = ConvertMonthNameToQuarter(month);
            Color outputColor = Colors.Magenta;
            if (balance == decimal.Zero)
            {
                outputColor = Colors.Black;
            }
            else if (balance > decimal.Zero)
            {
                outputColor = Colors.Green;
            }
            else
            {
                switch (quarter)
                {
                    case 1:
                        outputColor = Colors.Yellow;
                        break;
                    case 2:
                        outputColor = Colors.DarkOrange;
                        break;
                    case 3:
                        outputColor = Colors.OrangeRed;
                        break;
                    case 4:
                        outputColor = Colors.Red;
                        break;
                    default:
                        outputColor = Colors.Magenta;
                        break;
                }
            }
```

```
                return outputColor;
        }

        private int ConvertMonthNameToQuarter(string month)
        {
            DateTime monthDateTime = DateTime.MinValue;
            DateTime.TryParseExact(month, "MMMM", CultureInfo.CurrentCulture.↵
DateTimeFormat, DateTimeStyles.AssumeUniversal, out monthDateTime);
            return (monthDateTime.Month + 2) / 3;
        }
    }
```

This code will be familiar: it is almost exactly the same as before, albeit with minor refactoring here and there.

As Listing 2–21 shows, the XAML will now change rather significantly because we no longer require a multibinding or converter.

Listing 2–21. XAML Markup Showing How to Bind to a Method of a POCO Using ObjectDataProvider

```xml
<Window x:Class="MultiValueConverterExample.MainWindow"
        xmlns="http://schemas.microsoft.com/winfx/2006/xaml/presentation"
        xmlns:x="http://schemas.microsoft.com/winfx/2006/xaml"
        xmlns:system="clr-namespace:System;assembly=mscorlib"
        xmlns:local="clr-namespace:MultiValueConverterExample"
        Title="MainWindow" Height="350" Width="525">
    <Window.Resources>
        <ObjectDataProvider x:Key="myDomainObjectMethod" ObjectType="{x:Type↵
local:DomainObject}" MethodName="ConvertQuarterAndBalanceToColor">
            <ObjectDataProvider.MethodParameters>
                <system:String>April</system:String>
                <system:Decimal>-150.00</system:Decimal>
            </ObjectDataProvider.MethodParameters>
        </ObjectDataProvider>
        <local:BalanceQuarterColorConverter x:Key="myBalanceQuarterColorConverter" />
    </Window.Resources>
    <StackPanel>
        <TextBlock Text="{Binding Source={StaticResource myDomainObjectMethod},↵
BindsDirectlyToSource=True, Path=MethodParameters[1]}">
            <TextBlock.Foreground>
                <SolidColorBrush Color="{Binding Source={StaticResource↵
myDomainObjectMethod}}" />
            </TextBlock.Foreground>
        </TextBlock>
    </StackPanel>
</Window>
```

The only piece of this code that should provide any surprises is the TextBlock's Text binding. This is an example of the BindsDirectlyToSource parameter that was outlined earlier. Now that the DomainObject no longer exposes the Balance value as a property, we need to find some alternative way of binding to the Balance. Thankfully, the ObjectDataProvider itself exposes this value via the MethodParameters array. As mentioned, ObjectDataProviders implicitly pass bindings on to their underlying objects, so we override this behavior by setting BindsDirectlyToSource to True. We pass the Balance in as the second parameter, so we use an index of 1 in the binding's Path property.

Bear in mind that the result displayed is exactly the same as when a data converter was used, but the method used to achieve that result has drastically changed.

Asynchronous Methods

The ConvertQuarterAndBalanceToColor method is trivial, as well as CPU-bound. There is no real reason for this method to run on a separate worker thread. However, if we were to bind to a method that crossed a network boundary—perhaps accessing a database on a separate server, for example—we could ask the ObjectDataProvider to perform that work on a worker thread so as not to block the rest of the view's binding.

This is as simple as setting the ObjectDataProvider's IsAsynchronous property to True:

```
<ObjectDataProvider x:Key="myDomainObjectMethod" ObjectType="{x:Type local:DomainObject}"↵
  MethodName="ConvertQuarterAndBalanceToColor" IsAsynchronous="True">
```

Concurrency and threading are discussed in more detail in Chapter 4.

Binding to Enumerations

Sometimes you may wish to show a list of the possible values of an enumeration. We can leverage the System.Enum type's GetValues method to achieve exactly that, as Listing 2–22 shows.

Listing 2–22. Binding a List Box to the Values in the System.Windows.Visibility Enumeration

```
<Window x:Class="MultiValueConverterExample.EnumerationBindingExample"
        xmlns="http://schemas.microsoft.com/winfx/2006/xaml/presentation"
        xmlns:x="http://schemas.microsoft.com/winfx/2006/xaml"
        xmlns:system="clr-namespace:System;assembly=mscorlib"
        xmlns:windows="clr-namespace:System.Windows;assembly=PresentationCore"
        Title="EnumerationBindingExample" Height="300" Width="300">
    <Window.Resources>
        <ObjectDataProvider x:Key="visibilityValues" ObjectType="{x:Type system:Enum}"↵
MethodName="GetValues">
            <ObjectDataProvider.MethodParameters>
                <x:Type TypeName="windows:Visibility" />
            </ObjectDataProvider.MethodParameters>
        </ObjectDataProvider>
    </Window.Resources>
    <ListBox ItemsSource="{Binding Source={StaticResource visibilityValues}}"↵
SelectionMode="Single" />
</Window>
```

This is exactly like any other method binding, with the caveat that the GetValues method accepts a Type parameter so that it knows which enumeration's values it should return.

Debugging DataBindings

So far, we have assumed that our bindings all behave themselves and, when they do misbehave, we simply output something friendly to the user. But, if a binding acts out during development, there are a number of options for debugging that can point to the underlying problem so we can fix it.

Default Debug Output

Take a look at the markup in Listing 2–23. The object that is being used as the binding source does not have a property called ErroneousProperty. This will compile fine and will not make a stink at runtime. Instead, the window is blank, without any text in the TextBlock.

Listing 2–23. *Binding to a Property that Does Not Exist*

```
<Window.Resources>
        <local:DomainObject x:Key="myDomainObject" />
</Window.Resources>
<Grid>
    <TextBlock Text="{Binding Source={StaticResource myDomainObject},
 Path=ErroneousProperty}" />
</Grid>
```

However, provided we run the application with the debugger attached, we can check the Debug Output window in Visual Studio and see the error message.

```
System.Windows.Data Error: 40 : BindingExpression path error: 'ErroneousProperty' ⏎
property not found on 'object' ''DomainObject' (HashCode=13742435)'. ⏎
BindingExpression:Path=ErroneousProperty; DataItem='DomainObject' (HashCode=13742435); ⏎
target element is 'TextBlock' (Name=''); target property is 'Text' (type 'String')
```

The key part of this message is "'ErroneousProperty' property not found on 'object' 'DomainObject'". In many situations, this is where you can stop your debugging process, but some applications write so much to the Debug window that tracking down a specific binding error can quickly become laborious. Do not fear, though, as there are other options available.

TraceSources

Instead of writing the binding errors to the Debug console, we can write them to a text file of our choosing. TraceSources are set up in the application configuration (App.config) file. By default, WPF and Silverlight applications do not have an App.config file generated, so you may have to add it manually. Listing 2–24 shows the contents of a sample App.config file with some error-logging facilities configured.

Listing 2–24. *The Application Configuration File with System Diagnostics Listeners Added*

```
<?xml version="1.0" encoding="utf-8" ?>
<configuration>
  <system.diagnostics>
    <sources>
      <source name="System.Windows.Data" switchName="SourceSwitch">
        <listeners>
          <add name="textFileListener" />
        </listeners>
      </source>
    </sources>

    <switches>
      <add name="SourceSwitch" value="All" />
```

```
    </switches>

    <sharedListeners>
       <add name="textFileListener" type="System.Diagnostics.TextWriterTraceListener"↵
 initializeData="DebugTrace.txt" />
       </sharedListeners>

    <trace autoflush="true" indentsize="4" />

  </system.diagnostics>
</configuration>
```

We are creating a trace source that will catch debug information from the System.Windows.Data namespace. Each trace source can be configured to output two levels of debug information: warnings, errors, or both (as specified in this example). Also, each trace source can have one or more listeners that are targets for the debug output. A single listener is configured in the example: a System.Diagnostics.TextWriterTraceListener, which will output errors to the DebugTrace.txt file. You can have a trace source output debug data to the console or to an XML file with ConsoleTraceListener and XmlWriterTraceListener, respectively.

When the application runs, the exact same output seen in the Debug window is written to the file DebugTrace.txt in the current working directory. This logging method is not just useful for debugging bindings; it can be reused to log any problems that occur in other areas of your application.

PresentationTraceSources

The System.Diagnostics namespace provides an attached property called PresentationTraceSources.TraceLevel that can be used on your bindings to generate a complete picture of the steps taken by the binding, as shown in Listing 2–25.

Listing 2–25. Using PresentationTraceSources.TraceLevel to Output Binding Debug Data

```
<Window x:Class="DebuggingBindingsExample.MainWindow"
        xmlns="http://schemas.microsoft.com/winfx/2006/xaml/presentation"
        xmlns:x="http://schemas.microsoft.com/winfx/2006/xaml"
        xmlns:local="clr-namespace:DebuggingBindingsExample"
        xmlns:diagnostics="clr-namespace:System.Diagnostics;assembly=WindowsBase"
        Title="MainWindow" Height="350" Width="525">
    <Window.Resources>
        <local:DomainObject x:Key="myDomainObject" />
    </Window.Resources>
    <Grid>
        <TextBlock Text="{Binding Source={StaticResource myDomainObject},↵
 Path=ErroneousProperty, diagnostics:PresentationTraceSources.TraceLevel=High}" />
    </Grid>
</Window>
```

The output to the console window is much more in-depth, allowing you to track down the bugs in more problematic bindings. This option also lets you target the specific bindings that are misbehaving, rather than logging all binding interaction, which can be quite verbose.

■ **Tip** When referencing the `System.Diagnostics` namespace, remember to target the `WindowsBase` assembly, which is where `PresentationTraceSources` resides.

Value Converter

Value converters sit in between the two ends of a binding and we can reappropriate a pass-through converter to assist in our debugging efforts. By placing a breakpoint inside the `Convert` or `ConvertBack` methods, we can inspect the value that is being passed in and ensure that it is what we expected (see Listing 2–26).

Listing 2–26. *Facilitating a Breakpoint by Implementing a Pass-Through Value Converter*

```
public class PassThroughValueConverter : IValueConverter
{
    public object Convert(object value, Type targetType, object parameter,↩
 System.Globalization.CultureInfo culture)
    {
        return value;
    }

    public object ConvertBack(object value, Type targetType, object parameter,↩
 System.Globalization.CultureInfo culture)
    {
        return value;
    }
}
```

The added advantage is that we can debug a multibinding by inserting a proxy `IMultiValueConverter` that, despite doing no conversion, allows us to break in to the middle of the binding process.

Templating

WPF and Silverlight have a unique take on the concept of separating data from its representation. It is simultaneously more intuitive and more expressive than something like Windows Forms, and is reminiscent of the fluid design process that web sites exhibit.

Much of this capability comes from `ControlTemplates`: the ability to specify structure and style on a per-control basis, while retaining the behavioral essence of the control. Not only can we apply a template to individual controls, we can also add a `DataTemplate` to our domain objects, which would otherwise have no visual representation.

The Logical and Visual Trees

Key to understanding templating is discovering a little bit about how WPF and Silverlight work under the hood.

The logical tree is, typically, made up of the XAML elements you edit day-to-day. Admittedly, there are often implied objects that do some work behind the scenes that you can safely omit, but what you create as XAML can be said to constitute the logical tree. Listing 2–27 gives an example.

Listing 2–27. The Logical Tree of a Typical View

```
<Window x:Class="LogicalAndVisualTreeExample.MainWindow"
        xmlns="http://schemas.microsoft.com/winfx/2006/xaml/presentation"
        xmlns:x="http://schemas.microsoft.com/winfx/2006/xaml"
        Title="MainWindow" Height="350" Width="525">
    <StackPanel Orientation="Horizontal" Height="30" VerticalAlignment="Top">
        <!-- implied: <StackPanel.Children> -->
        <Label Content="My Label" />
        <ComboBox SelectedIndex="0">
            <ComboBox.Items>
            <!-- implied: <ListBox.Items> -->
            <ComboBoxItem Content="Item 1" />
            <ComboBoxItem Content="Item 2" />
            <ComboBoxItem Content="Item 3" />
            <!-- implied: </ListBox.Items> -->
            </ComboBox.Items>
        </ComboBox>
        <Button Content="My Button" />
        <!-- implied: </StackPanel.Children> -->
    </StackPanel>
</Window>
```

As Listing 2–27 shows, we can omit some elements and the parser will proceed happily with creating an object graph that is synonymous with this layout.

While this markup is reasonably brief, there are many, many other objects that are required to render this view to the screen. Each of these objects belongs to the visual tree, which describes the visual representation of objects that derive from the System.Windows.Media.Visual, such as System.Windows.UIElement. This, in turn, is the base class for System.Windows.FrameworkElement: the parent of nigh on all WPF controls.

The ComboBox in Listing 2–27 has its own default control template that dictates its visual representation. Were you so inclined, you could replace the default styling of all controls so that they are not just colored slightly differently, but composed in an entirely new fashion.

ControlTemplate

Let's demonstrate the drastic changes that can be made to controls using templating with an example. The default button structure is fairly boring and we are going to jazz it up a bit by making it look like a rounded rectangle, as shown in Listing 2–28.

Listing 2–28. Altering an Individual Button's Appearance Using a ControlTemplate

```
<StackPanel>
    <Button Content="Hello World!" Width="100" Height="30">
        <Button.Template>
            <ControlTemplate>
                <Grid>
                    <Rectangle Fill="{TemplateBinding Background}" RadiusX=↵
"5" RadiusY="5" />
                    <Border BorderBrush="Black" BorderThickness="1">
                        <ContentPresenter HorizontalAlignment="Center"↵
 VerticalAlignment="Center" Content="{TemplateBinding Button.Content}" />
                    </Border>
```

```
            </Grid>
        </ControlTemplate>
      </Button.Template>
   </Button>
</StackPanel>
```

Currently, this feature is of limited use because your XAML files would quickly become gargantuan if you had to specify the structure of each Button, or other control, in situ. It would be much more useful if we could apply a template to *all* buttons in our application, or even target certain buttons with a reference for ControlTemplate to use in each case. Of course, this is absolutely possible, as Listing 2–29 shows.

Listing 2–29. Targeting All Button Controls with a New ControlTemplate

```
<StackPanel>
    <StackPanel.Resources>
        <Style TargetType="Button">
            <Setter Property="Template">
                <Setter.Value>
                    <ControlTemplate>
                        <Grid>
                            <Rectangle Fill="{TemplateBinding Background}" />
                            <Border BorderBrush="Black" BorderThickness="1">
                                <ContentPresenter HorizontalAlignment="Center"↵
 VerticalAlignment="Center" Content="{TemplateBinding Button.Content}" />
                            </Border>
                        </Grid>
                    </ControlTemplate>
                </Setter.Value>
            </Setter>
        </Style>

        <Style x:Key="newButtonStyle" TargetType="Button">
            <Setter Property="Template">
                <Setter.Value>
                    <ControlTemplate>
                        <Grid>
                            <Ellipse Fill="{TemplateBinding Background}" />
                            <ContentPresenter HorizontalAlignment="Center"↵
 VerticalAlignment="Center" Content="{TemplateBinding Button.Content}" />
                        </Grid>
                    </ControlTemplate>
                </Setter.Value>
            </Setter>
        </Style>

    </StackPanel.Resources>
    <Button Content="Hello" Width="100" Height="30" />
    <Button Content="World!" Width="100" Height="30" Style="{StaticResource↵
 newButtonStyle}" />
</StackPanel>
```

Here, the two buttons are styled separately. The first has the style applied that is global to all `Buttons` that are children of this `StackPanel`. The second selects the `newButtonStyle` by referencing it in the `Style` property. In this way, we can have a number of different types of `Button` represented by very different styles.

DataTemplate

Whereas `ControlTemplates` specify a visual structure for a particular `control`, the `DataTemplate` can provide a visual structure for our good friend, the Plain Old CLR Object.

By way of example, you may often wish to bind to a list of domain objects. If you do this without a `DataTemplate`, the class's `ToString` method is called, which, by default, returns the class name qualified by the namespace, as Figure 2–7 demonstrates.

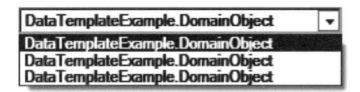

Figure 2–7. Binding to a list of domain objects without specifying a `DataTemplate`

This is not much use to us, but we can easily remedy the situation by applying a `DataTemplate`. Listing 2–30 shows the `DataTemplate` declaration, while Figure 2–8 shows the result.

Listing 2–30. Applying a DataTemplate to a Domain Object

```
<Window x:Class="DataTemplateExample.MainWindow"
        xmlns="http://schemas.microsoft.com/winfx/2006/xaml/presentation"
        xmlns:x="http://schemas.microsoft.com/winfx/2006/xaml"
        xmlns:local="clr-namespace:DataTemplateExample"
        Title="MainWindow" Height="350" Width="525">
    <Window.Resources>
        <x:Array x:Key="domainObjectsList" Type="{x:Type local:DomainObject}">
            <local:DomainObject />
            <local:DomainObject />
            <local:DomainObject />
        </x:Array>
    </Window.Resources>
    <StackPanel Width="250">
        <ComboBox SelectedIndex="0" ItemsSource="{Binding Source={StaticResource↵
domainObjectsList}}">
            <ComboBox.ItemTemplate>
                <DataTemplate>
                    <TextBlock Text="{Binding Path=DisplayText}" />
                </DataTemplate>
            </ComboBox.ItemTemplate>
        </ComboBox>
    </StackPanel>
</Window>
```

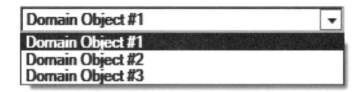

Figure 2–8. *The result of applying a* `DataTemplate`

This merely hints at the potential of `DataTemplates`, which will be fully unlocked in subsequent chapters.

Summary

This chapter has only slightly more than scratched the surface of databinding and all of the myriad scenarios that you may come across in a real-world project. However, you should now be well-equipped to investigate these possibilities with confidence.

It may appear that this chapter had little to do with MVVM, but it has laid some valuable foundations that MVVM necessarily builds upon. The ViewModel, for instance, must make extensive use of the databinding features available to WPF and Silverlight if it is to be at all relevant. Subsequent chapters will flesh out the bones of databinding and explore further the *why* and *how* of databinding, as opposed to the *what* addressed thus far.

■ ■ ■

CHAPTER 3

Model-View Separation

In a software product there are two distinct modules whose responsibilities are well-defined and should be clearly demarcated. The model is a software representation of a solution to a known problem whereas the view allows the user to interact with the model to solve a specific problem.

Before discussing the specifics of MVVM, it is necessary to consider why we need to separate the model and the view, how they can be separated, and what their respective roles are in a software product. There can be significant workload added to a project in keeping these two subsystems disconnected, and all stakeholders must be committed to the cause. It is easy to start cutting corners when under the pressure of deadlines, but adherence to principles pays dividends when it comes to product quality and code maintenance.

This chapter will highlight the importance of model-view separation and explain why it is considered such a significant paradigm as well as outlining potential options for separating the two in a WPF or Silverlight application. The problems that can occur when not separating the model and view—such as tightly coupled code with low cohesion—will also be explored.

Separation of Concerns

Separation of concerns (also known as SoC) is not a new term, although it has recently garnered a buzzword reputation. It simply means ensuring that code has a single, well-defined purpose—and that it does not assume any superfluous responsibilities. This applies at all levels of code, from individual methods up to entire subsystems, which should all focus on accomplishing their one aim, or "concern."

Dependencies

A code dependency does not necessarily refer to an assembly reference. There is a dependency wherever one unit of code needs to "know" about another. Should one class need to use another class, the former becomes dependent on the latter. Specifically, the dependency is on the class's interface—its methods, properties, and constructor(s). It is recommended practice to separate a class's interface from its implementation, as Listing 3–1 and Listing 3–2 contrast.

Listing 3–1. A method referring to a class implementation

```
public class ShapeRenderer
{
    private IGraphicsContext _graphicsContext;

    public void DrawShape(Circle circleShape)
    {
        _graphicsContext.DrawCircle(circleShape.Position, circleShape.Radius);
    }
}
```

Listing 3–2. *A method referring to an interface*

```
public class ShapeRenderer
{
    private IGraphicsContext graphicsContext;

    public void DrawShape(IShape shape)
    {
        shape.Draw(graphicsContext);
    }
}
```

It is worth noting that both listings have the same intent—to draw a shape. Let's take a moment to consider the differences between the two listings and the implications of both options.

With Listing 3–1, the only shape that is accepted is a Circle. In order to support alternative shapes, the method must be overloaded to accept each additional shape type as a parameter. Each time a new shape is added, the DrawShape code must also be changed, increasing the maintenance burden. The Circle class, plus any additional shapes, must also be visible at compile time to this code. Finally, the DrawShape method knows too much about the implementation of the Circle class. Granted, in this brief example, it is reasonable to assume that Circles would have Position and Radius properties. However, they are publically readable by anyone, and this unnecessarily breaks encapsulation.

The data that the Circle object contains should not be revealed to third parties, if possible. Perhaps, in future iterations, the Position property is split into its constituent X and Y components—this code would subsequently fail to compile due to such a breaking change. Encapsulation is intended to protect client code from interface changes such as this.

Listing 3–2 corrects a number of problems with the original code by using various techniques to achieve a separation of concerns. The DrawShape method now accepts an interface, IShape, rather than a single concrete implementation of a shape. Any class that implements the IShape interface can be passed into this method without any changes to the method at all.

Another technique is then used to preserve encapsulation of each shape: inversion of control (also known as IoC). Rather than querying the shape's members in order to draw the shape, the method instead asks the shape to *draw itself*. It then uses Dependency Injection (DI) to pass the shape the IGraphicsContext interface that it requires to draw itself. From a maintenance point of view, this implementation is much more extensible. Adding a new shape is easy—merely implement the IShape interface and write its Draw(IGraphicsContext) method. It is important to note that there are no changes required to the DrawShape method or its class whenever a new shape is introduced.

Of course, there is an obvious drawback to the code in Listing 3–2. It is more complex and less intuitive than the code in Listing 3–1. However, these problems are not insurmountable—given time, the latter can become more intuitive than the former.

A key objective in SoC is to limit dependencies as far as is possible and, where a dependency must exist, abstract it away so that the client code is protected from changes. Code that is too interdependent is hard to maintain because a single change can break innumerable parts. The worst kind of code dependency is a cyclic dependency, whereby two methods, or two classes, are mutually dependent on each other.

In order to solve the problem of cyclic dependencies, we must ensure that dependencies are properly *directed*. In other words, that the code forms a hierarchy from bottom to top, with code at higher levels dependent on code at lower levels. Figure 3–1 illustrates this using the MVVM architecture used in this book.

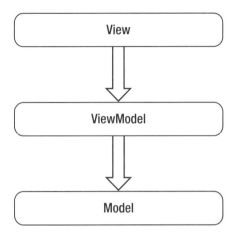

Figure 3–1. *MVVM layers with arrows depicting the dependency direction*

The view has no knowledge of the model. Instead, it acquires everything it needs from the ViewModel. In turn, the ViewModel acquires everything it needs from the model, decorating the data and operations with interfaces that the view can understand and utilize. Changes in the view are entirely irrelevant to the model, which has no concept of the existence of the view. Changes in the model are mitigated by the ViewModel, which the view uses exclusively. Ideally, the view assembly will not even include a reference to the model assembly, such is the separation afforded by the ViewModel.

Partitioning Dependencies with Assemblies

Assemblies form natural boundaries around code. They neatly encapsulate a subsystem of interrelated classes and are easily reused. While it is viable to use a single assembly for an application, this can lead to a confusing mixture of code types. In a WPF or Silverlight application, mixing XAML files with code (.cs or .vb) files is indicative of an underlying structural problem.

It is often more advisable to split the functionality of an application into more manageable pieces and decide where the dependencies occur. In order to replicate the MVVM layers in Figure 3–1, start up Visual Studio 2010 and create a new solution with a WPF application or Silverlight application as the project type. Then add two class libraries: one called Model and one called ViewModel. The result should look something like Figure 3–2 in Solution Explorer.

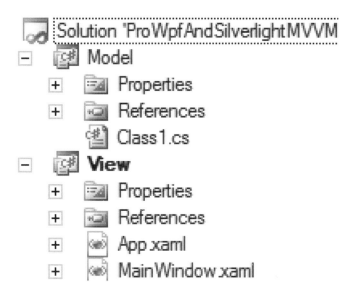

Figure 3–2. The Model, View, and ViewModel assemblies in Solution Explorer

As you can see, these are default assemblies, and the View project is set as the start-up project; the entry point to the application. However, the assemblies currently do not reference each other. Right-click on the View project and select "Add Reference…" to select the ViewModel project, as shown in Figure 3–3.

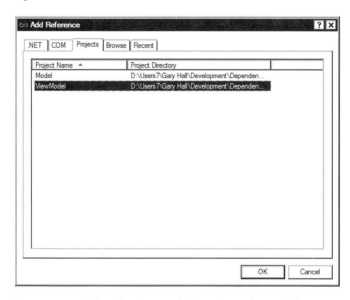

Figure 3–3. Adding the ViewModel as a dependency of the View

Once the ViewModel has been set as a dependency of the View, go ahead and repeat the process with the ViewModel project—this time setting the Model project as the dependency—as shown in Figure 3–4. Effectively, the three projects are in a chain with the View at the top, the Model at the bottom, and the ViewModel in between.

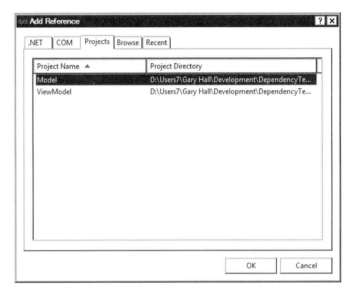

Figure 3–4. *Adding the Model as a dependency of the ViewModel*

In a general sense, the model is not dependent on either the view or the ViewModel. It sits alone and is isolated from them both, as models should be. The ViewModel depends on the model but not the view, and the view depends on the ViewModel and not the model. This is a typical starting point for most MVVM applications.

It is not entirely necessary to split the three component parts into their own assemblies, but it makes sense to do this most of the time. The three can happily coexist in the one assembly—there are no technical reasons why this would not work. The problem comes with human fallibility. Even with the best intentions, the fact that the view will be able to access the model classes is likely to lead to shortcutting past the ViewModel at some point. The term middleman generally has a negative connotation, but not in this case. The ViewModel is a middleman that should not be bypassed.

MVVM Alternatives

Smaller software products, such as trivial in-house tools or proof-of-concept prototypes, rarely require a framework in order to be functional, and the development effort required to set up MVVM can be a drain on time better spent solving the real problems. Thus, it is sometimes useful to develop to another style, using just code behind of XAML documents or a more trivial separation of model and view. Of course, these options are for smaller projects, and they both have their significant drawbacks. MVVM may be better suited to your particular needs.

■ **Tip** You may wish to develop a simple prototype using one of the two methods outlined here and then refactor it to a full MVVM architecture later. This can be especially useful when trying to persuade management that WPF and/or Silverlight are mature enough for production code—some companies believe change is expensive!

XAML Code Behind

Figure 3–5 displays the view uniting the XAML markup and the application code into one assembly. This is the simplest and quickest solution, but it is not suitable for anything other than the most trivial of applications.

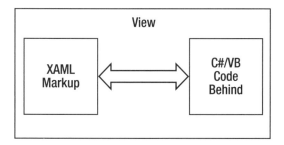

Figure 3–5. The view amalgamates the XAML markup and the application code into one assembly

Each XAML `Window`, `Page`, or `UserControl` has its own code-behind file, which can be used to hook into the click events of buttons and so forth. In these event handlers, you can do any heavy-lifting that is applicable to the program, such as connecting to databases, writing to files, and performing financial calculations. There is nothing wrong with this design, up to a point. Identifying the juncture where something more scalable and robust is required is an art intended for the pragmatic programmer. When introducing a new feature proves more difficult than it really should be, or there are numerous bugs introduced due to a lack of code clarity, it is likely time to switch to an alternative design.

Figure 3–6 shows a screenshot from a very simple application that takes as input a port number from the user and, when the Check Port button is clicked, displays a message box informing the user whether the port is open or closed.

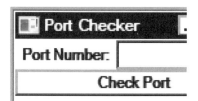

Figure 3–6. A trivial application to check whether a port on the local machine is open

It is so simple that it took about 10 minutes to write—it would have taken at least twice that if an MVVM architecture was used. Listing 3–3 shows the XAML code, and Listing 3–4 shows its corresponding code-behind file.

Listing 3–3. XAML that Constructs the Port Checker User Interface

```xml
<Window x:Class="ProWpfAndSilverlightMVVM.MainWindow"
        xmlns="http://schemas.microsoft.com/winfx/2006/xaml/presentation"
        xmlns:x="http://schemas.microsoft.com/winfx/2006/xaml"
        Title="Port Checker" Height="100" Width="200">
    <StackPanel Orientation="Vertical">
        <StackPanel Orientation="Horizontal">
            <Label Content="Port Number:" />
            <TextBox Name="portNumber" Width="95" />
        </StackPanel>
        <Button Content="Check Port" Click="CheckPortClick" />
    </StackPanel>
</Window>
```

Listing 3–4. The Code Behind that Responds to the Check Port Button

```csharp
using System.Net.Sockets;
…
public partial class MainWindow : Window
{
    public MainWindow()
    {
        InitializeComponent();
    }

    private void CheckPortClick(object sender, RoutedEventArgs e)
    {
        int portNumberInt = -1;

        if (int.TryParse(portNumber.Text, out portNumberInt))
        {
            Socket sock = new Socket(AddressFamily.InterNetwork, SocketType.Stream,
ProtocolType.Tcp);
            try
            {
                sock.Connect(System.Net.Dns.GetHostName(), portNumberInt);
                if (sock.Connected)
                {
                    MessageBox.Show("This port is closed :(");
                }
            }
            catch (SocketException ex)
            {
                if (ex.SocketErrorCode == SocketError.ConnectionRefused)
                {
                    MessageBox.Show("This port is open =D");
                }
            }
            finally
            {
                sock.Close();
            }
        }
```

```
        else
        {
            // invalid port number entered
            MessageBox.Show("Sorry, the port number entered is not valid.");
        }
    }
}
```

This code is already a little bit muddled, but it is acceptable as long as the application is fairly static and does not require many future features. If someone requested that it accepts a hostname or IP address, as well as a port, so that remote ports could be queried, perhaps that would be the limit of this code's utility.

If someone requested that it list all of the open ports on a machine, I would be tempted to move to the next stage, which is a separate model and view.

Model View

If the work required in the model is more involved than updating a database row or displaying the result of a simple mathematical equation, you may wish to decouple the model from the view but omit the ViewModel. The model will then perform two tasks in one: both model and ViewModel. Figure 3–7 shows the view and model split into two assemblies.

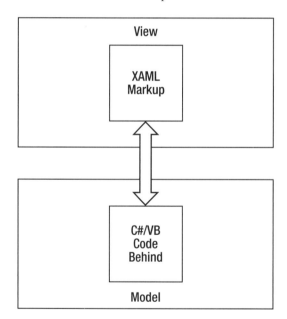

Figure 3–7. The view and model are split into two assemblies

Rather than having the purity of a model, which only solves the software problem at hand, the model realizes that it is to be consumed by a WPF or Silverlight view, and includes specific ViewModel code: commands, bindable properties and collections, validation, and so forth.

This architecture is actually quite scalable and will suffice for many in-house tools and prototypes. Its main problem is the confusion between model and ViewModel, which will naturally introduce problems as the code is trying to serve two purposes at once.

Let's take the Port Checker example and extend it to list all of the open ports on a given machine but use a separate model and view to achieve this goal.

The application takes as input a machine name or an IP address. In Figure 3–8, the IP address of the localhost has been entered and the Check Ports button has been clicked.

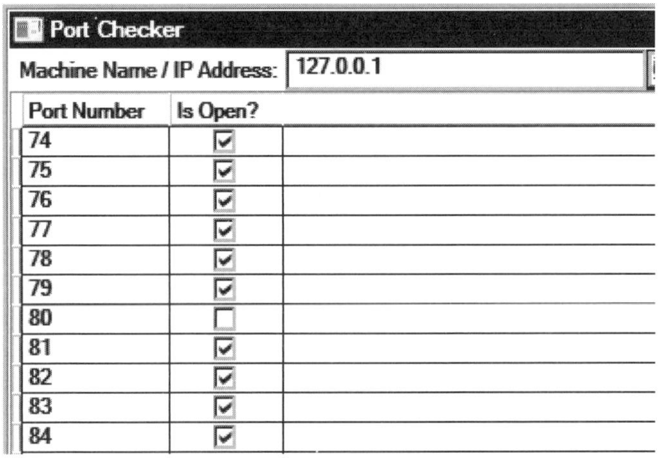

Figure 3–8. *Extended Port Checker application, which checks the state of multiple ports*

The DataGrid shown lists a port number and the port's status in a CheckBox. The port's status is a three-state value: open (checked), closed (unchecked), and indeterminate (filled). We will see how the model provides this value later. As you can see, port 80 is currently closed on my machine—which makes sense as I have a web server bound to that port.

Listing 3–5 displays the XAML code for this window. There is nothing particularly remarkable about this code; it is fairly self-explanatory. It is sufficient to note that the "Is Open?" column is bound only one way because this field is read-only. We cannot uncheck a port to close it or check a port to open it.

Listing 3–5. *XAML Code for the Port Checker*

```
<Window x:Class="PortChecker.View.MainWindow"
        xmlns="http://schemas.microsoft.com/winfx/2006/xaml/presentation"
        xmlns:x="http://schemas.microsoft.com/winfx/2006/xaml"
        Title="Port Checker" Height="350" Width="525">
    <DockPanel>
        <StackPanel Orientation="Horizontal" DockPanel.Dock="Top">
            <Label Content="Machine Name / IP Address:" />
            <TextBox Width="200" Name="machineNameOrIpAddress" />
            <Button Content="Check Ports" Click="CheckPortsClick" />
        </StackPanel>
        <DataGrid Name="ports" AutoGenerateColumns="False">
            <DataGrid.Columns>
                <DataGridTextColumn Header="Port Number" Binding="{Binding Number}" />
                <DataGridCheckBoxColumn Header="Is Open?" Binding="{Binding Mode=OneWay,↵
Path=IsOpen}" IsReadOnly="True" IsThreeState="True" />
            </DataGrid.Columns>
```

```
            </DataGrid>
        </DockPanel>
</Window>
```

The code behind this XAML file is very simple indeed. In fact, it is boiled down to just a single method—the click handler for the Check Ports button. Listing 3–6 shows that it is very simple in comparison to the previous Port Checker's code behind, despite the application becoming significantly more complex.

Listing 3–6. The Code Behind for the Check Ports Button's Click Event Handler

```
private void CheckPortsClick(object sender, RoutedEventArgs e)
{
    PortChecker.Model.PortChecker portChecker = new PortChecker.Model.PortChecker();

    portChecker.ScanPorts(machineNameOrIpAddress.Text);

    ports.ItemsSource = portChecker.Ports;
}
```

So, the button handler merely:

- constructs a PortChecker object

- requests that the PortChecker scans the ports on the machine name or IP address that the user has entered into the text box

- sets the PortChecker object's Ports property as the DataGrid's ItemsSource

It is clear that the heavy-duty port-scanning code has been moved into a dedicated object: the PortChecker, which is part of a separate PortChecker.Model namespace. Listing 3–7 shows the model code for the PortChecker.

Listing 3–7. The Model Code for the PortChecker

```
using System.Collections.ObjectModel;
using System.Net;
using System.Net.Sockets;

namespace PortChecker.Model
{
    public class PortChecker
    {
        public PortChecker()
        {
            Ports = new ObservableCollection<Port>();
        }

        public ObservableCollection<Port> Ports
        {
            get;
            private set;
        }

        public void ScanPorts(string machineNameOrIPAddress)
        {
```

```
            if (!IPAddress.TryParse(machineNameOrIPAddress, out ipAddress))
            {
                // assume machine name
                IPHostEntry hostEntry = Dns.GetHostEntry(machineNameOrIPAddress);
                if (hostEntry.AddressList.Count() > 0)
                {
                    ipAddress = hostEntry.AddressList[0];
                }
            }

            for (int currentPort = 1; currentPort <= 100; ++currentPort)
            {
                TestPort(currentPort);
            }
        }

        private void TestPort(int currentPort)
        {
            Socket socket = new Socket(AddressFamily.InterNetwork, SocketType.Stream,↩
ProtocolType.Tcp);
            try
            {
                socket.Connect(ipAddress, currentPort);
                if (socket.Connected)
                {
                    Ports.Add(new Port(currentPort, false));
                }
            }
            catch (SocketException ex)
            {
                Ports.Add(new Port(currentPort, ex.SocketErrorCode ==↩
SocketError.ConnectionRefused));
            }
            catch (Exception)
            {
                Ports.Add(new Port(currentPort, null));
            }
            finally
            {
                socket.Close();
            }
        }

        private IPAddress ipAddress;
    }
}
```

The PortChecker is rather limited. It is hardcoded to scan only the first hundred ports, it sets the port to an indeterminate state if there is an exception that it does not recognize, and it only performs minimal validation on the user's input. However, all of these details are self contained and can be changed without touching the view code. As long as the PortChecker's public interface remains constant, any changes can be made to this code without breaking the view.

This is where most WPF and Silverlight examples end: with a model and a view separated into two parts. The model, as in this example, makes use of the ObservableCollection or

INotifyPropertyChanged—it may even expose some commands. However, these are in addition to performing its primary duty, which is solving the domain problem. As we will see throughout this book, whenever code is tasked with more than one duty, its quality, comprehensibility, and (critically) deadlines suffer.

The Model

The model is the system that concentrates solely on solving a particular problem with a software solution. At all times, it should be completely ignorant of the context in which it will be used—as part of an ASP.Net application, a Windows Forms application, a Silverlight application, and so forth. It is common practice that the most business-aware software engineers are given the task of implementing the domain model, using object-oriented best practices to create a scalable, yet manageable, software solution.

Some of these practices are idiomatic and followed because of the belief that they are worth the effort further down the line. Others are axiomatic and are followed because their benefits make intuitive sense in any software context. We will explore a few of these principles here because a clean model implementation is a very important part of all professional software, not only in WPF and Silverlight applications.

■ **Note** These principles are more than suggestions, but they are not quite laws (although one of them claims to be law!) Being principled and sticking to best practices is a laudable aim that will pay dividends over the lifetime of a software product. However, do not be afraid to be pragmatic and contravene any of them at any time. Just be prepared to justify yourself if required.

Encapsulation

Encapsulation is synonymous with the concept of information hiding; encapsulation is the method used to hide information. The goal of many best practices is to maintain encapsulation and protect information from prying eyes. In code, information is formed by the classes and their public methods, properties, fields, and constructors. Some of this data is read-only, whereas some of the data is also writeable. If the data within a class is writeable directly, this can be indicative of an underlying problem. Listing 3–8 exemplifies this.

Listing 3–8. Promoting an Email Address to Its Own Class

```
public class EmailAddress
{
    public string emailAddressString;
}
```

This trivial example is a naive first attempt to encapsulate the concept of an EmailAddress in its own class. There is nothing wrong with such an undertaking—in fact, it is commendable—but the implementation is flawed.

The underlying string representation is publically writeable, and, because of this, there is no guarantee that any EmailAddress instance is in a valid state. The string could literally contain anything. Encapsulation attempts to hide the implementation details away so that the user of the class has no knowledge of how the email address is internally represented. Let's look at a second attempt, which is displayed in Listing 3–9.

Listing 3–9. A Second Attempt at an Email Address Class

```
public class EmailAddress
{
    private string emailAddressString;

    public EmailAddress(string emailAddress)
    {
        emailAddressString = emailAddress;
    }
}
```

Now, the email address' underlying representation—a string—is hidden from view.

This extends to all elements of classes, including methods and constructors, and even the classes themselves. This implementation is still flawed and requires further refactoring which will be performed later.

Don't Repeat Yourself (DRY)

One of the cardinal sins in writing software is code duplication. If you have written the same piece of code more than twice, and that piece of code needs to change, you have already doubled your maintenance effort. What is worse, if you do not remember the second instance of the code, you have then introduced a bug into the application. Vigilance is required at all times to ensure that repeated code is factored out into its own method that can then be reused as many times as is required, with only one place that needs maintaining.

Sometimes, of course, the patterns are slightly more difficult to spot and may require parameterizing the resultant factored method. Listing 3–10 exemplifies this.

Listing 3–10. A Method that Repeats Itself

```
public IDictionary<Area, Money> CalculatePrimaryAreaSalesTotals(IEnumerable<Sale> sales)
{
    IDictionary<Area, Money> areaSalesTotals = new Dictionary<Area, Money>();

    foreach(Sale sale in sales)
    {
        if(sale.Area == Area.NorthAmerica)
        {
            areaSalesTotals[Area.NorthAmerica] += sale.Value;
        }
    }

    foreach(Sale sale in sales)
    {
        if(sale.Area == Area.WesternEurope)
        {
            areaSalesTotals[Area.WesternEurope] += sale.Value;
        }
    }
    return areaSalesTotals;
}
```

The two loops in this method are redundant—only one would suffice. Their underlying intent is to total the sales in a single Area, which is probably quite a common scenario. Even if it is not a common scenario, this loop can be factored out into its own method, eliminating the maintenance effort should the CalculatePrimaryAreaSalesTotals method change in the future. The factored method and the rewritten CalculatePrimaryAreaSalesTotals method are shown in Listing 3–11.

Listing 3–11. The Refactored Method No Longer Duplicates Code

```
public IDictionary<Area, Money> CalculatePrimaryAreaSalesTotals(IEnumerable<Sale> sales)
{
    IDictionary<Area, Money> areaSalesTotals = new Dictionary<Area, Money>();

    areaSalesTotals[Area.NorthAmerica] = CalculateAreaSalesTotal(sales, Area.NorthAmerica);
    areaSalesTotals[Area.WesternEurope] = CalculateAreaSalesTotal(sales,↵
 Area.WesternEurope);

    return areaSalesTotals;
}

private Money CalculateAreaSalesTotal(IEnumerable sales, Area area)
{
    Money salesTotals = 0;
    foreach(Sale sale in sales)
    {
        if(sale.Area == area)
        {
            salesTotals += sale.Value;
        }
    }
    return salesTotals;
}
```

The newly implemented method does exactly what the original loop did, but it is more generic thanks to the Area parameter that is supplied. The intent is the same, but this code is reusable wherever an area's sales total is required. The method can then be written without impacting the code where it is used. For instance, it may be preferable to rewrite the method using IEnumerable extension methods, as shown in Listing 3–12.

Listing 3–12. The CalculateAreaSalesTotals Method Rewritten

```
private Money CalculateAreaSalesTotal(IEnumerable<Sale> sales, Area area)
{
        return sales.Sum(sale => new decimal?(sale.Area == area ? sale.Value : null));
}
```

Without having to alter any of the code locations that use this method, its internal implementation has been rewritten. What is not possible without external changes is editing the method's interface. For example, if the method was to return an alternative object, rather than a Money instance, the choices would be either ensure that the new return value could be implicitly cast to a Money object, or change all of the individual invocations of this method.

You Ain't Gonna Need It (YAGNI)

This is a colloquial way of saying "implement only what you need, nothing more." Read requirements carefully and pay attention to the context of the problem domain. Sometimes, a class's name is so evocative that it conjures up all sorts of cool and interesting possibilities, most of which may be completely unnecessary. Try to avoid the temptation to include anything that is superfluous to the requirements.

Refer back to the `EmailAddress` class in Listing 3–9. Two side-effects occurred as a result of hiding the underlying representation in this example:

- The email address can never be edited once constructed—it is *immutable*

- The email address can no longer be read as a string

Depending on the requirements for the email address, we may wish to develop this further. Perhaps the only requirement for an email address is to use it for validation purposes. For this, Listing 3–13 will suffice. Perhaps we wish to compare email addresses for logical equality, in which case Listing 3–14 is more appropriate.

Listing 3–13. An EmailAddress Class for Validating Email Addresses

```
public class EmailAddress
{
    private string emailAddressString;
    private Regex validEmailAddressRegex = new Regex("…");

    public EmailAddress(string emailAddress)
    {
        emailAddressString = emailAddress;
    }

    public bool IsValid
    {
        get
        {
            return validEmailAddressRegex.IsMatch(emailAddressString);
        }
    }
}
```

Listing 3–14. An EmailAddress Class for Email Address Comparison

```
public class EmailAddress
{
    private string emailAddressString;

    public EmailAddress(string emailAddress)
    {
        emailAddressString = emailAddress;
    }

    public override bool Equals(EmailAddress otherEmailAddress)
    {
        return emailAddressString.Equals(otherEmailAddress.emailAddressString, ↵
    StringComparison.InvariantCultureIgnoreCase);
    }
}
```

As you can see, the two implementations serve very different purposes. There would be no need to include this behavior if it was not necessary to solve part of the domain problem. Conversely, both of these implementations may be required and could be aggregated into one class. It is critical that only classes or methods that are directly addressing the problem at hand are implemented.

■ **Tip** The `EmailAddress` class in Listing 3–14 should probably also overload the equality operator (==). Microsoft's guidelines for overriding the Equals() method suggests that "when a type is immutable … overloading operator == to compare value equality instead of reference equality can be useful because … they can be considered the same as long as they have the same value."

The Law of Demeter

The Law of Demeter—sometimes referred to as the Principle of Least Knowledge—is designed to stringently promote loose coupling. The fact that it is called a law implies bad things will happen for transgressions against Demeter, but this is where a delicate balancing of code purity and circumstantial practicality is required. If your zeal for enforcing the Law of Demeter results in a missed milestone, unfulfilled iteration, or, at worst, a delayed product delivery, perhaps it is time to consider a more pragmatic approach. That said, the Law of Demeter protects encapsulation and has a positive impact on maintainability.

The Law of Demeter states that a given method of an object may only access the public properties, methods, or fields of certain objects available to it. Those objects that are:

- the object to which the method belongs and its fields, properties, and methods

- the parameters that are passed to the method

- constructed within the method

While this might be intuitive enough, the restriction comes when you try to access a property that is further down the object graph. For clarity, Listing 3–15 shows a method that breaks the Law of Demeter.

Listing 3–15. A method that Breaks the Law of Demeter

```
public void PrintReceipt(IEnumerable<StockKeepingUnit> purchases)
{
    Money subTotal = 0;
    Money salesTax = 0;
    Money total = 0;
    foreach(StockKeepingUnit sku in purchases)
    {
        this.ReceiptPrinter.AddLine(sku.Product.Name + ``: `` + sku.Price);

        subTotal += sku.Price;
        salesTax += this.CurrentLocale.Taxes.SalesTaxPercentage * sku.Price;
        total = subTotal + salesTax;
    }
    this.ReceiptPrinter.AddLine(``SubTotal: `` + subTotal);
    this.ReceiptPrinter.AddLine(``Sales Tax: `` + salesTax);
    this.ReceiptPrinter.AddLine(``Total: `` + total);
}
```

■ **Note** A Stock Keeping Unit (SKU) is distinct from a Product. An SKU is an individual, physical instance of Product that can be purchased. An iPod Touch is an example of a product, whereas a Black 8GB iPod Touch (no engraving) is an example of an SKU.

This method takes a list of SKUs that have been purchased (most likely by a `Customer`) and prints a receipt. There are two instances where the Law of Demeter has been broken: lines 8 and 11.

Line 8 accesses the `Name` property of a `Product`, but the `Product` is part of the `StockKeepingUnit`. A dependency has been implicitly added between this method and the interface of the `Product` class. If the `Product`'s `Name` changes (perhaps it is split into `FullName` and `ShortName`), this code will have to be changed. The second example, line 11, is an obvious and egregious breaking of encapsulation. Not only does it access the `CurrentLocale`'s `Taxes`' `SalesTaxPercentage` property—which would be sufficient to warrant refactoring according to the Law of Demeter—the calculation of sales tax should be hidden away. It is highly likely that sales tax will be calculated all over a model such as this; without implementing the calculation in one location, code duplication becomes a necessity.

For all of this, the first example is still an example of breaking the Law of Demeter. It could be argued that circumventing the problem is not really worth the benefits. In contrast, line 11 should definitely be fixed to look more like what is shown in Listing 3–16.

Listing 3–16. Sales Tax Calculation Refactored

```
salesTax += this.CurrentLocale.CalculateSalesTax(sku.Price);
```

The method now does not need to know of the `CurrentLocale`'s `Taxes` property at all, it merely delegates the calculation to the `CurrentLocale`. If the method of calculating sales tax changes, it changes in one place only.

Test-Driven Development

Test-Driven Development is a key characteristic of agile methodologies, especially extreme programming (XP). However, it has gained popularity outside of XP and is often quoted as a desirable on job specifications. It holds the view that writing a unit test before any production code is beneficial for a number of reasons. Here are just four of the big ones.

Unit Tests Are Proof that Code Works

Without a unit test, developers do not know that the code that they have written works. Sure, they might know that it *compiles*, which is certainly a start. But, they cannot be sure that the code that they have written works unless it is tested. With a unit test in place, you can verify that the code does exactly what was intended. The corollary to this is that *code is only as good its unit tests*—if you have a bug in your unit test, and the test passes, there is likely to be a bug in the production code.

Regression Tests Are Built-In

If you need to rewrite a method, either by refactoring to eliminate redundancy or because profiling has revealed an unacceptable inefficiency, once you have finished reimplementing the method you can run its unit tests and verify that you have not introduced any breaking changes. This makes refactoring almost risk-free and eliminates any excuses not to refactor liberally.

Unit Tests Are First-Class Clients

Before a single line of production code has been written, developers are thinking from a different perspective—perhaps the most important perspective—that of the code's client. They will concentrate almost entirely on the code's *interface*, rather than the details that the client code does not need to worry about. This yields cleaner, more succinct interfaces and helps maintain encapsulation with hardly any effort. Imagine being able to run the code deep within the bowels of a huge subsystem merely seconds after writing it. No need to run that behemoth user interface and contrive some edge-case scenario that makes your code run. Simply run the unit test directly and it executes the exact code required, with the precise parameters passed in. This plus alone is worth the effort of testing first.

Retrofitting Unit Tests Is Difficult

Unit tests are notoriously difficult to write after the production code has been implemented. Start as you mean to go on and you will quickly have tens of unit tests, eventually growing into an entire suite of unit tests that cover even the trickiest of scenarios. Do not be tempted to "put it off until later." Mañana is a synonym for never; write your tests first or you will not write them at all!

Why Many Do Not Test First

There seem to be plenty of reasons that programmers concoct in order to avoid adopting a test-first approach. Thankfully, they are generally fallacious and can be refuted quite easily!

- "Writing unit tests first is too slow"

  This is the most common complaint against testing first, and it comes exclusively from those who have never tested first. It is an argument from personal conviction; the claimant cannot conceive of a situation where writing *more* code could possibly be faster. However, he is failing to take into account the vast amount of time that he will spend in a debug-test-rewrite cycle toward the end of the project. This is the time that you are saving by writing your tests first.

- "It takes too long to run the unit tests"

  This is pure excuse—it really should not take long at all. Visual Studio 2010 contains built-in unit testing facilities and can run hundreds of unit tests in mere seconds. Microsoft Test Manager can manage the lifetime of bugs from reporting through to closing. NUnit works with all versions of Visual Studio, including Visual Studio Express. Unless you are manually executing each individual unit test, or you are so diligent as to have millions of unit tests, running the tests should not take nearly as long as a full recompile of the application.

- "I am paid to *write* code, not *test* code"

  Perhaps there are test analysts in your team who are paid to test code. However, as programmers, we are paid to write *working* code. It is our responsibility to write code that works as per requirements. In a team that habitually writes their tests first, the test analysts will spend more time with the programmer who refuses to test first. In these days where bug tracking is a project requirement, it is not unusual for management to request reports on who is responsible for introducing the most bugs. Ensure that it is not you by testing first.

The View

While the model provides the means to solve the software problem at hand, the view makes this code usable by anyone—without requiring the coding knowledge to use the model. It is required to perform two main roles: represent the data that the model provides and accept input from the user before handing it to the model.

It is important that the view does only these two things, never ceding to temptation by adding business or domain logic.

Data Representation

There are lots of different ways of representing data. User interface—and modern user experience—design is a specialization within the software engineering discipline. However, although some larger teams will have a dedicated UI or UX developer, it more commonly fits into the remit of a generic developer. Just as you may be called upon to create stored procedures in some flavor of SQL, you may be asked to design and implement a user experience. Data representation is a key part of the skills required to design intuitive and powerful user experiences.

If the model (or, hopefully, ViewModel) offers you a list of data to work with, there are many options for how to represent the data contained within. You could use the standard controls available to WPF or Silverlight that handle lists of data—the ListBox, ListView, perhaps even a DataGrid. If you need more control over how data is displayed to the user, you could even create your own DataTemplate and dictate exactly the format that you wish to use for the list. The same applies to individual objects or elements—a string within the model can be represented in innumerable different ways: a Label, a TextBlock, or, if the string is publically editable, with a TextBox. And these are just the obvious examples.

It is also possible to represent a single datum in multiple different ways. Take, for example, a URI to an image: you can use a TextBox to show the path of the URI as a string, a Button which displays a local file selection dialog to change the URI and then an Image control to display a preview of the selected image. You have then used multiple controls which work in harmony to form a user interface.

User Input

It is possible that your application merely reports the status of various objects and the user cannot affect any of the objects directly, but it is far more probable that you will want to enable meaningful interaction between the user and the model. Otherwise, you might as well just print out a physical report!

Events

In WPF and Silverlight, there are two ways to respond to user interaction: with events and with commands (see Listing 3–17 and Listing 3–18). Most controls will support both of these methods of interaction, but it seems more common for events to be exposed—especially in third-party controls.

This is somewhat of a shame, as events are fairly limited in their abilities. Sure, they can be handled elsewhere in the code, but they usually expose very view-specific data through their EventArgs.

Listing 3–17. Hooking Up a Click Event Listener on a Button

```
<Button Content="Click me" Click="ButtonClicked" />
```

Listing 3–18. Handling the Click Event

```
private void ButtonClicked(object sender, RoutedEventArgs e)
{
        MessageBox.Show("Hello World!");
}
```

As you can see, responding to a control's event is simple, but this simplicity should not outweigh architectural organization.

Commands

WPF and Silverlight make extensive use of the Command design pattern. Figure 3–9 shows the classes and interfaces involved in a typical Command pattern scenario.

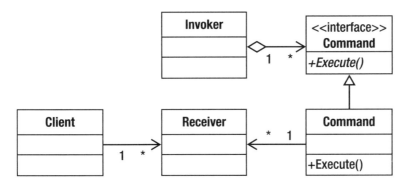

Figure 3–9. UML class diagram of the Command pattern

The goal of the Command pattern is to separate the Receiver from the Invoker and introduce an object that is dedicated to handling any state that may be required by the command.

Commands are examined in much closer detail in Chapter 5.

Data Binding

Data binding was covered in further detail in Chapter 2, but for now let's take an overview of data binding in WPF and Silverlight.

To readers who are familiar with Windows Forms or ASP.NET WebForms, data binding will be a recognized term. To others, data binding is—briefly—the ability of user interface controls to listen to object properties for changes in state and also to enact changes in state on those object properties, without the need for manual synchronization through coding. Until WPF and Silverlight, that was largely theory because data binding in Windows Forms and ASP.NET WebForms was fraught with caveats that prompted many developers to subclass their own controls with more customized data binding.

Data binding is intended to alleviate the repetitive coding effort that would otherwise occur whenever you wanted to synchronize the values of view controls and the values within the model. Even a merely adequate data binding system can be a great timesaver, but a powerful data binding system (such as the system used by WPF and Silverlight) requires a significant paradigm shift—which is exactly what this book addresses!

Separating Model from View

Programmers have seen the value of splitting model and view for a long time. By separating the model and the view, you achieve the first phase in fencing off the disparate responsibilities of major subsystems within a software product.

However, that is not usually enough—the view is not insulated sufficiently from changes in the model and, vice versa, the model must make concessions to enable the view to use its services properly. Contemporary implementations of model-view separation follow a Model-View-X pattern, where the X is a mediator between the two major subsystems.

The Mediator Pattern

Once again, we have an example of a design pattern—this time, the mediator pattern. Figure 3–10 illustrates the mediator pattern.

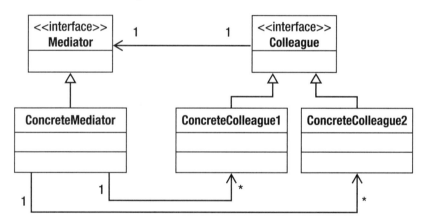

Figure 3–10. UML Class diagram of mediator pattern

The individual Colleagues cannot communicate directly with each other. Instead, they all "know" about the mediator that they should use and communicate *indirectly* through it. The original Gang of Four book on Design Patterns describes the mediator's intent thusly:

> *"Define an object that encapsulates how a set of objects interact. Mediator promotes loose coupling by keeping objects from referring to each other explicitly, and it lets you vary their interaction independently."*

[GoF, p273]

This is exactly the scenario that is encountered in a Model-View-X architecture. The mention of loose coupling is pertinent at this point as it justifies the inclusion of this extra level of abstraction.

Coupling and Cohesion

In software, it is generally accepted practice that a modular design is better than a monolithic design. However, it is true that some modular designs are better than others. There are two specific aspects that are common among good modular designs—loose coupling and high cohesion. Coupling and cohesion are distinct but related metrics used to measure the strength of dependencies between modules and the internal consistency within individual modules, respectively.

Coupling strength is measured from tight (bad) to loose (good). Two modules are tightly coupled when they have strong dependencies between them. If one module changes, it is inevitable that the second module will also change, such is their reliance on each other. However, if modules are loosely coupled, they are insulated from many changes that can be made without a concomitant impact. In a world of fluid requirements with an emphasis on refactoring, this protection is invaluable.

Cohesion, on the other hand, is measured from weak (bad) to strong (good). A module is considered to have weak cohesion if it performs too many irrelevant functions that it should not concern itself with. For example, it is very common for modules to log certain diagnostic messages to the debug console or to a file, but this is irrelevant to the problem that the module is intended to solve. Instead, the logging functionality should be factored out into its own module and such cross-cutting requirements should be implemented as aspects. A highly cohesive module focuses solely on its main intent and does not deviate from it or dilute it in any way.

Figure 3–11 shows a hypothetical graph that plots coupling against cohesion.

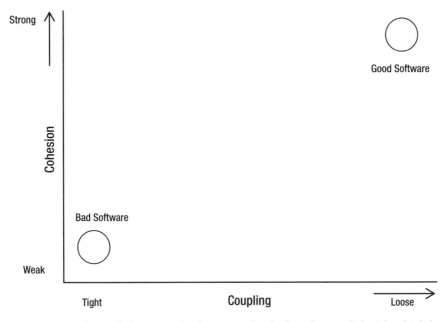

Figure 3–11. *The modules in good software tend to be loosely coupled with a high level of cohesion*

The bottom-left corner of the graph represents Bad Software, which is composed of modules which are tightly coupled with weak cohesion. The top-right of the graph is where we wish to be, producing Good Software with strongly cohesive, loosely coupled modules.

It is worth noting that the term *module* does not specifically refer to an assembly. A module can be an individual class or even a single method. The less that each separate code unit knows about another and the more rigor applied to their focus, the better designed they will be. The end result of all of this is code that is easier to maintain and test in the future.

Other Model-View-X Implementations

Model-View-Presenter (MVP) and Model-View-Controller (MVC) may well be familiar to some readers. However, for others who are new to the concepts presented in this chapter, a summarization of MVP and MVC is useful in order to clarify the reasoning behind model-view separation and demonstrate how it applies to more established .Net user-interface technologies such as ASP.Net, Windows Forms, and ASP.Net MVC.

Figure 3–12 indicates that the code forms a model, the view encompasses the user interface, and the mediator sits between the two layers.

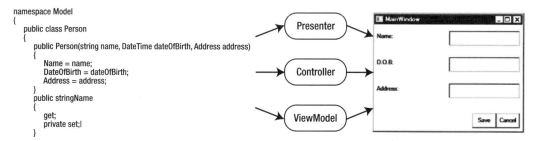

Figure 3–12. The model code, the view user interface, and the different options of mediator

The mediator differs in name and in the minutiae of implementation, but its principle responsibility remains: service input from the user and provide data that the view can use without any extra processing required.

Model-View-Presenter

In MVP, the presenter acts as the mediator between the view and the model. It receives user input requests from the view and enacts changes on the model in response. The presenter is able to query the view for data, which implies that it must contain knowledge of both the view and the model and indicates a dependency in two directions between the view and presenter. However, the presenter is decoupled from the view by holding a reference to the view's interface, rather than its implementation. The view, in turn, references the presenter by interface. In UML, this looks like the illustration displayed in Figure 3–13.

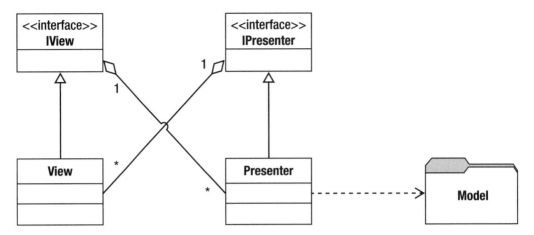

Figure 3–13. *Class diagram showing a generic MVP architecture*

There are a number of notable details in this diagram. Firstly, there will be multiple IViews, ViewImplementations, IPresenters, and PresenterImplementations, typically one per user interface view. The model is referenced by each PresenterImplementation and is represented here by a package. As seen previously, models are often complex beasts that need to be wrapped in some kind of façade for external use. In this example, the implementation of the presenter references the view's interface via *aggregation*, rather than *composition*. Quite often the latter will be enforced through accepting an IView as a constructor parameter in each PresenterImplementation, thus tying the lifetime of the view to that of the presenter. This is a valid option, but, by relaxing the association to aggregation, the view can be switched out at run time.

This architecture is used with both ASP.Net and Windows Forms. In fact, it is so flexible that the same PresenterImplementations can be used with both technologies. All that the developers require is implementing each IView as a System.Web.UI.Page or a System.Windows.Forms.Form, respectively.

Model-View-Controller

MVC has gained popularity recently with the release of ASP.Net MVC. Although it may appear similar to MVP, there are some key distinguishing features that set them apart. Firstly, in MVP, the view receives the requests from the user and dispatches them on to the presenter. In MVC, the controller is the entry point to each request, and it decides whether it will handle some user input or whether it will forward it on to a view.

Another difference is that views in MVP can be stateful, binding directly to the model—although this breaks the aforementioned encapsulation rule. In MVC, views are always dumb and merely display the data provided to them. Although these differences may be subtle, they are important because they dictate the interactions between each layer in the application.

You Gotta Keep 'Em Separated

Whether using MVP, MVC, or MVVM, the key tenet of model-view separation is that all developers on the team must endeavor to maintain the separation. In order to aid the developer in this battle against architectural osmosis, here are some rules as they apply to MVVM:

- The view must not call methods directly on the model or even bind to data on the model. All interaction must be delegated through the ViewModel. Do not reference the model assembly from the view.

- The view must not compute values manually, even if it uses the ViewModel to retrieve the inputs. The computation must be pushed back into the ViewModel (for view-specific calculations) or into the model and subsequently exposed by the ViewModel. This extends to the comparison of values that are exposed by the ViewModel.

- The data exposed by the model must not include formatting information— `string.Format` and such must be saved for the ViewModel or even the view.

This list is by no means exhaustive, but it goes some way to demonstrating how the model and view can be routed through the ViewModel, which, at all times, must act as the intermediary. Any contravention of these rules could start a slippery slope into project paralysis.

Summary

MVVM is intended for projects of a certain scale. If you are a single developer working on a project estimated to take only a week or so, it may be overkill to implement an MVVM solution and the significant infrastructure required to make it work. Each XAML file's code behind can be used to achieve rapid results given a trivial problem to solve, although this can quickly become cumbersome. For projects of a slightly more complex nature, the model and the view can be decoupled. The view then uses the model directly, but the model must make allowances for this and is effectively equal parts model and ViewModel. With the model performing more than one function at once, this can also become a confusing mess.

For more serious software products, a fully fledged MVVM architecture is recommended. This decouples the pure domain problem-solving aspect of the model from WPF and Silverlight's infrastructure requirements. The result is a three-layered system where each layer is highly cohesive— sticking rigidly to its defined purpose—and loosely coupled—containing minimal, abstract interdependencies.

With the ViewModel and model separated, each can be verified with automated unit testing. The code can be tested in isolation without the confusion of a user interface and can fit in with an existing automated build process. The result is a correctly architectured software product that contains less bugs, is easier to comprehend and maintain, and has a much greater chance of being shipped on time and within budget.

CHAPTER 4

■ ■ ■

The ViewModel

In Chapter 3, we looked at the reasons for splitting model and view responsibilities and implementing a ViewModel to mediate between these layers.

Now we'll focus more closely on the responsibilities of the ViewModel, which is, arguably, the most important component of the MVVM pattern, as well as the least familiar. We will look at the overall structure of an application built around MVVM, including a deeper explanation of how each layer operates. Concentrating more fully on the ViewModel, we will examine its lifecycle—from construction to destruction. We will also see that the .NET Framework provides a number of interfaces and classes that can help us produce a rounded ViewModel with enduring utility. Finally, we'll look at effectively wrapping the model while offering the correct services to the view.

First ViewModel

Even with the release of Microsoft Visual Studio 2010, the MVVM pattern has not been elevated to first-class citizen status: there is no project template for creating an application using the MVVM pattern, even as there are seemingly innumerable options for project templates. Even ASP.NET MVC received the honor of a project template.

As we saw in Chapter 3, it is very much possible to create an MVVM project manually by creating a WPF or Silverlight application and adding two class libraries to the project. However, of those two class libraries, the one that forms the ViewModel layer requires extra assembly references so it can use the intermediary interfaces and classes that facilitate view binding and commanding.

Thankfully, this book provides a project wizard that walks through the process of creating a functional MVVM application—using either WPF or Silverlight *or both*.

The MVVM Template Project

Installing the project template is simple, but it requires administrator privileges on your machine. Once it's installed, load Visual Studio and select *New Project,* as shown in Figure 4–1. The project template appears in the Other Project Types subcategory because we will configure it via the wizard, rather than select the language or view type up front.

Figure 4–1. The Model-View-ViewModel Project template in the Visual Studio New Project dialog

Go ahead and select the Model-View-ViewModel Project from the dialog and, as Figure 4–2 shows, you will be presented with a choice of language.

Figure 4–2. Language selection in the MVVM project wizard

The language you select here will be the language that *all* of the generated projects will use. While it is entirely feasible that the model uses Visual Basic and the ViewModel uses C#, it makes more sense for new projects to stick to one language throughout.

The next page of the wizard asks what type of view or view*s* you'd like to include in the solution (Figure 4–3). You can target a WPF application, a Silverlight application, or both, all with the same ViewModel and model code. For now, ensure that you include the WPF view as this example will walk through a WPF application.

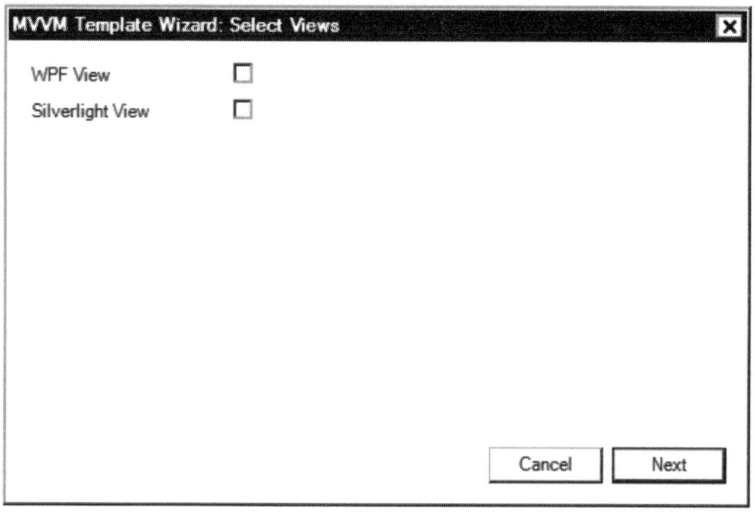

Figure 4–3. The view selection step of the MVVM project wizard

The penultimate page of the wizard will generate a test project for each corresponding project of the solution. We'll cover unit testing in more detail in Chapter 7, so you can safely deselect all of these options, so that the generated solution is clearer (Figure 4–4).

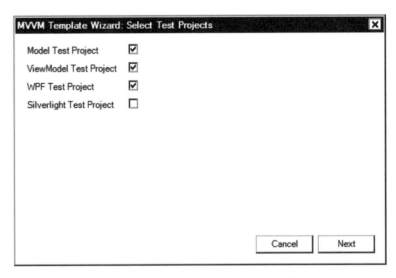

Figure 4–4. The Test Project generation step of the MVVM project wizard

The final page asks whether to generate a skeleton application, which will fill in some model, view and ViewModel code for us (Figure 4–5). Be sure to select this option as we will examine it here.

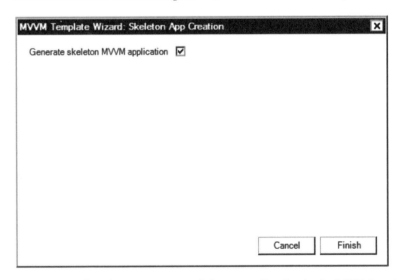

Figure 4–5. Choosing to generate a skeleton application in the MVVM project wizard

Once the final step is complete, the wizard generates your new application. In Solution Explorer, you should have at least three projects that look something like what's shown in Figure 4–6.

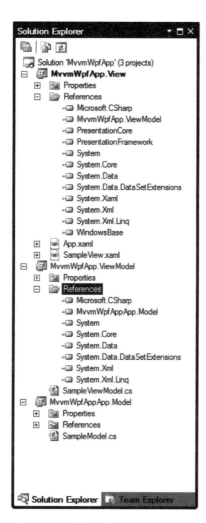

Figure 4–6. The Solution Explorer view of the generated MVVM application

Notice that the ViewModel project has some additional references—notably PresentationCore and WindowsBase—as well as referencing the application's Model assembly. The PresentationCore and WindowsBase assemblies provide interfaces and classes that allow the View to data bind to various properties within the ViewModel.

The View references the ViewModel assembly, while the ViewModel assembly references the Model assembly. It is absolutely essential that you do not add a reference from the View project to the Model. Any such reference, either explicit or implicit, will break the MVVM pattern and may lead to problems in the future.

The Model

Now open the SampleModel.cs file and view its contents. Remember we asked the wizard to generate a simple skeleton application? Well, Listing 4–1 shows what it generated for the model.

Listing 4–1. The Default Model Created by the Project Template

```
namespace MvvmWpfApp.Model
{
    public class SampleModel
    {
        public double CalculateSquareRoot(double number)
        {
            return Math.Sqrt(number);
        }
    }
}
```

This model is extremely simple; it merely wraps around the Math library's Sqrt method, which accepts a double precision floating-point number and returns the square root of that number. Notice that the method is an instance method, rather than static, and that the default constructor is left intact.

This model has no external dependencies—it relies only on the Math library that has been part of the .NET Framework since its inception. While the wizard generated the project to target .NET Framework version 4 (or 3.5 if you ran the wizard in Visual Studio 2008), we could just as easily lower the threshold to .NET Framework version 2.0. The Model assembly could then be used by developers or end users who only have version 2.0 installed.

■ **Tip** If you do retarget an assembly for an earlier version, you will lose all of the functionality present in later versions of the .NET Framework. If you targeted .NET Framework 2.0 for this assembly, you'd have to remove some .NET Framework 4 and 3.5 references. The most noticeable functionality you'd lose is the LINQ library and the IEnumerable extension methods, which can prove extremely useful in a model.

The View

The wizard sets the WPF view to the startup project, so press F5 to start debugging the application. You can enter a number into the text box and click Calculate, and you should see the square root of the number you entered, as in Figure 4–7.

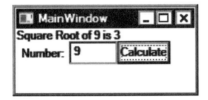

Figure 4–7. The skeleton MVVM application in operation

The skeleton view is almost as simple as the model, because it delegates everything to the ViewModel. The XAML markup in Listing 4–2 shows how simple this view really is.

Listing 4–2. The XAML Markup for the Default MVVM Sample View

```
<Window x:Class="MvvmWpfApp.MainWindow"
        xmlns="http://schemas.microsoft.com/winfx/2006/xaml/presentation"
        xmlns:x="http://schemas.microsoft.com/winfx/2006/xaml"
        xmlns:viewModel="clr-namespace:MvvmWpfApp.ViewModel;assembly=MvvmWpfApp.ViewModel"
        Title="MainWindow" Height="100" Width="200">
    <Window.Resources>
        <viewModel:SampleViewModel x:Key="sampleViewModel" />
    </Window.Resources>
    <StackPanel Orientation="Vertical">
        <TextBlock Text="{Binding Source={StaticResource sampleViewModel}, Path=Result}" />
        <StackPanel Orientation="Horizontal">
            <Label Content="Number:" />
            <TextBox Text="{Binding Source={StaticResource sampleViewModel}, Path=Number}"
Width="50" />
            <Button Content="Calculate" Command="{Binding Source={StaticResource
sampleViewModel}, Path=CalculateSquareRootCommand}" />
        </StackPanel>
    </StackPanel>
</Window>
```

We've made the lines we are particularly interested in bold for clarity. Taking each in turn, let's now see each line's purpose.

The ViewModel XML namespace declaration is the XAML synonym for a C# using statement or Visual Basic Imports statement. This particular namespace references the ViewModel project's namespace within the ViewModel's assembly. By including this namespace declaration, we can reference any of the classes within that namespace elsewhere in this XAML file.

The Window's Resources section makes use of the viewModel namespace and declares an instance of the SampleViewModel class. The x:Key attribute allows us to reference this specific object elsewhere in the XAML – analogous to a variable name. It's important to note that we have declaratively instantiated the SampleViewModel class and effectively assigned it the variable name of sampleViewModel.

This particular variable is then referenced in three bindings within the Window:

- A TextBlock's Text property is bound to the Result property.

- A TextBox's Text property is bound to the Number property.

- A Button's Command property is bound to the CalculateSquareRootCommand property.

This is all that the view contains; if you open up the code-behind file, you'll see that there is no further glue tying this view together. Listing 4–3 proves this.

Listing 4–3. Proof that the View Has the Most Basic of Code-Behind Files

```
namespace MvvmWpfApp
{
    /// <summary>
    /// Interaction logic for MainWindow.xaml
    /// </summary>
    public partial class MainWindow : Window
    {
```

```
    public MainWindow()
    {
        InitializeComponent();
    }
  }
}
```

All of the functionality provided to the View is achieved through XAML's extraordinarily powerful data-binding capabilities, the explanation of which will form much of the rest of this book.

The ViewModel

The final piece of the jigsaw is the most important: the ViewModel. Listing 4–4 is the longest of the three, so pay close attention to the new concepts at work.

Listing 4–4. The ViewModel Code Interacts with both the View and the Model

```
using MvvmWpfApp.Model;

namespace MvvmWpfApp.ViewModel
{
    public class SampleViewModel : INotifyPropertyChanged
    {
        #region Constructors

        public SampleViewModel()
        {
            _model = new SampleModel();
        }

        #endregion

        #region Properties

        public double Result
        {
            get { return _result; }
            private set
            {
                if(_result != value)
                {
                    _result = value;
                    if (PropertyChanged != null)
                    {
                        PropertyChanged(this, new PropertyChangedEventArgs("Result"));
                    }
                }
            }
        }

        public double Number
        {
            get;
```

```
            set;
        }

        public ICommand CalculateSquareRootCommand
        {
            get
            {
                if (_calculateSquareRootCommand == null)
                {
                    _calculateSquareRootCommand = new RelayCommand(param =>↵
    this.CalculateSquareRoot());
                }
                return _calculateSquareRootCommand;
            }
        }

        #endregion

        #region Methods

        private void CalculateSquareRoot()
        {
            Result = _model.CalculateSquareRoot(Number);
        }

        #endregion

        #region Fields

        public event PropertyChangedEventHandler PropertyChanged;

        private double _result;
        private RelayCommand _calculateSquareRootCommand;
        private SampleModel _model;

        #endregion
    }
}
```

There's a lot to take in here, so let's break it down, piece by piece.

The using statement allows us to reference the model code, specifically the SampleModel class that performs the actions we wish to expose to the view.

For readability, the #region directives demarcate the various sections of the class, with the most commonly required public elements at the top and the private fields at the bottom.

The Fields region contains a reference to the SampleModel, to which we will delegate the calculation of the square root. The ViewModel is not responsible for carrying out such a process even if, at this stage, it might appear simpler to implement that functionality directly.

The properties region holds the three properties that are bound from the view's XAML markup: the Result, Number and CalculateSquareRootCommand.

The Number is a simple double auto-property that is both readable and writeable by the view, which is necessary because we want to take the Number as input from the user. Note that the Number is a double, because that's the type the model requires. If the user enters an invalid value, we will see a red border around the TextBox in the view—just one example of automatic validation that XAML provides. Data validation is covered in further detail in Chapter 6.

The `Result` property is also a double, but it is read-only because it has a private setter. The user can't change this value, only the ViewModel can. The view, of course, will read this property and display it to the user. The `SampleViewModel` class implements `INotifyPropertyChanged` and fires the `PropertyChanged` event whenever the value of `Result` changes. We will cover the whys and wherefores of this interface in more detail later in this chapter.

The final property is the `CalculateSquareRootCommand`. For now, it is enough to know that whenever the user clicks the Calculate button, the ViewModel's `CalculateSquareRoot()` method is called. This method is where the model is asked to calculate the square root from the input `Number` and return the value into the `Result` property. Commands are covered in Chapter 5.

.NET Framework Interfaces and Classes

The .NET Framework provides a number of interfaces and classes that the ViewModel can implement or use to integrate properly with a View that is driven by XAML data binding. Most of these helpers are implementations of the *Observer* pattern, which will be familiar to readers who have experience with design patterns, authored by the famous Gang of Four (GoF).

Observer Pattern

> *"Define a one-to-many dependency between objects so that when one object changes state, all its dependents are notified and updated automatically."*
>
> Design Patterns: Elements of Reusable Object-Oriented Software [GoF, p293]

In .NET CLR languages, such as Visual Basic and C#, the Observer pattern is built into the language in the form of events. Events follow a publish/subscribe model whereby one object will fire its event and any objects that are registered listeners will receive notification that the event has fired. The subscriber list is managed internally by the event and there is even some syntactic sugar so that events can be registered and unregistered using the += and -= operators.

The Observer pattern enables loose coupling between the publisher and the subscriber: the publisher has absolutely no knowledge of its subscribers, while the subscriber references the publisher. So, we can say that the dependency is directed from subscriber to publisher.

Without this pattern, if you wanted to be informed of a state change on an object, you'd have to continually check its value for changes. This process is called *polling*, and it's the opposite of *observing*. In order to poll for changes, you'd have to continually loop until a change was discovered and then act upon that change. This can be extremely inefficient, so an event-based model is often preferred.

In UML, the class diagram for the Observer pattern looks like the one in Figure 4–8.

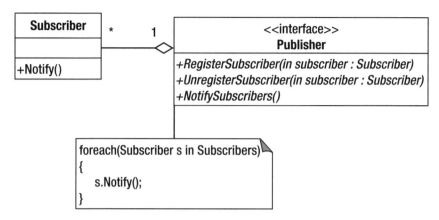

Figure 4–8. A generic Observer pattern implementation

■ **Note** The .NET Framework provides interfaces for explicit Observer pattern implementation—the IObserver<T> and IObservable<T> interfaces—but the event mechanism is an implicit implementation of this pattern.

INotifyPropertyChanged Interface

The INotifyPropertyChanged interface is part of an implementation of the Observer pattern for a specific purpose: to inform subscribers that the value of a property on the publisher has just changed. Without this interface, the subscribers would have to continually poll the properties of the publisher in order to determine that the value had changed.

To implement the interface, you need to include a using System.ComponentModel statement at the top of your class's source file. The interface itself includes merely one single event that must be implemented, shown in Listing 4–5.

Listing 4–5. The PropertyChanged Event

```
event PropertyChangedEventHandler PropertyChanged
```

The PropertyChangedEventHandler is a delegate that accepts a sender object and a PropertyChangedEventArgs instance. As with all interface members, this event must be public. The event's associated arguments class, as with all EventArgs derivations, is extremely simple, merely an immutable wrapper around the event's context—in this case, the name of the property that has changed value (see Listing 4–6).

Listing 4–6. The PropertyChangedEventArgs Constructor

```
public PropertyChangedEventArgs(
        string propertyName
)
```

For those classes that implement the `PropertyChanged` event, it makes sense to write a small helper method that simplifies firing the event. Such a helper method, called `OnPropertyChanged`, is shown in Listing 4–7.

Listing 4–7. Common OnPropertyChanged Helper

```
protected void OnPropertyChanged(string propertyName)
{
        If(PropertyChanged != null)
        {
                PropertyChanged(this, new PropertyChangedEventArgs(propertyName));
        }
}
```

You can then fire the event within the class—or, due to the protected accessor, its subclasses—simply by calling this method with the name of the property that has changed. However, be careful to call the method only if the property in question has changed, as shown in Listing 4–8.

Listing 4–8. OnPropertyChanged Use

```
public string Result
{
        get { return _result; }
        set
        {
                if(_result != value)
                {
                        _result = value;
                        OnPropertyChanged("Result");
                }
        }
}
```

Clients that subscribe to the `PropertyChanged` event specify a local method that responds to a change in the property value. What the client does in response depends entirely on the client in question. Many .NET Framework classes automatically detect the presence of the `INotifyPropertyChanged` interface in order to react to property changes. Windows Forms controls do this and the XAML-based user interfaces, WPF and Silverlight, also automatically detect changes in the value of properties. In this case, their reaction is to refresh the data they are bound to, without having to either poll for changes or be directly informed that something has changed.

`INotifyPropertyChanged` is used throughout the ViewModel to inform the view that some value somewhere has changed and that it should rebind to the applicable data. It is so common that a base ViewModel class can be written to expose the `OnPropertyChanged` method. There are many other useful helpers that can be added to a base ViewModel class, as we will see throughout this book.

It is not ordinarily recommended to implement `INotifyPropertyChanged`, or any other observer pattern interfaces within the model. This is because the model should be used directly by the ViewModel and should not require a further level of abstraction in between. The ViewModel should know that a property has changed in the model simply *because the ViewModel changed the property!*

Observable Collections

It is not just individual object instances that need to inform the view of data changes. Collections also need to inform their bound-view elements that their contents have changed. This does not only include triggering events when a new item has been added or an existing item removed, but also when an item held by the collection has changed. As long as the items contained by the collection implement INotifyPropertyChanged, propagating this change should be relatively simple.

INotifyCollectionChanged

INotifyCollectionChanged is similar to the INotifyPropertyChanged interface, but it applies to collections of objects rather than a single property. INotifyCollectionChanged is part of the Systems.Collections.Specialized namespace, as of .NET Framework 3.0.

The CollectionChanged event uses the NotifyCollectionChangedEventHandler delegate, which accepts a sender object and a NotifyCollectionChangedEventArgs instance. All are shown in Listing 4–9.

Listing 4–9. The CollectionChanged Event, NotifyCollectionChangedEventHandler, and the CollectionChangedEventArgs

```
event NotifyCollectionChangedEventHandler CollectionChanged

public delegate void NotifyCollectionChangedEventHandler(
        Object sender,
        NotifyCollectionChangedEventArgs e
)
```

Unlike a property, whose value is simply different from what it previously was, there are a number of ways that a collection can change. The event will be fired for any of the change types, and the manner in which the collection changes is dictated by the NotifyCollectionChangedEventArgs.Action property—one of the values of the NotifyCollectionChangedAction enumeration (see Table 4–1).

Table 4–1. The Values of the NotifyCollectionChangedAction Enumeration and Their Respective Meanings

Action Value	Action Meaning
Add	At least one new item was added to this collection.
Remove	At least one item was removed from this collection.
Replace	At least one item was replaced within this collection.
Move	At least one item was moved within this collection.
Reset	This collection has changed significantly; consider a full refresh.

When you are firing the event from within your own collection, you need to collate extra data pertaining to the action that has occurred. For example, if new values have been added to the collection, the Action would be Add, the NewItems list would be filled with the newly added items, and the NewStartingIndex would be set to the index where the new items had been added. With collections of a certain size, this is much more efficient than forcing the subscriber to perform a total refresh, which is what the Reset action recommends.

ObservableCollection<T>

All of this is merely a prelude to the class that you will likely use instead of manually implementing the INotifyCollectionChanged interface. Just as you are more likely to use the List<T> class rather than implementing a new IList<T> class, you will probably use the ObservableCollection<T> class for collections that are, well, observable! This class resides in the `System.Collections.ObjectModel` namespace.

The `ObservableCollection<T>` class does all of the heavy-lifting for you: responding to changes within the collection by firing the `NotifyCollectionChanged` event with the correct `Action` and applicable data. The XAML controls that bind to collections of data will automatically detect that the collection you have provided will inform them that changes have been made to the list of items contained therein. However, be advised that, should the individual items within the collection change, you will have to ensure that they properly implement the aforementioned `INotifyPropertyChanged` interface so that individual rows within a list are automatically updated.

As with all generic collection classes in .NET, you may subclass the `ObservableCollection<T>` to constrain it to a specified type. Listing 4–10 shows such a collection that is constrained to `Products` only. Maintaining the Observable prefix informs clients that this collection implements the `INotifyCollectionChanged` interface.

***Listing 4–10.** A Collection that Can Be Observed that Is Also Constrained to a Certain Item Type*

```
public class ObservableProductsCollection : ObservableCollection<Product>
{

}
```

ReadOnlyObservableCollection<T>

All of the methods that edit a `ReadOnlyObservableCollection<T>` are overridden to throw a `NotSupportedException`. This class is useful when you want to disallow a View from adding or removing items from the list but would like the view to be informed of any changes to the list. Initially, these two requirements sound like they are at odds with each other—how can you inform anyone of changes to a list that can't be changed!?

Well, you can wrap an ordinary `ObservableCollection<T>` in a `ReadOnlyObservableCollection<T>` and expose only the read-only collection to the view, maintaining the writeable collection within the ViewModel.

It is advisable to do this whenever the requirements indicate that all views *must not* edit the underlying list. If the views *may* edit the list, allow the view to specify whether it is read-only in the XAML markup.

CollectionViewSource

So far, we have looked at how to propagate changes in properties and collections from the ViewModel to the view, without directly informing the view. Sometimes, you need to provide more functionality with collections, such as the ability to group, sort, filter, or select the underlying data. The `CollectionViewSource` does exactly that: you provide a `Source` collection and specify how you want the data to be displayed.

■ **Note** While there's a case for putting `CollectionViewSource` instances in the XAML markup, the fact that the filtering is provided by the `Filter` *event* means that we should implement this collection wrapper in the ViewModel. If we didn't, we'd have to handle the event in the view's code behind, which we'd like to avoid if possible.

Grouping

Sometimes, it's useful to take a flat list of items and group them by one or more properties. The CollectionViewSource's GroupDescriptions property accepts a list of, predictably, GroupDescription objects. However, this object is abstract and there's only one usable subclass provided by the .NET Framework: PropertyGroupDescription.

Listing 4–11. *Grouping a List of Objects by One of Its Properties*

```
public CollectionViewSource AppointmentsByDate
{
        get
        {
                CollectionViewSource appointmentsByDate = new CollectionViewSource();
                appointmentsByDate.Source = appointments;
                appointmentsByDate.GroupDescriptions.Add(new
                PropertyGroupDescription("Date"));
                return appointmentsByDate;
        }
}
```

Listing 4–11 shows a concrete example of using the CollectionViewSource for grouping. The Source property is a simple object, but it should be an existing list that will be used for the source data. The GroupDescriptions property is an instance of our new friend the ObservableCollection, with the templated parameter GroupDescription. Here, we are adding a PropertyGroupDescription, which accepts the name of a property that belongs to the Source list items.

Sorting

Sorting is implemented in a very similar way to grouping, and, in much the same way, you can specify multiple criteria to sort by and they will be applied in the given order.

Listing 4–12 demonstrates how to sort the aforementioned appointments list, first by location and then by attendee surname.

Listing 4–12. *Sorting a CollectionViewSource*

```
public CollectionViewSource AppointmentsByDate
{
        get
        {
                CollectionViewSource appointmentsByDate = new CollectionViewSource();
                appointmentsByDate.Source = appointments;
                appointmentsByDate.SortDescriptions.Add(new SortDescription("Location",
        ListSortDirection.Ascending));
                appointmentsByDate.SortDescriptions.Add(new
        SortDescription("AttendeeSurname", ListSortDirection.Descending));
                return appointmentsByDate;
        }
}
```

Notice that each SortDescription accepts a ListSortDirection enum value, which specificies whether the sort is Ascending or Descending. The underlying property must implement IComparable in order to be sortable.

IComparable

The IComparable interface defines a single method–CompareTo–which accepts the object that is being compared as a parameter (see Listing 4–13).

Listing 4–13. The Generic IComparable Interface

```
public interface IComparable<in T>
{
    int CompareTo(T other);
}
```

The integer return value has three significant and orthogonal meanings. If it is less than zero, this object is less than the object parameter. If it is greater than zero, this object is greater than the object parameter. If the two are equal, a zero value is returned.

Filtering

The way filtering is implemented in the CollectionViewSource is the reason that it is included as part of the ViewModel, rather than being declared in the XAML markup of the view. The Filter property is an event that requires a FilterEventHandler delegate, which accepts a FilterEventArgs object. Subscribing to this event in the view's code-behind would result in ViewModel logic leaking into the view, something we are at great pains to avoid. Listing 4–14 continues our appointments example and shows only those appointments that are organized within the next month.

Listing 4–13. Filtering a CollectionViewSource

```
private void AppointmentsWithinTheNextMonth(object sender, FilterEventArgs e)
{
        Appointment appointment = e.Item as Appointment;
        if(appointment)
        {
                e.Accepted = DateTime.Now.AddMonths(1) > appointment.Date;
        }
}
```

The FilterEventArgs contains the current Item in the list that is being tested against. If the current date plus a month is later than the appointment's Date, we accept this item and it will be included in the filtered list.

Constructing ViewModels

There's a subset of design patterns whose goal is to abstract the process of constructing an object of a given type or that fulfills a given interface. These are creational design patterns and they are ubiquitous wherever the exact class of an object needs to be hidden from the client code. This is especially useful in the model where you may have a subsystem you wish to expose only through a well-defined interface, but keep the implementation details under wraps. However, there is another good reason to use creational design patterns for the construction of ViewModels—to hide the inherent complexity away from the view.

Let's take a look at the places where you'll need to create a new ViewModel instance and how best to do this.

The Application

Strictly speaking, the application itself is not a view. However, it has a XAML file (`App.xaml` by default) and some useful events that can help us manage our ViewModels.

Listing 4–15. A Sample ApplicationViewModel

```
namespace MvvmWpfApp.ViewModel
{
    public class ApplicationViewModel
    {
        public void Startup()
        {
            // Place application intialization code here
        }
    }
}
```

The `ApplicationViewModel` in Listing 4–15 doesn't look particularly useful right now, but it provides an important starting point. The ViewModel as a subsystem can sometimes require explicit initialization, and an `ApplicationViewModel` can form an intuitive façade for this purpose. Perhaps the ViewModel will just delegate to the model and pass on the message that the application has started. After all, our entry point is the view in a WPF or Silverlight application.

The XAML file for the application (Listing 4–16) imports the ViewModel namespace and declares the `ApplicationViewModel` as a resource, with its own unique key. The reason we declare the `ApplicationViewModel` in this way is so that all other views within the application can access this ViewModel and use the top-level services it offers. Perhaps we wish to store the application name in the `ApplicationViewModel`; there are plenty of places we may want to reference such information and we can do so entirely with data binding as long as we declare the `ApplicationViewModel` in the application's XAML file.

Listing 4–16. The App.xaml file, Containing the ApplicationViewModel Declaration

```
<Application x:Class="MvvmWpfApp.App"
             xmlns="http://schemas.microsoft.com/winfx/2006/xaml/presentation"
             xmlns:x="http://schemas.microsoft.com/winfx/2006/xaml"
             xmlns:viewModel="clr-
namespace:MvvmWpfApp.ViewModel;assembly=MvvmWpfApp.ViewModel"
             Startup="Application_Startup">
    <Application.Resources>
        <viewModel:ApplicationViewModel x:Key="applicationViewModel" />
    </Application.Resources>
</Application>
```

Notice that the XAML has registered a listener for the application's Startup event. A look in the code-behind file will show what occurs when this event is fired (see Listing 4–17).

Listing 4–17. Handling the Application.Startup Event and Passing the Message on to the

ApplicationViewModel

```
using MvvmWpfApp.ViewModel;

namespace MvvmWpfApp
{
```

```
public partial class App : Application
{
    private ApplicationViewModel _appViewModel;

    private void Application_Startup(object sender, StartupEventArgs e)
    {
        _appViewModel = Resources["applicationViewModel"] as ApplicationViewModel;

        if(_appViewModel != null)
        {
            _appViewModel.Startup();
        }
    }
}
}
```

We have a private `ApplicationViewModel` that is set to refer to the instance declared in the XAML file. We could have constructed an `ApplicationViewModel` manually but, as previously mentioned, we declare it as a resource so it can be referenced in all other XAML files in the project.

Finding a resource by key is very simple; we just index the dictionary with the string key we supplied in the XAML and cast the returned object to an `ApplicationViewModel`.

■ **Tip** The `as` keyword attempts to cast the object on the left to the type on the right. However, whereas a normal cast will throw an `InvalidCastException` on failure, if an `as` cast fails it merely returns a null reference. This is why we check that the returned object is not null before calling any methods or properties on it.

Once we have a valid `ApplicationViewModel` instance, we call its `Startup()` method to pass on the message that the application has started.

We could stop here if we wanted, with no further contextual data passed to the ViewModel. Or, we could pass in extra arguments to inform the `ApplicationViewModel` of various relevant view-related states. One common addition would be to pass in any command-line arguments that may have been supplied if the application was executed from the console or a shortcut. The `StartupEventArgs` supplied to the `Application_Startup` event handler contains an `Args` property, which is a string array of the supplied arguments.

The Main Window

It is likely that your `Main` window will be split into a number of different sections, each with its own ViewModel. This avoids the maintenance effort of one monolithic ViewModel with a number of disparate responsibilities that can all too easily become unwieldy. Instead, the main ViewModel will hold other ViewModels that service distinct sections of the view—such as a dedicated `ToolBarViewModel`, `MenuViewModel`, or `TabbedWindowsViewModel`.

You may have noticed that Listing 4–17 did not include a `StartupUri` in the application XAML. Ordinarily, the `StartupUri` contains the name of the XAML view you wish to show on application startup. However, we often require more control over the construction of our views in MVVM, because they are sometimes useless without an accompanying ViewModel. The initial construction of the `MainViewModel` is, then, delegated to the `ApplicationViewModel`, as shown in Listing 4–18.

Listing 4–18. Constructing the MainViewModel and the MainWindow.

```
using MvvmWpfApp.ViewModel;

namespace MvvmWpfApp
{
    public partial class App : Application
    {
        ApplicationViewModel _appViewModel;

        private void Application_Startup(object sender, StartupEventArgs e)
        {
            _appViewModel = Resources["applicationViewModel"] as ApplicationViewModel;
            if (_appViewModel != null)
            {
                _appViewModel.Startup();

                MainViewModel mainViewModel = _appViewModel.CreateMainViewModel();
                MainWindow mainWindow = new MainWindow();
                mainWindow.DataContext = mainViewModel;
                this.MainWindow = mainWindow;
                this.MainWindow.Show();
            }
        }
    }
}
```

We have expanded on the previous example and asked the ApplicationViewModel to create a MainViewModel. It is free to construct the MainViewModel however it likes; the application view does not really care. We then manually instantiate a MainWindow, rather than having it created automatically via the StartupUri. The next line was covered in more detail in Chapter 2, which focused on data binding: this is how we link the view and the ViewModel. The application view has its own MainWindow property. This must be a Window subclass and affects the behavior of the application in a ways that we will explore later. Without the final line we would have no idea that our application was running because the main window would not be visible!

Dialogs

In WPF, dialogs are just ordinary windows that are displayed using the ShowDialog() method. Previously, in Silverlight 2, implementing a dialog involved rolling your own solution. Thankfully, Silverlight 3 introduced the ChildWindow class, which does everything a dialog should.

The example in Listing 4–19 shows the dialog when a button is clicked. In much the same way that the MainViewModel was created by the ApplicationViewModel, the MainViewModel, in turn, creates the DialogViewModel.

Listing 4–19. Creating a Dialog Window

```
private void Button_Click(object sender, RoutedEventArgs e)
{
    MainViewModel mainViewModel = DataContext as MainViewModel;
    if (mainViewModel)
    {
        DialogViewModel dialogViewModel = mainViewModel.CreateDialogViewModel();
```

```
            DialogView dialogView = new DialogView();
            dialogView.DataContext = dialogViewModel;
            bool? dialogResult = dialogView.ShowDialog();
            if (dialogResult)
            {
                // handle dialog OK
            }
        }
    }
}
```

After casting the MainView's DataContext to a MainViewModel—and ensuring that the cast succeeded—we request the creation of a DialogViewModel and construct the corresponding DialogView. Its DataContext is then set and the dialog shown, with code executed only on user acceptance of the dialog.

■ **Note** Adding a ? after a value type implicitly wraps the type in a Nullable<T> object, allowing value types to have a null value. In the case of a bool, bool? indicates a possible tertiary null value, signaling that this bool is neither true nor false, but some indeterminate third value.

Handling Concurrency

This section will presume a certain level of knowledge on behalf of the reader with respect to concurrency. Specifically, it is assumed the pitfalls of race conditions, deadlocking, and livelocking are already known because they will not be covered in great detail. A minimal introduction to concurrency using the shared-memory threading model is included, which explains why threads are sometimes useful as well as the complexities that they introduce.

The problems that are posed by using threads in a WPF or Silverlight application are then outlined before presenting two potential approaches to the solution.

Threading

Applications typically run in single processes on a single machine. In the course of a normal session, the user is likely to run more than one application at a time. For example, I am currently running Microsoft Word, two instances of Visual Studio 2010, and Google Chrome. The Windows operating system allows each of these processes to cooperate by running each for a certain amount of time—called a *timeslice*—before moving to the next process and running it for a little while. This happens so quickly that the user has no idea, giving the illusion of the processes being run concurrently.

Within an individual application's process, there can be multiple threads, which are analogous to processes but at a finer level of granularity. While the process is running, the operating system decides which thread is to be run and for how long. Each thread can progress through any amount of code before being interrupted and a new thread taking over.

In a single processor, single core machine, there is never any true concurrency—the CPU can only ever execute one machine code instruction at a time. Concurrency is an illusion without multiple processors. However, there are plenty of situations where threading can prove extremely useful, most commonly when trying to avoid blocking on a bound task.

Alleviating Bound Tasks

A bound task is a bottleneck within code that would be overcome if there were more of a certain resource. Tasks can be bound on a number of different resources including, but not limited to:

- CPU speed

- Input/Output resources:

  - Network

  - Console

  - CPU Cache

Network-bound code is probably the most common modern scenario for introducing threading into an application. Take a look at Listing 4–20.

Listing 4–20. Blocking on a Network Call

```
using System.Net;
using System.Net.Sockets;

namespace NetworkBlocking
{
    class Program
    {
        static void Main(string[] args)
        {
            IPAddress ipAddress = IPAddress.Parse("127.0.0.1");
            int portNumber = 1500;

            TcpListener server = new TcpListener(ipAddress, portNumber);
            try
            {
                server.Start();

                // This call blocks until a client is received
                TcpClient client = server.AcceptTcpClient();
                Console.WriteLine("Client connected!");
                client.Close();
            }
            catch(SocketException ex)
            {
                Console.WriteLine("Socket Exception caught: {0}", ex);
            }
            finally
            {
                server.Stop();
            }

            Console.ReadKey();
        }
    }
}
```

The code starts a TCP server on port 1500 of the local machine. The call to `TcpListener.AcceptTcpClient()` is called a blocking call. The next line of code will not be executed until `AcceptTcpClient()` returns, which is dependent on when a TCP client connects to that port. This might be immediately or it might be in a few hours, days or perhaps they never connect. While the call is blocked, the application just sits around waiting and cannot do anything else to occupy this dead time. This is where threading helps. The call to `AcceptTcpClient` can be run on a different thread so the rest of the process is free to continue doing something useful. The thread that makes the call will block while the main thread will continue. Thankfully, the framework provides facilities for calling blocking methods asynchronously. The TcpListener class exposes the `BeginAcceptTcpClient` and `EndAcceptTcpClient` methods. The former is a non-blocking version of the `AcceptTcpClient`, so it will return immediately. It accepts a callback delegate that will fire once the call finally returns—whenever a client connects to the listened port. Listing 4–21 shows an example.

Listing 4–21. Asynchronous Network Calls

```
using System.Net;
using System.Net.Sockets;

namespace NetworkBlocking
{
    class Program
    {
        static void Main(string[] args)
        {
            IPAddress ipAddress = IPAddress.Parse("127.0.0.1");
            int portNumber = 1500;

            TcpListener server = new TcpListener(ipAddress, portNumber);
            try
            {
                server.Start();

                // This call returns immediately, but there is no guarantee when a client
connects
                server.BeginAcceptTcpClient(new AsyncCallback(ClientConnected), server);
            }
            catch(SocketException ex)
            {
                Console.WriteLine("Socket Exception caught: {0}", ex);
                server.Stop();
            }

            Console.ReadKey();
        }

        private static void ClientConnected(IAsyncResult asyncResult)
        {
            TcpListener server = asyncResult.AsyncState as TcpListener;

            TcpClient client = server.EndAcceptTcpClient(asyncResult);
            Console.WriteLine("Client connected!");

            server.Stop();
        }
```

```
    }
}
```

This is just one of many ways that the server could listen for connections on a different thread so that the application is not blocked and can continue processing.

In a situation where a process is CPU-bound, the only way to increase processing speed is by adding a new CPU (or core) to the machine. As a quick thought experiment, imagine an application that calculates prime numbers. It accepts no input and prints to console only when a new prime number is discovered. Given that the machine running the application has only a single CPU with a single core and the application is CPU-bound, will threading make any difference to processing speed? The answer is: no. In fact, threading the application is not only redundant, but it adds the overhead that comes with threading as well as the complexities that are introduced by threading. The only way to speed up CPU-bound application is by adding processing power. Threads *may* then become useful, if they could distribute the workload evenly between cores or CPUs.

Increased Complexity

Threading may allow bound tasks to remain functional and responsive, but this comes at a high price. Not only is it much more difficult to understand, the problems that multi-threaded applications introduce are extremely hard to debug. Developers are most comfortable when their code is executed in a predictable order without any odd inconsistencies. Threading means that code can be stopped at any time and run by a different thread before returning to the original thread to continue, which greatly complicates matters.

Shared Memory

The problems occur primarily when there is memory shared between two or more threads, which is mutable. If the shared memory can only be read, there is not much of a problem because all reads across all threads will be consistent. However, if one thread can write to memory, the threads that can read from it may receive data that is inconsistent. This is best overcome by ensuring that any shared memory is immutable, which obviously limits how useful the threads can be. If shared memory *must* be writeable, then access to the data for reading or writing must be mediated so that data remains consistent across all threads.

Race Conditions

If the code in Listing 4–22 is run on more than one thread, it will randomly crash. It is not possible to know deterministically whether the code will throw an `ArgumentOutOfRangeException`. Sometimes it will, sometimes it won't.

Listing 4–22. *Example of a Race Condition*

```
IList<string> list = new List<string>();
list.Add("Hello");
…
// multi-threaded code
if(list.Count > 0)
{
    list.RemoveAt(0);
}
```

The problem is that the list is shared between the two threads. Imagine that there are two threads running the code, T1 and T2. T1 checks the Count property of the list and returns the value 1. At this point, the operating system halts execution of T1 and switches execution to T2. T2 now checks the value of Count and also receives the value 1. T2 continues execution into the if statement and removes the first string in the list. T1 takes over at this point and also continues execution into the if statement because it previously received a value of true from the boolean condition. It also tries to remove the first element of the list, but it has already been removed. The code throws an ArgumentOutOfRangeException and crashes.

To prevent a race condition, a lock can be taken around a block of code, which ensures that access is limited to one thread at a time, as shown in Listing 4–23.

Listing 4–23. *Adding Locks to Prevent Concurrent Access*

```
object lockObj = new object();
IList<string> list = new List<string>();
list.Add("Hello");
…
// multi-threaded code
lock(lockObj)
{
    if(list.Count > 0)
    {
        list.RemoveAt(0);
    }
}
```

The list is now protected from concurrent access. The if statement and the RemoveAt call are considered to be an atomic action that a thread must complete in its entirety before another thread can gain a lock on the lockObj. The question now is, "What has threading gained us except for a headache?" It is extremely important that code is multi-threaded only when there is a proven requirement to do so.

Deadlock

Locks do not magically solve the problems of threads. In fact, they add a whole slew of problems of their own. The most egregious locking problem is that of deadlock. Deadlock occurs when there are at least two threads that try to gain locks on two different lock objects in an order that prevents either from proceeding. Rather than explore this with code, it is much easier to explain with a thought experiment.

Imagine you are sitting at a dining table with a friend. You both have a bowl of rice in front of you, and there are two chopsticks on the table. In order to start eating, either one of you will require both chopsticks. If you pick up one chopstick and your friend picks up the other, neither of you can start eating and you have entered a deadlock situation.

Instead of two people, think of two threads, and instead of chopsticks think of locks. There are solutions to this problem—having more mediation between the two threads and the locks that they require is one possibility—but it adds ever more complexity to a situation that is already difficult to comprehend.

Threading Problems In WPF and Silverlight

WPF and Silverlight introduce their own problems when dealing with multiple threads. Thankfully, the solution is relatively simple and does not require the developer to manage locks manually.

Dispatcher and DispatcherObjects

A vast majority of the classes in the System.Windows namespace inherit from
System.Windows.Threading.DispatcherObject. This includes all of the user interface controls. A
DispatcherObject ties a normal System.Object instance to a specific Dispatcher. What this means in
practical terms is that only the thread that the Dispatcher was created on can access this object. WPF
generally has two threads running—one for rendering and one for handling the UI and application code.
Note that this second thread has more than one responsibility. If you try calling
System.Threading.Thread.Sleep(10000) within the click event of a button, the whole user interface
becomes completely unresponsive for 10 seconds. This is because the same thread that is responsible for
updating the user interface is currently handling the button click event, which has instructed the thread
to sleep. Ordinarily, this is not a problem. However, if your model or ViewModel receives an event from a
thread that is not the UI thread, any attempt to update the UI will fail with an
InvalidOperationException.

In many situations, WPF and Silverlight will automatically marshal the differences between the
threads. Listing 4–24 shows an example.

Listing 4–24. Letting the Framework Marshalling Thread Boundaries Automatically

```csharp
using System.Timers;

namespace DispatcherFailure
{
    public class ViewModel : INotifyPropertyChanged
    {
        public ViewModel()
        {
            _timer = new Timer(5000D);
            _timer.Elapsed += new ElapsedEventHandler(TimerElapsed);
            _timer.Enabled = true;
            _timer.Start();
        }

        private string _message;
        public string Message
        {
            get { return _message; }
            private set
            {
                if(_message != value)
                {
                    _message = value;
                    if(PropertyChanged != null)
                    {
                        PropertyChanged(this, new PropertyChangedEventArgs("Message"));
                    }
                }
            }
        }

        void TimerElapsed(object sender, ElapsedEventArgs e)
        {
            Message = "Timer elapsed!";
        }
```

```
            public event PropertyChangedEventHandler PropertyChanged;

            private Timer _timer;
        }
}
```

For brevity, the corresponding XAML is omitted. All it does is bind a Label's Content DependencyProperty to the Message property of the ViewModel. When a System.Timers.Timer elapses, the registered event fires on a new worker thread. The reason why the Message assignment works is because the framework internally detects whether the correct thread is being executed in order to update the UI. If it is not, it executes the code on the correct thread and neither the user nor the developers need to know about it. However, this does not always work, and there may be common situations where the marshalling needs to be done manually.

Listing 4–25. *The Framework Cannot Always Auto-Marshal*

```
using System.Timers;
namespace DispatcherFailure
{
    public class ViewModel
    {
        public ViewModel()
        {
            Messages = new ObservableCollection<string>();

            _timer = new Timer(5000D);
            _timer.Elapsed += new ElapsedEventHandler(TimerElapsed);
            _timer.Enabled = true;
            _timer.Start();
        }

        public ObservableCollection<string> Messages
        {
            get;
            private set;
        }

        void TimerElapsed(object sender, ElapsedEventArgs e)
        {
            Messages.Add("Timer fired!");
        }

        private Timer _timer;
    }
}
```

In the example in Listing 4–25, the Messages property is bound to a ListView in the XAML. When a new Message string is added to the ObservableCollection, the framework throws a NotSupportedException because the wrong thread is executing. It does not marshal to the correct thread automatically. Thankfully, the marshalling is relatively simple, but organizing which layer should be responsible for marshalling requires some explanation.

Updating the UI

There are a few architectural choices available that facilitate executing arbitrary ViewModel code on the UI dispatcher thread. Both have their pros and cons, and it is up you to decide which. The only constraint is that it is probably best to be consistent within an individual project to avoid confusion.

Executing code on the dispatcher is simple enough, but a reference to the UI dispatcher is needed, and this complicates matters somewhat (see Listing 4–26).

Listing 4–26. Executing Code on the Dispatcher Thread

```
void TimerElapsed(object sender, ElapsedEventArgs e)
{
    _uiDispatcher.Invoke(
        (Action)delegate
        {
            Messages.Add("Timer fired!");
        }
    );
}
```

This code requests that the UI dispatcher call the supplied anonymous delegate on the correct thread. There are a number of overloads for Invoke that allow parameterization of the task's priority, a timeout for signalling that the operation has failed, and parameters to pass into the delegate.

Pass Dispatcher to the ViewModel

The problem with Listing 4–26 is that the _uiDispatcher reference must be supplied to the ViewModel. Dependency injection can be used for this, so that the ViewModel's constructor accepts a Dispatcher as a parameter (see Listing 4–27).

Listing 4–27. The ViewModel Requires a Dispatcher for Construction

```
public ViewModel(Dispatcher dispatcher)
{
    _dispatcher = dispatcher;
}
```

The ViewModel is now free to call Invoke on the _dispatcher at will. The positive aspect of this method is that the details of *what* the Dispatcher is supposed to run are hidden in the ViewModel, which is good. However, the question remains whether the ViewModel should be concerned at all with the Dispatcher. Perhaps it could be aware that some of its code needs to be run through a mediator, but that the mediator should be a Dispatcher instance is problematic.

Imagine trying to unit test this code. Even the unit tests would have to inject a Dispatcher into this, and that would be problematic very quickly. Perhaps an improvement to this example would accept a delegate so that the tests could pass in a mocked method and the view could pass in the Invoke method. However, if more than one overload of the Invoke method was required, more constructors would have to be added, so this is not particularly extensible.

Factor Out View Functionality

An alternative could be to factor out view-specific functionality and have the ViewModel delegate cross-thread calls to the view. This would replicate MVP inasmuch as the ViewModel would hold a reference to an interface that the view would fulfil (see Listing 4–28).

Listing 4–28. Passing the View Interface into the ViewModel

```
public ViewModel(IView view)
{
    _view = view;
}

void TimerElapsed(object sender, ElapsedEventArgs e)
{
    _view.AddMessage("Timer fired!");
}
```

The IView interface exposes a method per operation that requires running on the UI dispatcher. The Window, Page, or UserControl that this ViewModel is bound to will implement the interface (refer to Listing 4–29).

Listing 4–29. Implementing the IView Interface on the View

```
public partial class MainWindow : Window, IView
{
    public MainWindow()
    {
        InitializeComponent();
    }

    public void AddMessage(string message)
    {
        ViewModel viewModel = DataContext as ViewModel;
        Dispatcher.Invoke(
            (Action)delegate
            {
                viewModel.Messages.Add(message);
            }
        );
    }
}
```

The problem with this approach is two-fold. Firstly, we have added a requirement to all views that need to be updated on the dispatcher thread where the framework does not automatically marshal across the thread. Also, the view merely calls back into the ViewModel to do the work because the message is still data bound to the view. The positives are that the view is abstracted away into an interface so unit testing is still possible and the dispatcher does not cross into the ViewModel layer.

Using a Mediator

The best answer lies somewhere between the two previous examples. A mediator can be created that will fulfil all of the requirements while limiting the negative impact. The dispatcher should stay in the view layer, only one implementation is required for the entire view, and the interface is passed into all ViewModels that require cross-thread marshalling.

Subclassing ObservableCollection

An alternative is to internalize the solution so that client code does not need to concern itself at all. To do this, the ObservableCollection is subclassed and furnished with a Dispatcher so that the methods that edit the collection are executed on the correct thread.

Aspect Oriented Programming

Aspect Oriented Programming (AOP) takes the separation of concerns principle to its logical conclusion when dealing with cross-cutting concerns. Cross-cutting concerns are ubiquitous features that must be implemented in multiple modules and end up polluting the focused intent of the module. Intuitive examples include logging, authentication, and authorization. AOP factors out the common functionality into its own module and then applies it in a less-intrusive method than mixing it with imperative code. For example, all methods that need to be logged are decorated with an attribute that implicitly calls the logging module on entry. This attribute could even be applied to the assembly as a whole, with an assembly attribute, and the specific methods to be targeted are specified using a string regular expression.

To solve the UI dispatcher problem, an aspect could be developed that will run an arbitrary method on the UI thread. The AddMessage method could then be decorated with the ExecuteOnUIThreadAttribute (see Listing 4–30).

Listing 4–30. Using AOP to Specify Which Thread Must Execute a Method

```
using System.Windows.Threading;

using PostSharp.Aspects;

namespace DispatcherFailure
{
    [Serializable]
    public class ExecuteOnUIThreadAttribute : MethodInterceptionAspect
    {
        public static Dispatcher Dispatcher { get; set; }

        public override void OnInvoke(MethodInterceptionArgs args)
        {
            if (Dispatcher != null && !Dispatcher.CheckAccess())
            {
                Dispatcher.Invoke((Action)delegate { args.Proceed(); });
            }
            else
            {
                args.Proceed();
            }
        }
    }
}
...
[ExecuteOnUIThread]
```

```
void TimerElapsed(object sender, ElapsedEventArgs e)
{
    Messages.Add("Timer fired!");
}
```

The attribute's static `Dispatcher` property can then be set at application startup. It is probably best that the reference be factored out into an interface as in the previous examples so that the decorated methods can be run in a unit testing environment with no ill effects.

■ **Note** Listing 4–30 uses an Aspect Oriented Programming framework for .Net called PostSharp, which weaves MSIL code into the decorated method.

Summary

The ViewModel is the mediator between the view and the model in an MVVM application. It has a key responsibility that is just as important as that of the view or model, arguably more so. ViewModels should not be mere adapters wrapped around models. They should expose the model's functionality in a way that aggregates its utility into a feature the view can use.

There are multiple options available for developing an individual ViewModel. Choices need to be made as to whether the ViewModel should service a single view—transitively created and destroyed whenever the view is used—or whether the ViewModel maps more closely to an individual model class instance—created on application startup and persisting until the user requests that the application exits.

The .NET Framework supplies a number of helpful interfaces, classes, and collections that aid the creation of a feature-rich ViewModel that can be used by views in a number of ways. These Framework helpers are mainly catalysts for data binding, which is the ViewModel glue to which views… erm, bind!

We have also looked at various methods for overcoming the limitation that ViewModel data must be edited from the same thread that owns the UI components to which they are bound. In many cases, the framework will handle marshalling the changes onto the correct thread, but interacting with the `ObservableCollection` is a classic example where the framework does not come to our aid.

CHAPTER 5

Events and Commands

Events

An event is a programming construct that reacts to a change in state, notifying any endpoints that have registered for notification. They are ubiquitous in .NET generally, and this continues in WPF and Silverlight. Primarily, events are used to inform of user input via the mouse and keyboard, but their utility is not limited to that. Whenever a state change is detected, perhaps when an object has been loaded or initialized, an event can be fired to alert any interested third parties.

Events in .NET

In .NET, events are first-class citizens: they are represented by delegates and declared with the event keyword (see Listing 5–1).

Listing 5–1. Declaring a Plain Event in .NET

```
delegate void MyEventHandler();
...
public event MyEventHandler EventOccurred;
```

The code in Listing 5–1 declares a delegate that both accepts and returns no values and then declares an event that requires a receiver that matches that delegate. Events can be subscribed to using the += operator, and unsubscribed with the -= operator, as in Listing 5–2.

Listing 5–2. Subscribing and Unsubscribing to an Event

```
MyEventHandler eventHandler = new MyEventHandler(this.Handler);

EventOccurred += eventHandler;
EventOccurred -= eventHandler;
```

The event can then be fired by calling it as if it were a method. However, if there are no subscribers to the event it will be null, so this must be tested for first, as shown in Listing 5–3.

Listing 5–3. Firing an Event

```
if(EventOccurred != null)
{
    EventOccurred();
}
```

This calls all of the subscribed handlers. With this brief example, it's easy to see that events separate the source of a state change from the target handlers. Rather than have the source maintain a list of references to the subscribers, the event itself is in charge of this registration. The source is then free to invoke the event, sending a message to all of the disparate subscribers that this event has occurred.

■ **Tip** An alternative to checking the event against `null` is to declare the event and initialize it with an empty handler:

```
public event EventHandler EventOccurred = delegate { };
```

There will now always be at least one handler registered and the `null` check becomes superfluous. This also has the happy side effect of alleviating a race condition that could yield a `NullReferenceException` in a multi-threaded environment.

This is an invaluable paradigm that is used throughout the framework, with WPF and Silverlight similarly leveraging this functionality to provide notifications about user input and control state changes.

Events in WPF and Silverlight

Controls in WPF and Silverlight expose events that can be subscribed to, just like Windows Forms and ASP.NET. The difference is in how these events are implemented and, consequently, how they behave.

WPF and Silverlight do not use plain CLR events, but instead use *routed events*. The main reason for the different approach is so there can be multiple event subscribers within an element tree. Whereas CLR events directly invoke the handler on the event subscriber, routed events may be handled by any ancestor in the element tree.

Listing 5–4. Declaring a Routed Event in WPF

```
public static readonly RoutedEvent MyRoutedEvent =
    EventManager.RegisterRoutedEvent(
        "MyEvent", RoutingStrategy.Bubble, typeof(RoutedEventHandler), typeof(MyClass));
```

Listing 5–4 shows very clearly the difference in defining a routed event. The `EventManager` class is used as a factory for events, with the `RegisterRoutedEvent` method returning a `RoutedEvent` instance. However, there should be only one instance of each event per class, so it is stored in a static variable. The `RegisterRoutedEvent` method's signature is shown in Listing 5–5.

Listing 5–5. The RegisterRoutedEvent Method Signature

```
public static RoutedEvent RegisterRoutedEvent(
        string name,
        RoutingStrategy routingStrategy,
        Type handlerType,
        Type ownerType
)
```

Here's a brief explanation:

- `name`: This is the name of the event; it must be unique within the class that owns the event.

- `routingStrategy`: The routing strategy dictates how the event moves through the element tree.

- `handlerType`: A delegate type that defines the signature for the event's handler.

- `ownerType`: This is the type that owns the event, typically the class that the event is defined in.

The event is then exposed as a CLR instance property, as shown in Listing 5–6.

Listing 5–6. Declaring a CLR Property Wrapper Around the Routed Event

```
public event RoutedEventHandler Tap
{
        add { AddHandler(MyRoutedEvent, value); }
        remove { RemoveHandler(MyRoutedEvent, value); }
}
```

Note that the type of this property matches the delegate `handlerType` from the `RegisterRoutedEvent` method. The `AddHandler` and `RemoveHandler` methods are inherited from the `UIElement` class, which is an ancestor of all WPF and Silverlight control classes. They are used to forward the CLR event add and remove functionality, allowing the routed event to intercept and handle subscribers.

Routing Strategies

The `RoutingStrategy` enumeration indicates to the `EventManager` how the events should travel though the event hierarchy. There are three possible values that can be used, as shown in Table 5–1.

Table 5–1. The Possible Strategies Used for Routing Events

Bubbling	The event starts at the owner class and bubbles upward through all parent elements until handled or the root element is found.
Tunneling	The event starts at the root element and tunnels downward through each control until handled or the source element is found.
Direct	Event routing is circumvented but other `RoutedEvent` functionality is still supported.

The difference between the three options is quite simple. With bubbling, the event is dispatched and starts from the event owner. If the owner does not handle the event (and it very well may not), the event continues upward to the owner's parent control. This control could then handle the event, but the event could be passed upward once more. This pattern continues until a control handles the event or the event reaches the root node and has not been handled.

Tunneling is the opposite approach in that the event starts with the root node and, if not handled there, is passed down to the next descendent that is the ancestor of the event owner. The ending condition in this scenario is when the event is unhandled and arrives at the event owner.

The direct method circumvents event routing for instances in which the direction of an event is irrelevant. However, when using the direct method, you can still use other `RoutedEvent` functionality in your code.

Limitations

Events in WPF and Silverlight are problematic for one very good reason: they must be handled by an instance method on the code-behind class. This means that the event can't be handled in another class, limiting the event-handling code to being written inside the code-behind file. This is much less than ideal because domain-logic code needs to be kept away from view code.

While there have been many attempts to circumvent this limitation with some clever use of attached properties and adapters to force an event to be handled by a separate class, two possible approaches are much simpler to implement.

The first option is to not handle the event and prefer data binding instead. Take a look at Listing 5–7.

Listing 5–7. Hooking Up to the TextChanged Event

```
<TextBox Text="{Binding Source={StaticResource myDomainObject}, Path=StringProperty}"↵
  TextChanged="TextBox_TextChanged" />
```

This is quite a common scenario: enact some logic whenever the TextBox's Text has been changed by the user, but the TextChanged property is an event so we must handle it in the code behind, leaking domain logic into the view. However, as Chapter 2 demonstrated, the Text property only updates the binding source when the TextBox loses input focus—*this* is the real limitation, here. We can request that the binding update the StringProperty as soon as the Text property changes with the UpdateSourceTrigger parameter, as shown in Listing 5–8.

Listing 5–8. Requesting That the Text Property is Updated as Soon as It Has Changed

```
<TextBox Text="{Binding Source={StaticResource myDomainObject}, Path=StringProperty,↵
 UpdateSourceTrigger=PropertyChanged}" />
```

As Listing 5–9 shows, the domain object's StringProperty setter can then perform the domain logic that was originally required.

Listing 5–9. Responding to Changes in the StringProperty

```
public string StringProperty
{
    get { return _stringProperty; }
    set
    {
        _stringProperty = value;
        ProcessNewStringProperty(_stringProperty);
    }
}
```

So, by changing the focus of the problem, we found a viable solution that made the original requirement of responding to the TextChanged event obsolete. But, what if there is no databinding solution? In that case, the code-behind must be used—but only to delegate the request to the ViewModel, as shown in Listings 5–10 and 5–11.

Listing 5–10. Registering the MouseEnter Event

```
<TextBlock Text="Mouse over me" MouseEnter="TextBlock_MouseEnter" />
```

Listing 5–11. Handling the MouseEnter Event

```
private void TextBlock_MouseEnter(object sender, MouseEventArgs e)
{
```

```
    MyViewModel viewModel = DataContext as MyViewModel;
    if (viewModel)
    {
        viewModel.ProcessMouseEnter(e.LeftButton);
        e.Handled = true;
    }
}
```

This event handler does not do any processing of its own—it acquires the ViewModel from the `DataContext` of the `Window` and forwards the message on to it, marking the event as handled to prevent further bubbling. The ViewModel is then free to process this just as it would any other message or command.

■ **Tip** If you require contextual information from the event's `EventArgs` instance, considering passing in just what you require to the ViewModel's methods. This keeps the interface clean, reduces coupling between the ViewModel and external dependencies, and simplifies the unit tests for the ViewModel.

Commands

In Chapter 3, we briefly touched upon commands and the purpose they serve. The Command pattern [GoF] encapsulates the functionality of a command—the action it performs—while separating the invoker and the receiver of the command, as shown in Figure 5–1.

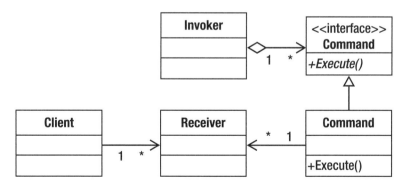

Figure 5–1. *UML class diagram of the Command pattern*

This helps us to overcome the limitations of events because we can fire a command in the view and elect to receive it in the ViewModel, which knows what processing should occur in response.

Not only that, the multiplicity of Invokers to Commands ensures that we can define interaction logic once and use it in many different places without repetition. Imagine a command that exits an application: the exit code is written once but there are multiple different locations in the user interface this command can be invoked from. You can click the exit cross on the top right of the screen, select Exit from the File menu, or simply hit Alt+F4 on the keyboard when the application has the input focus. All of these are different Invokers that bind to exactly the same command.

Command Pattern

The Command pattern is implemented in WPF and Silverlight via interfaces that are analogous to the Gang of Four Invoker, Receiver, and Command interface. Understanding how these entities collaborate will highlight why the default commanding implementations—RoutedCommand and RoutedUICommand—are not entirely suitable for our purposes.

Instead, an alternative implementation is provided that is a better fit for the MVVM architecture.

ICommandSource

The Invoker of a command is represented by the ICommandSource interface, the definition of which is shown in listing 5–12.

Listing 5–12. Definition of the ICommandSource Interface

```
public interface ICommandSource
{
    ICommand Command { get; }

    object CommandParameter { get; }

    IInputElement CommandTarget { get; }
}
```

What should be immediately apparent from this design is that each class that implements ICommandSource can expose only a single command. This explains why we must rely on events much of the time—even if the Control *wanted* to expose multiple commands, the architecture prevents this. With controls, this typically follows the most common associated action: all ButtonBase inheritors fire their Command when the button is pressed. This applies to vanilla Buttons, CheckBoxes, RadioButtons, and so forth.

The Command property is an instance of ICommand, which is covered in more detail later. Controls should expose this as a DependencyProperty so that it can be set with databinding.

CommandParameter is a plain object because it could literally be anything and is specific to an individual Command implementation.

CommandTarget, of type IInputElement, is used only when Command is a RoutedCommand. It establishes which object's Executed and CanExecute events are raised. In the default scenario—where CommandTarget is left null—the current element is used as the target. As we will not be using RoutedCommands, this is out of scope for our purposes.

ICommand Interface

All commands are represented by the ICommand interface, which establishes a contract that each command implementation must fulfill (see Listing 5–13).

Listing 5–13. Definition of the ICommand Interface

```
public interface ICommand
{
    event EventHandler CanExecuteChanged;

    bool CanExecute(object parameter);

    void Execute(object parameter);
}
```

The Execute method is the crux of the Command pattern—it encapsulates the work the command will perform. Here, we can provide the Execute method with any kind of parameter we require, so that contextual data can be passed in and used to customize the command's execution.

The CanExecute method informs invokers whether or not this command can currently be executed. In practice, it is used to automatically enable or disable the Invoker. Reusing our previous example of exiting an application, imagine that a long-running process can't be interrupted and, consequently, the application can't be exited. Unless you provide a visual cue to the user that the application can't currently quit, he is going to be annoyed when attempting to exit has no discernable effect. This is in direct contravention to the Principle of Least Astonishment.

The way around this problem has been established by precedent: the menu item that enacts this command should be disabled and this should be represented in the user interface. Even just graying out the menu item is enough to tell the user that clicking this option will yield no effect. With a good user interface design, other visual cues on the application will indicate that the option is unavailable due to the long-running process.

■ **Caution** In all honesty, disallowing the user to cancel a long-running process is, in itself, contrary to usability rules.

The CanExecute method returns true only if the command is able to fully perform the Execute method. If there are certain preconditions for Execute that are not presently met, CanExecute should return false.

The Invoker is not perpetually polling the CanExecute method to see if the command can (or can't) currently be executed. Instead, the command must implement a CanExecuteChanged event, which serves to notify the Invoker that the command previously could not execute and now can, or vice versa.

Routed Command Implementations

WPF and Silverlight provide two implementations of ICommand: RoutedCommand and RoutedUICommand. Neither directly implements the Execute and CanExecute methods.

■ **Tip** The only difference between RoutedCommand and RoutedUICommand is that the latter has an additional string Text property. This enables the command's binding targets—or the sources of the command, if you like—to display the same textual name. Behaviorally, the two are identical, RoutedUICommand inheriting directly from RoutedCommand.

Figure 5–2 shows a UML sequence diagram showing the (somewhat convoluted) collaboration that occurs when a user interacts with a control, causing it to fire its command.

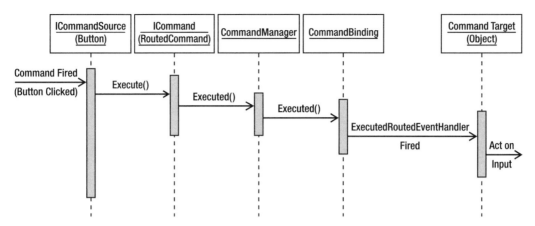

Figure 5–2. UML Sequence diagram showing the execution path of a fired command

There are a number of steps in this process that are useful for the purposes of RoutedCommand but are extraneous to our requirements.

The RoutedCommand calls the Executed method of the CommandManager, which subsequently searches the element tree for a suitable CommandBinding that links a Command with a target handler. The CommandBinding class acts as an association class that facilitates the many-to-many relationship that would otherwise occur between Commands and their target handlers, as exemplified by the UML class diagram in Figure 5–3.

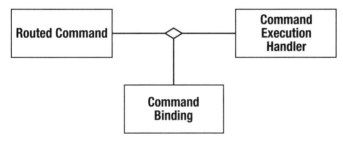

Figure 5–3. UML class diagram showing the relationship between Commands, CommandBindings, and target handlers

However, in MVVM, this poses a number of problems. MVVM commands reside on ViewModel classes that encapsulate the desired behavior of the corresponding View. The ViewModel is merely using the command as a notification system, asking the View to inform it whenever a command is fired. The CommandManager and CommandBinding are a couple of levels of indirection too far for the ViewModel's needs.

Listing 5–14. Attempting to Expose a RoutedCommand on a ViewModel Class

```
public class ViewModel
{
    public ViewModel()
    {
        SaveViewCommand = new RoutedCommand("SaveViewCommand", typeof(ViewModel));
    }

    public RoutedCommand SaveViewCommand
    {
        get;
        private set;
    }
}
```

Exposing RoutedCommand instances—as shown in Listing 5–14—on ViewModels will not work. Currently, the SaveViewCommand's Executed method will be called by whatever ICommandSource this command is bound to. In turn, this will call CommandManager's Executed method, which will scour the element tree for an applicable CommandBinding. This is the problem, the CommandBinding needs to be associated with the element tree. Proof of this is in the static CommandManager.AddExecutedHandler method:

```
public static void AddExecutedHandler(UIElement element, ExecutedRoutedEventHandler↩
  handler);
```

A UIElement instance is required to attach this binding to, which can't be provided from inside the ViewModel. What is needed is a specialized implementation of the ICommand interface.

The RelayCommand

Having established the problems with the RoutedCommand implementation, let's go about solving the problem by implementing a new ICommand. Skipping slightly ahead, the name of this particular command is the RelayCommand.

■ **Note** This implementation is not an original work—it is the implementation recommended by Josh Smith, which is, itself, a simplified version of the DelegateCommand found in the Microsoft Composite Application Library.

Requirements

There are a few requirements for the RelayCommand to fulfill:

- Keep the separation between controls as command invokers declared on the view and the handler that elects to respond to the user input.

- RelayCommands are generally declared as instance members of ViewModel classes.

- The response to a RelayCommand is normally handled in the same class—and, in fact, instance—that hosts the RelayCommand. If not directly there, the handler will be accessible *from* the instance via properties or fields.

- The CanExecute method and CanExecuteChanged event must be implemented and functional as intended: ensure that the ICommandSource is enabled or disabled as appropriate.

- The CanExecute constructor parameter is optional. Without specifying a handler the command should default to true.

- The CanExecute method will similarly be handled by the ViewModel or its constituents.

- Extra dependencies should be kept to an absolute minimum.

- The implementation may be as contrived as is necessary, but the interface should be extremely intuitive to use.

With these requirements in mind, the next step is to consider a potential technical design.

Technical Design

Figure 5–4 shows how the RelayCommand should interact with the ViewModel command target and any ICommandSource.

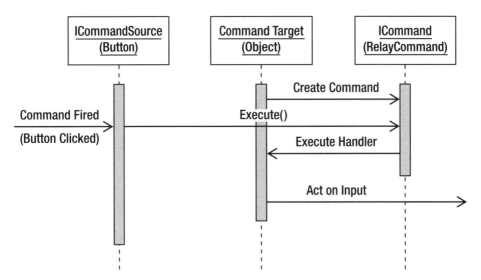

Figure 5–4. How the RelayCommand is envisaged to work

The command target (ViewModel) will create one RelayCommand for each command it wishes to handle. These commands will then be exposed via public properties for binding by the ICommandSources in the view. When the command source calls the Execute method on the RelayCommand, it should delegate the call to its owning ViewModel, which is then free to handle the command itself, or perhaps forward the message on to a more appropriate object.

The interesting code here is in specifying to the RelayCommand which method on the ViewModel should act as the handler. The encapsulation of a method that can be passed as an argument is a delegate, so this is an excellent candidate as a constructor parameter for the RelayCommand:

```
public delegate void CommandExecuteHandler(object parameter);
...
public RelayCommand(CommandExecuteHandler execute)
{
...
}
```

Recall that one of the requirements was that *extra dependencies should be kept to an absolute minimum*. The CommandExecuteHandler delegate is such a dependency that should prompt a refactor. Happily, the .NET Framework provides a templated delegate that will fit the bill perfectly:

```
public delegate void Action<in T>(T obj);
```

Excellent. With the template parameter as an object, this delegate is exactly what will serve as the signature for all command execution handlers.

Next, the ICommand.Execute method is implemented so that it simply delegates the call wherever the RelayCommand is instructed to forward it.

```
public void Execute(object parameter)
{
    _execute(parameter);
}
```

The parameter passed in to the Execute command is whatever was supplied as the CommandParameter on the ICommandSource.

This RelayCommand is not quite fit for our purpose just yet: the CanExecute method is part of the requirements and is not currently provided for. The delegate will be slightly different this time because the handler must return a Boolean.

```
public delegate bool CanCommandExecuteHandler(object parameter);
```

Again, this dependency can be factored out thanks to the framework:

```
public delegate bool Predicate<in T>(T obj);
```

The presence of a CanExecute is optional, so a second constructor is added with this parameter:

```
public RelayCommand(Action<object> execute, Predicate<object> canExecute)
{
...
}
```

■ **Note** In C# 4.0, although default values for method parameters have been added to avoid this kind of method overloading, the default value must be a compile-time constant, so we can't specify a default Predicate<object> that always returns true.

Now we can fulfill the CanExecute method of the ICommand contract:

```
public bool CanExecute(object parameter)
{
    return _canExecute == null ? true : _canExecute(parameter);
}
```

If the _canExecute field has not been specified, we can always execute the command, otherwise we delegate to the specified _canExecute predicate. Another requirement ticked, but the (apparently) trickiest remains.

The CanExecuteChanged event needs to fire whenever the CanExecute method changes its return value. Initially, all sorts of horrible thoughts occur: polling the _canExecute predicate for changes, for example. Thankfully, help is at hand. The CommandManager supplies an event called RequerySuggested, which fires when it believes that the CanExecute method may have changed. Not only that, but the event is static, so the RelayCommand does not have to be further parameterized to accept an instance of CommandManager. This does, of course, introduce a dependency: the benefits of using this approach, coupled with the fact that the dependency is encapsulated in the *implementation* and not the *interface*, makes it a winner.

What is needed is a way of transparently forwarding the registration of the CanExecuteChanged event to an implicit registration of the CommandManager.RequerySuggested event:

```
public event EventHandler CanExecuteChanged
{
    add { CommandManager.RequerySuggested += value; }
    remove { CommandManager.RequerySuggested -= value; }
}
```

Try to see past the syntactic sugar that is provided for events: instead of get and set, they have the event analogies of add and remove, respectively. Similarly, the += and -= are analogous to calling add and remove directly.

This works because CommandManager detects user interface changes, like the input focus moving to a different control, and fires off a RequerySuggested event. This pattern of delegating the CanExecuteChanged event to the CommandManager is implemented by the RoutedCommand class, so the RelayCommand is certainly in good company.

Implementation

Putting all of the technical design details together results in the full implementation of the RelayCommand class shown in Listing 5–15.

Listing 5–15. The Finished RelayCommand Implementation

```
public class RelayCommand : ICommand
{
    public RelayCommand(Action<object> execute)
        : this(execute, null)
    {
    }

    public RelayCommand(Action<object> execute, Predicate<object> canExecute)
    {
        if (execute == null)
            throw new ArgumentNullException("execute");
        _execute = execute;
```

```
            _canExecute = canExecute;
    }

    public bool CanExecute(object parameter)
    {
        return _canExecute == null ? true : _canExecute(parameter);
    }

    public event EventHandler CanExecuteChanged
    {
        add { CommandManager.RequerySuggested += value; }
        remove { CommandManager.RequerySuggested -= value; }
    }

    public void Execute(object parameter)
    {
        _execute(parameter);
    }

    private readonly Action<object> _execute;
    private readonly Predicate<object> _canExecute;
}
```

Usage

The new ICommand implementation can now be used in ViewModels and then bound to in view. The example in Listing 5–16 will display a typical log-in form, which will be handled by a RelayCommand on a ViewModel. The ViewModel will delegate to the model to assess the credentials supplied by the user. Listing 5–17 shows the XAML markup of the view that binds to the ViewModel.

Listing 5–16. The ViewModel Containing the Log-In RelayCommand

```
public class LogInViewModel
{
    public LogInViewModel()
    {
        _logInModel = new LogInModel();
        _logInCommand = new RelayCommand(param => this.AttemptLogIn(), param =>↵
 this.CanAttemptLogIn());
    }

    public string UserName
    {
        get;
        set;
    }

    public string Password
    {
        get;
        set;
    }
```

```
        public ICommand LogInCommand
        {
            get
            {
                return _logInCommand;
            }
        }

        private void AttemptLogIn()
        {
            _logInModel.LogIn(UserName, Password);
        }

        private bool CanAttemptLogIn()
        {
            return !String.IsNullOrWhiteSpace(UserName) && !String.IsNullOrWhiteSpace(Password);
        }

        private RelayCommand _logInCommand;
        private LogInModel _logInModel;
}
```

There are a few concepts at work here that require explanation. There are two string auto-properties, UserName and Password that will serve as storage for the user's input.

The _logInCommand is defined as a private field of type RelayCommand but is exposed publically via its ICommand interface. This allows the definition of the RelayCommand to remain internal. The _logInCommand is instantiated in the constructor and, because there is a condition wherein the user can't login, the constructor takes two arguments: the execute action and the canExecute predicate. Rather than wrapping these methods up in Action<object> and Predicate<object> instances, a lambda expression is used instead. This allows the methods to disregard the parameter, as in this example. If either the AttemptLogIn or CanAttemptLogIn method required access to the bound CommandParameter from the ICommandSource, the lambda expression would pass the parameter in like so:

```
param => AttemptLogIn(param)
```

■ **Tip** Lambda expressions are defined by the => syntax, which is read as "goes to." The left side of the goes-to operator holds the input parameters, possibly grouped by parentheses. The right side is an expression or a statement block. In this example, lambdas are used as a shorthand way of forwarding the delegates to an instance method.

LAZY INITIALIZATION

I have seen examples where the RelayCommand is lazy-initialized inside the public property. As RelayCommand construction is not a computationally intensive process, this seems like muddying the waters. There is no performance hit by constructing the RelayCommand before it is required, in the ViewModel's constructor. At least this way, future maintainers of the ViewModel will not be tricked into assuming that RelayCommand needs to be handled with kid gloves. One supporting argument for the lazy initialization is that it keeps the command declaration on its definition grouped.

The `AttemptLogIn` method is called when the command is fired and merely delegates to the contained `LogInModel.LogIn` method, which will—it is assumed—log the user in if the credentials are verified. This is illustrative of how the model is tasked with the heavy lifting and, as such, the result of this operation is not part of this example. The `LogInModel` is an external dependency and should be injected via the constructor to allow isolated unit testing of this ViewModel, as discussed in Chapter 7.

The `CanAttemptLogIn` method tests the `UserName` and `Password` strings that the user has entered and ensures that neither of them is null, empty, or contains only whitespace. If either of them does, the `ICommandSource` that binds to this `ICommand` will be disabled.

Listing 5–17. The XAML Markup of the View that Binds to the ViewModel

```
<Window x:Class="EventCommandExample.LogInWindow"
        xmlns="http://schemas.microsoft.com/winfx/2006/xaml/presentation"
        xmlns:x="http://schemas.microsoft.com/winfx/2006/xaml"
        xmlns:local="clr-namespace:EventCommandExample"
        Title="LogInWindow" Height="150" Width="300">
    <Window.Resources>
        <local:LogInViewModel x:Key="logInViewModel" />
    </Window.Resources>
    <Grid DataContext="{Binding Source={StaticResource logInViewModel}}">
        <Grid.ColumnDefinitions>
            <ColumnDefinition Width="100" />
            <ColumnDefinition />
        </Grid.ColumnDefinitions>
        <Grid.RowDefinitions>
            <RowDefinition />
            <RowDefinition />
            <RowDefinition Height="30" />
        </Grid.RowDefinitions>

        <Label Grid.Column="0" Grid.Row="0" Content="UserName:" />
        <TextBox Grid.Column="1" Grid.Row="0" Text="{Binding Path=UserName,↵
UpdateSourceTrigger=PropertyChanged}" />

        <Label Grid.Column="0" Grid.Row="1" Content="Password:" />
        <TextBox Grid.Column="1" Grid.Row="1" Text="{Binding Path=Password,↵
UpdateSourceTrigger=PropertyChanged}" />

        <Button Grid.Row="2" Grid.ColumnSpan="2" HorizontalAlignment="Right" Content="Log↵
In" Command="{Binding LogInCommand}" />

    </Grid>
</Window>
```

The bindings themselves are incredibly simple. Most of this markup is aimed at setting the controls out properly so that everything is nicely aligned and in the correct grid cell. All of the constituent parts (XML namespaces, ViewModel declaration, `DataContext` and bindings, `UpdateSourceTrigger`) have been covered, leaving only one major issue to clarify. The `Password` property is bound to a vanilla `TextBox`, which will display the contents of whatever the user types. This is a security risk and *should not* be used in production code.

Instead, the `PasswordBox` automatically masks the user input to hide the value entered. The trouble is, the `PasswordBox.Password` property is *not* a dependency property, so it can't be the target of a binding.

Attached Command Behavior

If commands are so useful and events lead to using the code-behind file and mixing logic into the view, then surely it would make sense to implement all control behaviors as commands, rather than events? Theoretically, this is correct. However, the framework does not follow this strictly; instead, it prefers events in places where a command would perhaps be more pertinent.

The answer to this problem is attached command behavior, which adapts an event and exposes it as a command that can be databound just the same as any other. An example of using attached command behaviour is shown in listing 5–18.

Listing 5–18. *Using Attached Command Behavior to Add Double-Click Functionality to a List Item*

```
<ListView ItemsSource="{Binding Names}">
    <ListView.ItemContainerStyle>
        <Style>
            <Setter Property="acb:AttachedCommand.Behaviors">
                <Setter.Value>
                    <acb:BehaviorBinding Event="MouseDoubleClick" Command="{Binding
ShowPersonCommand}" CommandParameter="{Binding}" />
                </Setter.Value>
            </Setter>
        </Style>
    </ListView.ItemContainerStyle>
 </ListView>
```

The implementation code that makes this work is, sadly, too long to reproduce here. It can be found on the Apress web site along with the rest of the code samples in this book.

Listing 5–18 adds a style to each ListViewItem in the ListView, setting the attached property AttachedBehaviors property, which is a list of BehaviorBinding instances. Each BehaviorBinding accepts three properties: an Event name, a Command to execute when the event fires, and a CommandParameter that will be passed to the Command on execution. This can be used in conjunction with the aforementioned RelayCommand so that events can be handled by the ViewModel and not in the code behind.

Avoiding Events Using Dependency Injection

Sometimes, the view provides services that the ViewModel needs to use. In these situations it is tempting to circumvent MVVM and handle this scenario in the code behind. However, by doing this, you lose the clean separation of concerns and testability that MVVM safeguards. There is a better way of achieving the same result.

One of the most common examples is in the display of standard Windows dialogs such as the OpenFileDialog and SaveFileDialog. A user interface may provide a MenuItem for opening a file, which is handled by a RelayCommand in the ViewModel. However, once inside the ViewModel, the temptation is to create an OpenFileDialog directly and show it from here. Of course, this introduces an implicit view dependency into the ViewModel. Instead, an interface should be required by the ViewModel class's constructor, which will provide the open file path whenever it is needed (see Listing 5–19).

Listing 5–19. *Injecting a IFilePathProvider Into the ViewModel*

```
public interface IFilePathProvider
{
    string GetLoadPath();

    string GetSavePath();
```

```
}
...
public MainWindowViewModel(IFilePathProvider filePathFinder)
{
    _filePathFinder = filePathFinder;
}

private void Load()
{
    string loadFilePath = _filePathFinder.GetLoadPath();
    if (loadFilePath != null)
    {
        // The user has selected a file to open
    }
}

private void Save()
{
    string saveFilePath = _filePathFinder.GetSavePath();
    if(saveFilePath != null)
    {
        // The user has selected a file to save
    }
}
```

The view layer can provide an implementation of this interface, which uses the OpenFileDialog and SaveFileDialog (see Listing 5–20).

Listing 5–20. Implementing the IFilePathProvider in the View

```
public class FilePathProvider : IFilePathProvider
{
    public string GetLoadPath()
    {
        OpenFileDialog ofd = new OpenFileDialog();
        ofd.Filter = "XML files (*.xml)|*.xml";
        string filePath = null;
        bool? dialogResult = ofd.ShowDialog();
        if(dialogResult.HasValue && dialogResult.Value)
        {
            filePath = ofd.FileName;
        }
        return filePath;
    }

    public string GetSavePath()
    {
        SaveFileDialog sfd = new SaveFileDialog();
        sfd.Filter = "XML files (*.xml)|*.xml";
        string filePath = null;
        bool? dialogResult = sfd.ShowDialog();
        if (dialogResult.HasValue && dialogResult.Value)
        {
            filePath = sfd.FileName;
```

```
        }
        return filePath;
    }
}
```

Of course, now the ViewModel cannot merely be default constructed as it has a constructor parameter. The `ObjectDataProvider` comes to the rescue here and acts as an inversion of control container, with the constructor parameter declaratively injected (see Listing 5–21).

Listing 5-21. *Constructing the ViewModel with an ObjectDataProvider*

```
<ObjectDataProvider x:Key="mainWindowViewModel" ObjectType="{x:Type
viewModel:MainWindowViewModel}">
    <ObjectDataProvider.ConstructorParameters>
        <view:FilePathProvider />
    </ObjectDataProvider.ConstructorParameters>
</ObjectDataProvider>
```

This can be used whenever the view provides a service that the ViewModel requires. If there is a WPF control or a third-party component that is not friendly to the MVVM pattern, exposes scant commands, and is not a candidate for attached command behavior, try to factor out the smallest dependency possible and create an interface that the view can fulfil.

Summary

This chapter has laid further groundwork that will enable you to write useful ViewModels that can expose domain functionality to the XAML view. It has been demonstrated that routed events, while separating the source of a trigger from its destination handler, are limited in that they must be caught by the controls in the element tree.

The alternative, wherever possible, is to allow the view to bind to commands that can be handled in the ViewModel. The default command implementations—`RoutedCommand` and `RoutedUICommand`—have limitations much the same as `RouteEvent`: they all require their destination handlers to be part of the element tree. A solution to this problem has been provided, which is a custom implementation of the `ICommand` interface. The `RelayCommand` accepts a delegate that should be invoked whenever the command is fired, and that delegate will typically be part of the ViewModel that hosts the command. This helps to centralize the behavior of commands while exposing them to the view for use in typical WPF and Silverlight binding scenarios.

CHAPTER 6

■■■

Validation

Data integrity is a very important part of developing a software product. Users of software are human beings and, being such, are universally fallible. Whenever requiring input from a user—especially free-text input—the values that are supplied should be treated with extreme suspicion. When it comes to user input, data lives in a totalitarian state: it is all guilty until proven innocent and must be vigorously validated before being trusted.

■ **Note** Much of this chapter is aimed at WPF. However, the "Validation In Silverlight" section deals with Silverlight directly, indicating which parts are common and what can be leveraged specifically in Silverlight. With the release of Silverlight 4, validation is much improved and the gap between the two technologies is ever decreasing.

The best way to eliminate bad data is with the preventative measure of data validation. Before the data is allowed to burrow deep into the model layer, it needs to be tested for *correctness*. Validation cannot unequivocally say that a piece of data is exactly the right piece of data—such bold claims are the remit of data *verification*. Validation simply informs whether data appears good enough on a more superficial level, answering questions such as:

- Is it of the correct data type?

- Is it within a certain range or set of values?

- Does it contain only characters that are acceptable?

- Is it of a specific length?

Even such seemingly shallow tests can directly prevent problems that can be introduced by validation errors. Imagine that an application wishes to provide a powerful reporting feature whereby users with SQL knowledge can construct queries directly on the data source. Without validating the free-text input received from the user, the nefarious ne'er-do-well user could enter the command in Listing 6–1 with disastrous effects.

Listing 6–1. A SQL Injection Attack

```
DROP TABLE Products;
```

This type of insecurity is so common that it has its own term: the SQL Injection Attack. One way of solving the problem would be to disallow the user from entering plain SQL commands at all, but validation can also be used to ensure that the entered command is harmless.

■ **Note** I once worked for a multinational corporation on a project for their client that they billed into the hundreds of millions of dollars. However, despite this vast expense, they not only opened themselves up to a SQL Injection Attack by running plain, user-input SQL directly on the database, the interface for the command was a *web service*. If they had gone live with that set up, it would not have been long before their database was irreparably destroyed.

The Validation Process

A binding's validation rules are fired when the source of the binding is updated. As explained in Chapter 2, the catalyst for updating a binding source can be set using the UpdateSourceTrigger property. Once the update has begun, validation progresses as outlined below. If a validation error occurs at any point during the process, the process stops.

1. The binding engine collates all ValidationRule objects whose ValidationStep value is RawProposedValue, calling their Validate method and halting if there is an error or continuing if all rules pass.

2. At this point, any data converters attached to the Binding are executed. The converter may fail at this point, stopping the validation process.

3. The binding engine then collates all attached ValidationRules whose ValidationStep value is set to ConvertedProposedValue, calling the Validate method and halting on an error.

4. At this point, the binding engine sets the binding source value.

5. The binding engine collates all the attached ValidationRules whose ValidationStep value is set to UpdatedValue, calling their Validate method and halting on an error. Any DataErrorValidationRules attached with a default ValidationStep value (which is also UpdatedValue) are collated and tested for validity at this point, too.

6. The final step is to call the Validate method on ValidationRules whose ValidationStep value is set to CommittedValue, and halt on a validation error.

Clearly, there are many ways in which the validation process can be customized. Mainly, allowances are made for testing the binding source value at a variety of stages during the binding process, with the aid of the ValidationStep value. A more thorough explanation of the participant classes involved in this process follows below.

Should a ValidationRule fail at any point during this process, the binding engine constructs a ValidationError instance and adds it to the Validation.Errors collection of the target Control. If, at the end of the process, this Validation.Errors collection contains at least one error, the Validation.HasError property is set to true. Similarly, if the NotifyOnValidationError property is set to true, the Validation.Error event is raised on the target Control.

Binding Validation Rules

Binding objects have a `ValidationRules` property that accepts a list of `ValidationRule` objects. As explained previously, these are iterated over to determine whether or not an input value is valid. There are two implementations of the `ValidationRule` class supplied, one for handling exceptions and another for hooking in to the `IDataErrorInfo` provision of validation. Of course, if neither of these facilities suffice, custom `ValidationRule` implementations can be created to suit specific situations. Listing 6–2 shows the definition of a binding that contains a single `ExceptionValidationRule`. Note that the binding is defined in long-form, because the `ValidationRules` value is a list.

Listing 6–2. Adding an Exception Handling Validation Rule to a Binding

```
<TextBox>
    <TextBox.Text>
        <Binding>
            <Binding.ValidationRules>
                <ExceptionValidationRule />
            </Binding.ValidationRules>
        </Binding>
    </TextBox.Text>
</TextBox>
```

ValidationRule Class

The `ValidationRule` class provides an abstract base class for the implementation of validation rules that can be applied to individual bindings. Although two implementations are provided, it may be necessary to define custom implementations that correspond to specific validation rules. For example, if the user is presented with a dialog for creating a new customer record, there may be a validation rule that disallows certain characters in the person's name, enforces a certain minimum or maximum age limit, or ensures the validity of a zip or postal code.

Validate Method

The `ValidationRule` class specifies a single abstract method that must be overridden by all subclasses (see Listing 6–3). It is supplied with the value of `object` type that requires validation and a `CultureInfo` object in case the validation rule requires knowledge of the current culture.

Listing 6–3. The ValidationRule Method Signature

```
public abstract ValidationResult Validate(object value, CultureInfo cultureInfo)
```

The return value is of type `ValidationResult`. It is a class created for the sole purpose of allowing validation methods to return two different values: a `Boolean` signifying the value's validity and an `object` that provides data about the error generated when the validation result is false. The `ValidationResult` constructor typically accepts a `'true, null'` pairing if the validation has succeeded, or a `'false, "explanation" '` pairing if the validation has failed, where "explanation" is a string of text informing the user what went wrong. Of course, a string explanation is not exclusively required; any sort of error data could be provided.

Listing 6–4 shows an example implementation of the `Validate` method. It ensures that the supplied input value is a `string` that can be parsed into an `integer` value. Note that the

`ValidationResult.ValidResult` static property is used as a shortcut for new `ValidationResult(true, null)`.

Listing 6–4. A Trivial Implementation of a Validation Rule

```
public override ValidationResult Validate(object value, CultureInfo cultureInfo)
{
    ValidationResult result = new ValidationResult(false, "An unknown validation error
occurred");
    if(value is string)
    {
        int integerValue = int.MinValue;
        if(int.TryParse(value as string, out integerValue))
        {
            result = ValidationResult.ValidResult;
        }
        else
        {
            result = new ValidationResult(false, "The string provided could not be parsed as
an integer value");
        }
    }
    else
    {
        result = new ValidationResult(false, "The value provided is not a string");
    }
    return result;
}
```

▦ **Tip** The example in Listing 6–4 uses the *Single Exit Pattern*, which can often result in more understandable code. The theory is that all methods should only contain a single `return` statement and it should be located right at the end. More often than not, this is easily achievable and code is consequently more comprehensible, but it is, as ever, a personal preference.

Constructors

The `ValidationRule` has two constructors. The default constructor is most commonly used and simply initializes the class to use default values for the two properties that affect the behavior of this rule. These are the `ValidatesOnTargetUpdated` and `ValidationStep` properties, which govern whether the validation rule runs when the target of the associated `Binding` is updated and in which part of the validation process the rule runs, respectively. Listing 6–5 shows an example.

Listing 6–5. Default ValidationRule Constructor

```
public ValidationRule()
{
    ValidationStep = ValidationStep.RawProposedValue;
    ValidatesOnTargetUpdated = false;
}
```

An alternative constructor is provided to supply these two values on creation (see Listing 6–6).

Listing 6–6. Alternative ValidationRule Constructor

```
public ValidationRule(ValidationStep validationStep, bool validatesOnTargetUpdated)
```

The default constructor is more likely to be used in binding situations, as the validation rule is declared in XAML. As the validation rule is constructed, the two properties can be set via the usual methods, as shown in Listing 6–7.

Listing 6–7. Constructing a ValidationRule and Setting Its Behavioral Properties

```
<TextBox>
    <TextBox.Text>
        <Binding>
            <Binding.ValidationRules>
                <local:MyValidationRule ValidationStep="UpdatedValue"
ValidatesOnTargetUpdated="True" />
            </Binding.ValidationRules>
        </Binding>
    </TextBox.Text>
</TextBox>
```

Exceptions for Validation

When the target control of a binding is updated, an exception is sometimes thrown somewhere in the process of setting the new value on the binding source. A common example is when the value entered does not match the value required by the binding source. Whenever an exception is thrown in this situation, it can be caught and handled as a validation error. The ExceptionValidationRule class is provided for this purpose and can be added to a binding's ValidationRules list, as shown in Listing 6–8.

Listing 6–8. Constructing a ValidationRule and Setting Its Behavioral Properties

```
<TextBox>
    <TextBox.Text>
        <Binding>
            <Binding.ValidationRules>
                <ExceptionValidationRule />
            </Binding.ValidationRules>
        </Binding>
    </TextBox.Text>
</TextBox>
```

If the user entered a string value that could not be automatically parsed into an integer, yet the binding source required an integer value, an exception would be thrown. Normally, this would present your user with an unhelpful message that would likely cause confusion or irritation. By presenting the exception as a broken validation rule, the user will readily understand the problem and can work to rectify the error without ruining their experience.

Filtering Validation Exceptions

There may be a situation whereby certain specific exceptions should be handled in different ways. Perhaps an InvalidCastException would prompt a different response than a DivideByZeroException.

Both should be caught, but the user should be presented with a different response for each. Listing 6–9 shows how to add an UpdateSourceExceptionFilter to a Binding, which will then call the specified UpdateSourceExceptionFilterCallback method in the code behind.

Listing 6–9. Filtering Exceptions that Occur When Updating a Binding Source

```
<TextBox>
    <TextBox.Text>
        <Binding UpdateSourceExceptionFilter="MyExceptionFilter">
            <Binding.ValidationRules>
                <ExceptionValidationRule />
            </Binding.ValidationRules>
        </Binding>
    </TextBox.Text>
</TextBox>
```

Listing 6–10 shows the method signature required for such callbacks.

Listing 6–10. The UpdateSourceExceptionFilterCallback Delegate

```
public delegate object UpdateSourceExceptionFilterCallback(object bindExpression,↵
 Exception exception)
```

The delegate returns an object instance that has a different intention depending on the returned value, as shown in Table 6–1.

Table 6–1. The Possible Exception Filter Return Values and Their Respective Intent

Return Value	Intent
Null	Creates a ValidationError using the exception as the ErrorContent property and adds the error to the bound control's Validation.Errors collection.
Any object	Creates a ValidationError using the returned object as the ErrorContent property and adds the error to the bound control's Validation.Errors collection.
A ValidationError instance	For fine-grained control of how the ValidationError is constructed (note that it is automatically constructed in the prior examples), merely add this ValidationError to the bound control's Validation.Errors collection.

The Exception object that is passed into the filter callback can then be used to determine the specific subclass thrown and the response varies on that, as shown in Listing 6–11.

Listing 6–11. Testing the Thrown Exception's Type so as to Respond Differently

```
public object MyExceptionFilter(object bindExpression, Exception exception)
{
    if (exception is InvalidCastException)
    {
        // Respond to an invalid cast
```

```
    }
    else if (exception is DivideByZeroException)
    {
        // Respond to a division by zero
    }
}
```

Note that this property is set on the `Binding`, not the `ExceptionValidationRule`, but it is specific to validation scenarios, so the `ExceptionValidationRule` must be present in the `Binding`'s `ValidationRules` list.

Exceptions Represent Exceptional Circumstances

There is a problem with using exceptions for validation: the term *exception* implies that it represents an *exceptional circumstance*. Conveying the contravention of arbitrary, business-oriented validation rules is not the intent of an exception. In fact, one major point of input validation is to *avoid* throwing an exception.

A Validation Framework

So far, I have looked at implementing custom `ValidationRule` classes and leveraging the usable, if flawed, `ExceptionValidationRule`. However, what is needed is a more robust validation framework, whereby the rules used for validation are in close proximity to the rest of the business logic. After all, validation rules *are* business rules.

The .NET Framework provides an interface that is used to supply user interfaces with custom error information. Windows Forms and ASP.NET MVC both make use of the `IDataErrorInfo` interface to present validation error messages that users can comprehend. WPF and Silverlight allow the adaptation of this interface for use as `Binding ValidationRules` with the use of the `DataErrorValidationRule` subclass.

If your project involves porting an existing Windows Forms application to WPF and the original code makes use of `IDataErrorInfo`, then it is advisable to reuse this code and hook the validation code to the user interface using `DataErrorValidationRule`.

IDataErrorInfo Interface

This interface has two properties, as shown in Listing 6–12.

Listing 6–12. The IDataErrorInfo Interface Definition

```
public interface IDataErrorInfo
{
    string Error { get; }

    string this[string columnName] { get; }
}
```

There are two getter properties that comprise this interface. The `Error` property returns a string explaining—in natural language for the user interface to present to the user—what is wrong with the object's current state.

The other property is an indexer that requires a property name as an argument. The property name matches a property on the implementing object and the returned string value explains what is wrong with this specific property.

So, the object itself can be in error and have its own error message. Individual properties can also be in error and have individual explanation strings as to what is wrong with them. The default return value for both is the empty string (string.Empty).

In an MVVM application, there are two possible places where you may wish to implement the IDataErrorInfo interface. Both have their merits, but the key is to be consistent: choose which layer will house the validation code, reconcile why this is the most applicable, and stick to it.

Model Implementation

One possible location to implement the IDataErrorInfo is in the model implementation. That is, along with the rest of the problem solution. This makes sense because validation is business logic and the two are interlinked. Listing 6–13 shows an example of implementing the IDataErrorInfo on a Customer class that disallows an Age value of less than 21.

Listing 6–13. Implementing the IDataErrorInfo in a Model Class

```
public class Customer : IDataErrorInfo
{
    public Customer(string name, int age)
    {
        Name = name;
        Age = age;
    }

    public string Name
    {
        get { return _name; }
        set { _name = value; }
    }

    public int Age
    {
        get { return _age; }
        set { _age = value; }
    }

    public string Error
    {
        get { throw new NotImplementedException(); }
    }

    public string this[string columnName]
    {
        get
        {
            string error = string.Empty;
            switch (columnName)
            {
                case "Name":
                    if (_name.IndexOfAny(IllegalCharacters) > 0)
```

```
                {
                        error = string.Format("The customer's name contains illegal↵
characters ({0})", new string(IllegalCharacters));
                }
                break;
            case "Age":
                if (_age < 21)
                {
                        error = "Customers must be 21 or over to shop here!";
                }
                break;
        }

        return error;
    }
}

    private string _name;
    private int _age;

    private static readonly char[] IllegalCharacters = new char[] {'_', '!', '@', '%'};
}
```

There is a problem with this approach: the strings being returned are for user interface consumption and the model classes should be ignorant of their use in a user interface. Furthermore, domain modeling purists would argue that the interface implementation requirement is too heavy a burden on the model and contravenes the Single Responsibility Principle. They would argue that model classes should be POCOs and should have no extraneous constraints. This is theoretically correct but, as ever, there is a time when purity becomes pedantry. As long as all stakeholders are aware of the potential risks or issues, the expediency of implementing the validation code in the model may well make it the right solution.

ViewModel Implementation

The alternative to implementing the IDataErrorInfo in the model is implementing it in the ViewModel classes, as shown in Listing 6–14.

Listing 6–14. Implementing the IDataErrorInfo in a ViewModel Class

```
public class CustomerViewModel : IDataErrorInfo
{
    public string Name
    {
        get;
        set;
    }

    public int Age
    {
        get;
        set;
    }
```

```
    public string Error
    {
        get { throw new NotImplementedException(); }
    }

    public string this[string columnName]
    {
        get
        {
            string error = string.Empty;

            switch (columnName)
            {
                case "Name":
                    if (Name.IndexOfAny(IllegalCharacters) > 0)
                    {
                        error = string.Format("The customer's name contains illegal↵
characters ({0})", new string(IllegalCharacters));
                    }
                    break;
                case "Age":
                    if (Age < 21)
                    {
                        error = "Customers must be 21 or over to shop here!";
                    }
                    break;

            }

            return error;
        }
    }

    public void CreateCustomer()
    {
        _customer = new Customer(Name, Age);
    }

    private Customer _customer;

    private static readonly char[] IllegalCharacters = new char[] { '_', '!', '@', '%' };
}
```

This makes sense for many practical reasons unrelated to an abstract notion of "code purity." Firstly, the intent of the ViewModel is to bridge the gap between the business logic that solves a programming problem and the user interface that interacts with the user. The IDataErrorInfo also mediates between the user interface and the domain layer by explaining errors to the user in natural language.

The interface does not provide any contract for implementing validation rules; it provides a contract for *reporting* validation rules that have already been broken. Notice, also, that the ViewModel implementation maintains the encapsulation of the Customer business object: the Customer's Name and Age properties can be immutable and the CreateCustomer method is only called when the data has been validated.

DataErrorValidationRule Class

Once the IDataErrorInfo interface has been implemented, the DataErrorValidationRule class is the adapter between a ValidationRule and the IDataErrorInfo.Error property. See Listing 6–15 for an example.

Listing 6–15. Enabling a Binding to Check for IDataErrorInfo Errors

```
<TextBox>
    <TextBox.Text>
        <Binding>
            <Binding.ValidationRules>
                <DataErrorValidationRule />
            </Binding.ValidationRules>
        </Binding>
    </TextBox.Text>
</TextBox>
```

If the source of the binding implements IDataErrorInfo and indicates that an error has occurred, the binding behaves just as it would for other broken validation rules, using the returned string as information to feed to the user. Altering how broken validation rules are displayed is covered later in this chapter.

■ **Caution** The DataErrorValidationRule class was introduced in .NET Framework version 3.5. If you are targeting the first version of WPF or Silverlight, introduced in version 3.0, you will not be able to use this class for validation scenarios.

A shortcut property is available on Bindings that will implicitly add the DataErrorValidationRule to the Binding's ValidationRules collection, shown in Listing 6–16.

Listing 6–16. Using the ValidatesOnDataErrors Property

```
<TextBox>
    <TextBox.Text>
        <Binding ValidatesOnDataErrors="True" />
    </TextBox.Text>
</TextBox>
```

Validation in Silverlight

Until the recent release of Silverlight 4, validation presented somewhat of a problem to developers of WPF's online brethren. Throwing an exception and marking the binding with ValidatesOnExceptions was the typical solution. As examined previously, this is not optimal.

Thankfully, with Silverlight 4, this situation has been remedied and IDataErrorInfo has been introduced, so ViewModel implementations could potentially be shared between WPF and Silverlight user interfaces.

One feature that Silverlight 4 possesses but WPF does not is the INotifyDataErrorInfo interface. As Silverlight is designed for client/server deployment, it is important to realize the implications of each approach. The IDataErrorInfo runs synchronously on the client whereas INotifyDataErrorInfo runs asynchronously on the server. Listing 6–17 outlines its contract.

Listing 6–17. *The Members of the INotifyDataErrorInfo Interface*

```
public interface INotifyDataErrorInfo
{
    IEnumerable GetErrors(string propertyName);

    bool HasErrors { get; }

    event EventHandler<DataErrorsChangedEventArgs> ErrorsChanged;
}

public sealed class DataErrorsChangedEventArgs : EventArgs
{
    public DataErrorsChangedEventArgs(string propertyName)
    {
        PropertyName = propertyName;
    }

    public string PropertyName
    {
        get;
        private set;
    }
}
```

Implementers of the interface will have to fulfill the GetErrors method, the HasErrors property, and fire the ErrorsChanged event under the appropriate conditions.

The GetErrors method requires a property name whose errors are to be returned and returns an untyped list representing those errors. If the property name is the empty string, the errors requested are those pertinent to the entity as a whole.

The HasErrors property indicates whether or not the object is currently in a state of validation error.

The ErrorsChanged event must be fired whenever the return value for GetErrors would yield a different value for any property. This is because the implementation is asynchronous with this portion run on the server and the user interface on the client side. Without a direct notification via an event such as this, the UI would have to poll across a network boundary, which would be very inefficient. The event should be fired once for each property whose errors have changed, with the property name supplied to the EventArgs subclass, DataErrorsChangedEventArgs.

It is not sufficient just to implement the interface on the ViewModel classes: support must also be turned on with the ValidatesOnNotifyDataErrors property (see Listing 6–18).

Listing 6–18. *Enable Support for Server-Side Validation*

```
<TextBox Text="{Binding Source=x, ValidatesOnNotifyDataErrors=true}" />
```

A sample implementation of the INotifyDataErrorInfo interface, using a ViewModel class, is provided in Listing 6–19.

Listing 6–19. Implementing Server-Side Validation in the ViewModel Layer of a Silverlight Application

```csharp
public class CustomerViewModel : INotifyDataErrorInfo
{
    public CustomerViewModel()
    {
        _propertyErrors = new Dictionary<string, IEnumerable>();
    }

    public string Name
    {
        get { return _name; }
        set
        {
            if (ValidateName(value))
            {
                _name = value;
            }
        }
    }

    public int Age
    {
        get { return _age; }
        set
        {
            if (ValidateAge(value))
            {
                _age = value;
            }
        }
    }

    public IEnumerable GetErrors(string propertyName)
    {
        return _propertyErrors[propertyName];
    }

    public bool HasErrors
    {
        get
        {
            return _propertyErrors.Count > 0;
        }
    }

    public void CreateCustomer()
    {
        _customer = new Customer(Name, Age);
    }

    private bool ValidateName(string name)
    {
```

```csharp
            bool nameIsValid = (name.IndexOfAny(IllegalCharacters) == -1);

            IEnumerable nameErrors = null;
            if (!nameIsValid)
            {
                List<string> errors = new List<string>();
                errors.Add(string.Format("Customer name contains illegal characters ({0})",↵
    new string(IllegalCharacters)));
                nameErrors = errors;
            }

            OnDataErrorsChanged("Name");

            _propertyErrors["Name"] = nameErrors;

            return nameIsValid;
        }

        private bool ValidateAge(int age)
        {
            bool ageIsValid = (age >= 21);

            IEnumerable ageErrors = null;
            if (!ageIsValid)
            {
                List<string> errors = new List<string>();
                errors.Add("Customer must be over 21 to shop here");
                _propertyErrors["Age"] = errors;
            }

            OnDataErrorsChanged("Age");

            _propertyErrors["Age"] = ageErrors;

            return ageIsValid;
        }

        private void OnDataErrorsChanged(string propertyName)
        {
            if (ErrorsChanged != null)
            {
                ErrorsChanged(this, new DataErrorsChangedEventArgs(propertyName));
            }
        }

        public event EventHandler<DataErrorsChangedEventArgs> ErrorsChanged;

        private string _name;
        private int _age;
        private IDictionary<string, IEnumerable> _propertyErrors;
        private static readonly char[] IllegalCharacters = new char[] {'!', '$', '%', '_'};
        private Customer _customer;
    }
```

This implementation prevents setting an invalid value for the `Name` and `Age` properties. The validation methods test whether the user input is valid and, if not, maintain the errors that were present. Any listeners to the `ErrorsChanged` event are then notified that the property's validation errors have changed. Note that this occurs even if the value is valid: it may have previously been invalid so its state has still changed.

Visually Formatting Validation Errors

Successfully detecting a validation error is one side of the validation reporting coin. Reporting the error to the user via the view is just as important—and is just as customizable.

Validation.ErrorTemplate Attached Property

Controls can use the `Validation.ErrorTemplate` attached property to specify an alternative `ControlTemplate` to display when the binding source has a validation error, as in Listing 6–20.

Listing 6–20. Specifying an Alternative ControlTemplate on a Control

```
<TextBox Text="{Binding Source=x, ValidatesOnDataErrors=True}"↵
 Validation.ErrorTemplate="{StaticResource validationFailedTextBoxTemplate}" />

<ControlTemplate x:Key="validationFailedTextBoxTemplate">
    <StackPanel Orientation="Horizontal">
        <AdornedElementPlaceholder />
        <TextBlock Foreground="Red">!</TextBlock>
    </StackPanel>
</ControlTemplate>
```

This should be familiar as control templating was covered in Chapter 2. However, the `AdornedElementPlaceholder` is new. It can be considered analogous to the `ContentPresenter` control but it's specifically for use in `ControlTemplates` that are intended for use as a `Validation.ErrorTemplate`. When the view is constructed, the placeholder is replaced with the original control (in this instance, a `TextBox`). This `ErrorTemplate` places a red exclamation mark after the `TextBox` if the binding source's `IDataErrorInfo` implementation indicates that there is a validation error.

Validation.HasError Attached Property

An alternative is to use a style trigger predicated on the `Validation.HasError` attached property, which will return true if a `Control` has any validation errors (see Listing 6–21).

Listing 6–21. Using Triggers to Alter the Appearance of an Erroneous Control

```
<Style TargetType="TextBox">
    <Style.Triggers>
        <Trigger Property="Validation.HasError" Value="True">
            <Setter Property="BorderBrush" Value="#FFFF0000" />
        </Trigger>
    </Style.Triggers>
</Style>
```

This style definition will apply to all of the TextBox controls in the application, applying a red border when validation fails. The textual value of the validation error can also be bound. Listing 6–22 shows how to use the ToolTip to show the error message to the user.

Listing 6–22. *Binding to the Validation Error's String Message*

```
<Style TargetType="TextBox">
    <Style.Triggers>
        <Trigger Property="Validation.HasError" Value="True">
            <Setter Property="ToolTip"
                Value="{Binding RelativeSource={RelativeSource.Self},↵
 Path=(Validation.Errors)[0].ErrorContent}" />
        </Trigger>
    </Style.Triggers>
</Style>
```

The setter's binding may look a little complicated, but it is fairly self-explanatory. The source is the control that this style is being applied to, and the path uses the Validation.Errors attached property that is the list of broken ValidationRules associated with the control. As this property is a collection, the first error is referenced using the indexing notation and the ErrorContent property contains the helpful string to display to the user.

Summary

All user-provided data should be handled with care and also treated with distrust until it proves that it is neither intentionally malicious nor accidentally erroneous. As such, validation is an important topic and should be integrated into an application at the earliest opportunity, not tacked on to the end of a project. WPF and Silverlight provide a robust technique for integrating validation into the user interface by adding ValidationRules to Bindings.

Custom validation rules can be written from scratch to perform any necessary checks and balances on data that has been input by the user. Exceptions can be caught and automatically converted into broken validation rules, further insulating the core of the solution from potentially harmful data.

If a more structured approach is desired, the existing component model that the .NET Framework supplies can be leveraged, allowing the integration of custom validation into the appropriate layer. Ideally, an application designed around the MVVM paradigm would implement its validation in the ViewModel, but it may be quicker and easier to include such rules directly in the model. Once a validation rule is broken, WPF and Silverlight allow developers to tailor how the errors are presented to the user in order to unify the look and feel of their applications.

■■■

CHAPTER 7

Unit Testing

The Importance of Testing

As a discipline, software engineering encompasses many different skills, techniques, and methods. Dabbling with database administration, setting up development and production environments, designing user interfaces are all occasional tasks aside from the primary role of implementing solutions, which is writing code.

One skill, above all, has a perceived malignancy that is directly proportional to its objective importance: testing. Software is absolutely useless if it does not—or, more accurately, cannot—carry out the tasks it was created to perform. Worse still is software which errs insidiously but purports to function correctly, undermining the trust of the end user.

Software failures can be merely a minor embarrassment to a business. However, if compounded, these failures slowly erode the goodwill and confidence that the client originally held. At their worst, depending on the application and environment, software failures are catastrophic and can endanger human life.

■ **Note** Ariane 5 Flight 501, an ill-fated space launch, is one of the most infamous examples of software failure. After just 37 seconds, the rocket veered off course due to a software error and subsequently self-destructed. The error was an uncaught arithmetic overflow exception caused by converting a 64-bit floating point value to a 16-bit integer value. The loss was estimated at $370 million (1996 U.S. prices, not adjusted for inflation).

Traditional Testing

Over the course of the past decade or so, there have been fundamental shifts in the methodologies and practices that define software engineering. From initial requirements gathering through deployment and maintenance, not only has each part of the process evolved but there has been a revolution in exactly *which* processes are performed to create a software product.

The Waterfall Methodology

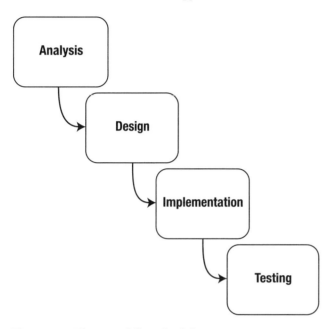

Figure 7–1. The waterfall methodology

Figure 7–1 shows a typical waterfall methodology, with the minimal phases of analysis, design, implementation, and testing. There may be additional fine-grained phases such as verification, deployment, or maintenance, depending on nature of the project. The most important flaw with this approach is the rigidity of the process: each phase follows directly from the last with a minimum possibility of revisiting the previous phase.

Notice also that the implementation of the software cannot even commence until both analysis and design (two significantly time-consuming and resource-intensive phases) have been completed. This has been given its own pejorative acronym: Big Design Up-Front (BDUF). It is one of many terms that have been coined to denigrate "outmoded" practices when a newer, more adaptable methodology emerges. Alongside BDUF is the prosaic "analysis paralysis" that manifests itself as a lack of tangible, demonstrable progress made on a project because of over-analyzing to the point that decisive action is never taken.

The rigidity of the waterfall method is explicable, if not excusable. Table 7–1 demonstrates that the relative cost of fixing bugs increases exponentially with the passing of each phase. The statistics show that bugs detected in the phase after their introduction cost orders of magnitude more than if the bug was detected during the phase in which it was introduced.

Table 7–1. The Multiplicative Costs of Fixing Bugs in Various Stages of the Software Lifecycle

		Phase Detected				
		Analysis	Design	Implementation	Testing	Maintenance
Phase Introduced	Analysis	1x	3x	5-10x	10x	10-100x
	Design	-	1x	10x	15x	25-100x
	Implementation	-	-	1x	10x	10-25x

The waterfall methodology's reaction to this table is to concentrate more effort on analysis and design to ensure that bugs are detected and corrected at these stages when the costs are relatively inexpensive. This is understandable, but the process itself is largely to blame because the costs are directly attributable to revisiting a previously "finished" phase.

A corollary of this rigidity is that the customer suffers directly: an analysis bug is an incorrectly specified chunk of functionality, often relating to a specific business process. As an example, a business rule in an online shopping website such as "Customers cannot apply more than one discount to their basket" may be neglected during analysis but the omission is discovered during the testing phase. According to Table 7–1, this would yield a cost of 10 times that of its correct inclusion during analysis. However, consider the implausible situation where the business analyst performed her job flawlessly. Instead, the "bug" is actually an oversight by the client, who would like the feature introducing once the testing phase is reached.

The reaction to this from the business implementing a waterfall methodology is this: the feature passes through analysis, design, and implementation before reaching testing and the costs are just as applicable, but the business does not mind because the "blame" for the omission lies with the client, who is billed accordingly. Considering that these sorts of changes (added or amended features) occur frequently, your client will quickly find their way to your competitor who can handle fluctuations in requirements *without* punitive costs.

■ **Caution** I cannot pretend to be wholly objective, being partisan to agile methodologies. This is merely what has worked for me; to use yet another idiomatic term, your mileage may vary.

The Testing Afterthought

In the waterfall methodology, testing is deferred until the end of the project, *after* implementation. As per the recurring theme of inflexibility, this implies that the whole implementation phase must complete before the testing process commences.

Assuming that the implementation is organized into layers with directed dependencies, separation of concerns, the single responsibility principle, and other such best practices, there will still be bugs in the software. The target is to lower the defect count while maintaining an expedient implementation time, not to eradicate all bugs, which will doubtless atrophy progress entirely.

If testing is left until after implementation has completed, it is difficult to test each module in isolation, as client code is consumed by more code further up the pyramid of layers until the user interface at the top obfuscates the fine-grained functionality. Testers start reporting defects, thus programmers are taken away from productive and billable work to start an often laborious debugging investigation to track down and fix the defect. It need not be this way.

Gaining Agility

This book is not directly about the agile methodology, but it is an advocate. Agile is based around iterative development: setting recurring weekly, fortnightly, or perhaps monthly deadlines during which new features are implemented in their entirety so that they can be released to the client for interim approval (see Figure 7–2). There is a strong emphasis on developing a feedback loop so that the client's comments on each iteration are turned into new features or altered requirements to be completed in the next or future iteration. This continues until the product is complete. There are many advantages to this approach for the development team as well as the business itself. Even the client benefits.

Figure 7–2. The agile methodology's iterative development cycle

The developers know their responsibilities for the next fortnight and become focused on achieving these goals. They are given ownership in, and accountability for, the features that are assigned to them. They realize that these features will reflect directly on their abilities and so gain job satisfaction from being in an efficient and effective working environment. Nobody likes to work on a project that is late, ridden with defects, and treated with disdain by both client and management.

With iterative development, the business stands a better chance of completing projects on-time and within budget. It can estimate and plan with greater accuracy, knowing that the methodology delivers. It gains a reputation for a high quality of work and customer satisfaction.

The client gains visibility as to how the project is progressing. Instead of being told with confusing technical jargon that "the database has been normalized, the data access layer is in place, and we are now working on implementing the domain logic," the client is *shown* working, albeit minimal, functionality. They are able to see their ideas and requirements put into action from a very early stage, and they are encouraged to provide feedback and constructive criticism so that the software evolves to meet their needs.

Testing needs to be performed before the release of every iteration, but it is often a time-consuming process that can detract from more productive work. Instead of deferring testing to the end of the iteration, much like the waterfall methodology defers testing to end of implementation as a whole, testing can be performed every day by every developer on all of the code that they produce.

■ **Note** There are many more facets to agile development that are recommended: planning poker, velocity charts, daily stand-up meetings, a continuous integration environment. If you do not currently use these practices, give them a try and find out for yourself how good they are.

What Is Unit Testing?

Having established that it is desirable to avoid deferring testing to one large, unmanageable chunk of unknowable duration at the end of the project, the alternative— unit testing—requires explanation.

Unit testing occurs concurrently with development and is performed by the developers. This is not to say that test analysts have suddenly become obsolete. Far from it, the quality of their input—the code produced by the developers—is of a higher quality and is more robust.

The unit tests themselves require a change in attitude and emphasis for the developer. Rather than interpreting the specification and diving straight into implementation, the specification is turned into unit tests that directly enforce the business rules, validation, or any conditional code.

Each unit test is merely code written to verify the expected behavior and outcome of other code. This often results in each method of the tested code having multiple tests written to cover the possible parameter values that could yield differing results.

Defining Interface Before Implementation

It is most beneficial if the unit tests are written *before* the accompanying code to be tested. This might seem very backward, almost purposefully masochistic, but it shifts the focus of the code from its implementation to its interface. This means that the developer is concentrating more on the purpose of the code and how client code interacts with it, rather than jumping straight into writing the body of the method with nary a thought for *how* it is to be used.

Automation

Being code themselves, unit tests are compiled just like the rest of the project. They are also executed by test-running software, which can speed through each test, effectively giving the thumbs up or thumbs down to indicate whether the test has passed or failed, respectively. The crux of the unit testing cycle is as follows:

1. Interpret the specification and factor it down to the method granularity.

2. Write a *failing* test method whose signature explains its purpose.

3. Verify that the test fails by running the test.

4. Implement the most minimal solution possible that would make the test pass.

5. Run the test again and ensure that the test has turned from "red" (failure) to "green" (success).

6. Repeat to completion.

Only the method being tested and the test itself need be compiled and run at steps 3 and 5, so there should be no bottlenecks in such a build/execute cycle.

Once functionality is implemented to a degree that it is usable—and useful—to others, it should be checked into whatever source control software is used. This is where the unit tests really demonstrate their utility. In a continuous integration environment, a separate build server would wait for check-ins to the source control repository and then spring into life. It would proceed to get the latest code, build the entire solution, and then run all of the tests that are present. A test failure becomes as important as a compilation failure, and the development team is informed that the build has broken, perhaps by e-mail or by stand-alone build monitoring software that correctly identifies the member whose code broke the build. This is not to foster a blame culture but serves to identify the most appropriate person nominated to fix the build.

■ **Tip** Source control, like unit testing, is another part of the development process that, though they feel it would be nice to have, clients often balk at diverting resources to implement. I believe that pulling out all of the stops to do so pays dividends for future productivity. It is also quite likely that some members of the development team would appreciate the new process so much that they would be willing to implement it out of hours—for suitable recompense, naturally.

The advantages of this should be obvious. The build server will, at any given point in time, either contain a fully working copy of the software that could feasibly be released, or it contains a broken copy of the software and knows who broke it, when, and via which change.

There is then an emphasis on developers checking in their code frequently—at least once each working day but preferably as soon as sufficient functionality is implemented. They are also focused on checking in code that is sufficiently tested so that a build failure does not subsequently occur.

Eventually, after only a handful of iterations of development, a significant body of regression tests will have been developed. If someone refactors some of the previously developed code, these regression tests will sound the alert should any erroneous code be introduced. This allows the developers to refactor without fear of potentially breaking important functionality.

Code Coverage

Code is only as good as its unit tests. The endless stream of green-light successful unit tests is by no means a panacea; it can't be relied upon to tell the full story. For example, what if there is only one unit test per method that tests only the best-case scenario? If no error paths are tested, it's likely that the code is not functioning as well as is believed.

Code coverage assigns a percentage value to a method, class, project, or solution, signifying the amount of code that has an accompanying unit test. The code coverage detection is also automated and integrated into the continuous integration environment. If the coverage percentage drops below a predefined level, the build fails. Although the software compiles, executes, and has passed those tests that are present, it does not have enough tests associated with it for the software to be fully trusted for release.

The level of code coverage required need not be 100% unless the software is safety critical, where this figure may well be necessary. Instead, a more pragmatic, heuristic approach may be adopted. More critical modules may opt for 90% test coverage, whereas more trivial modules could set 70% as an acceptable level.

Why Unit Test?

Perhaps you are still not convinced that unit testing can benefit you or your project. Donning the advocacy cape, here are some reasons why unit testing can be *for everyone*.

Spread the Effort

Statistically, more bugs are introduced during implementation than at any other time. This makes intuitive sense: writing code is a non-trivial and skilled practice that requires concentration and an acute awareness of the myriad scenarios in which the code may be used. Neglecting to realize that a fellow colleague may metaphorically throw your class or method against a wall will likely see the code smash horribly into pieces. Unit tests can help that code bounce gracefully.

Knowing that most bugs are created during implementation, it makes sense to expend a lot of effort at this stage to ensure that, as they are introduced, they are also detected and removed as quickly. However, some developers abhor testing and consider it to be anathema to their job description. They are paid to write code, not sit around testing all day. While this is generally true, they are paid to write working code—code that functions as required. Also, unit testing is writing code. These developers gain confidence in their own code, produce a better product, and all the while they are writing code. Ask any developer what they would prefer to do: implement new feature X, or debug bug Y. Implementing new features is far more rewarding and this is what the vast majority would choose. Debugging can be laborious, and applying a fix can have a ripple effect on higher level code, which can often be infuriating.

Enforce Better Design

Unit tests exercise code in isolation, without heavyweight dependencies in tow. If a method must access a database, file storage, or cross a process or network boundary, these operations are expensive and will confuse the intent of the unit test. If a method has an implicit dependency via a static class or global variable, the unit testing process forces an immediate redesign so that the dependency can be injected at will and all internal code paths covered.

Imagine that you wanted to test the method in Listing 7–1, which is a simple Save method of an Active Record [PoEAA, Fowler].

Listing 7–1. An Embedded Dependency Makes a Class Difficult to Test in Isolation

```
public class Customer : IActiveRecord
{
    #region Constructors

    public Customer(Name name, Address address, EmailAddress emailAddress)
    {
        _name = name;
        _address = address;
        _emailAddress = emailAddress;
    }

    #endregion

    #region IActiveRecord Implementation

    public int? Save()
    {
```

```
        return DataAccessLayer.SaveCustomer(_name.Title, _name.FirstName, _name.Surname,↵
  _address.Street, _address.City, _address.State, _address.ZipCode, _emailAddress);
    }

    public bool Update()
    {
        // ...
    }

    public bool Delete()
    {
        // ...
    }

    #endregion

    #region Fields

    private int _ID;
    private Name _name;
    private Address _address;
    private EmailAddress _emailAddress;

    #endregion
}
```

The Customer implements the IActiveRecord interface, which defines the three methods Save, Update, and Delete. Each of these methods secretly depends on the DataAccessLayer static class. Static classes are like global variables; they are not absolutely harmful but are often abused like this. Nowhere in the Customer's interface is the dependency explicitly mentioned. If you tried to run the Save method inside a unit test, the DataAccessLayer would be accessed directly and concomitantly the database would be accessed, which is both a major bottleneck to the speed of running unit tests and contravenes the purpose of testing code in isolation.

In the next section, you will see how this sort of problem is solved.

How to Unit Test

Unit testing is not particularly difficult. For a competent programmer, unit tests do not pose a significant challenge to write.

Unit Testing with Visual Studio 2010

Visual Studio 2010 comes with a Test Project template that uses the testing framework provided by the Microsoft.VisualStudio.QualityTools.UnitTestFramework assembly. It provides everything that is required to write and run unit tests, all from within the development environment.

NUnit is an alternative third-party framework that presents a couple of advantages over the Visual Studio offering, but is largely similar. NCover analyses the tests' coverage of the code to be tested, responding with a percentage of code covered.

Rhino Mocks is another third-party library that allows complex classes and expensive operations to be mocked-up with simplistic or transparent alternatives.

These are just some of the more common tools in the unit tester's arsenal, which will likely be used with each project.

Test Projects

Typically, a new test project is added that contains the tests for each existing project (Figure 7–3). So, the Domain project, which contains the business logic layer, has its tests in a new Domain.Tests project. This is neater and more scalable than having all of your tests inside one monolithic project. It also separates the test code from the production code so that you do not ship your tests with the product.

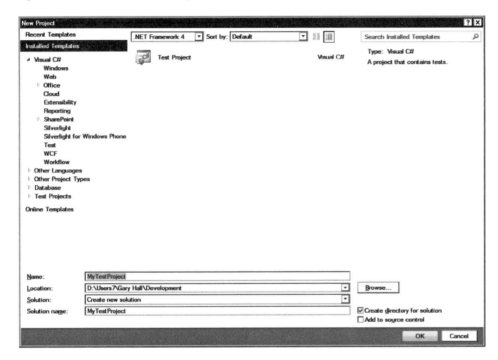

Figure 7–3. Creating a new test project

Once created, the skeleton test project contains a single unit test class and inserts some solution items for editing the test settings and running the tests, as shown in Figure 7–4.

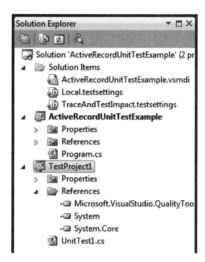

Figure 7–4. *The test project template adds items to Solution Explorer*

Listing 7–2 shows an empty unit test class. Test runners inspect assemblies that require testing and, via reflection, search for attributes on classes and methods that indicate tests that need to be run. The classes are marked with a TestClass attribute and each test method has the TestMethod attribute applied. The TestInitialize and TestCleanup methods are called before and after every test method is executed, respectively. They are used to initialize and release data for every single test because each test is executed in isolation. There should be no dependency on the order that tests are run; most test runners use an alphabetical ordering system rather than adhering to the order that the methods are defined in the class.

Listing 7–2. *A Minimal Unit Test Class*

```
[TestClass]
public class UnitTest1
{
    [TestInitialize]
    public void Initialize()
    {

    }

    [TestMethod]
    public void TestMethod1()
    {

    }

    [TestCleanup]
    public void Cleanup()
    {

    }
}
```

Initialization and cleanup can also be performed on a class and assembly level. Organizing the tests into logical units and grouping them into classes enables a more coarse-grained initialization that is run per module. By grouping the tests for an entire subsystem into their own assembly, the AssemblyInitialize attribute can perform any set up that is require across all tests in the assembly.

Selecting Run ➤ All Tests In Solution from the Test menu compiles the tests and runs them in the Visual Studio Test runner. Figure 7–5 shows that the empty test passes.

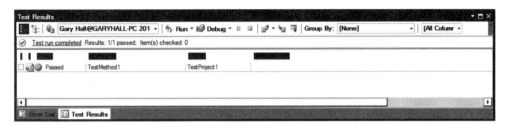

Figure 7–5. A passing (albeit empty) test

NUnit

NUnit is an alternative to using the Visual Studio test environment and can be downloaded from www.nunit.org. The two frameworks share similarities in that they make extensive use of attributes to label classes and methods as testable. Table 7–2 shows the analogous attributes between NUnit and Visual Studio Tests.

Table 7–2. The Similarity Between Testing Attributes in NUnit and Visual Studio Tests

Attribute Purpose	Visual Studio Test	NUnit
Indicate a test class	[TestClass]	[TestFixture]
Indicate a test method	[TestMethod]	[Test]
Per-test initialization	[TestInitialize]	[SetUp]
Per-test clean-up	[TestCleanup]	[TearDown]
Test categorization	[TestCategory]	[Category]
Modular initialization	[ClassInitialize]	[TestFixtureSetUp]
Modular clean-up	[ClassCleanup]	[TestFixtureTearDown]

The two frameworks differ in that Visual Studio tests are linked closely with the development environment so creating and running tests are integral to the development process. But, in order to benefit from the close relationship between tests and the development environment, the tests must be part of a stand-alone test project. NUnit does not impose such a restriction; the test runner will find tests that are present in any assembly and does not provide any Visual Studio integration. NUnit also has better support from continuous integration tools like TeamCity or Cruise Control.

■ **Tip** To integrate NUnit into Visual Studio and to be able to run the tests from Visual Studio's context menus, consider TestDriven.NET.

One of the most compelling reasons to choose NUnit is its constraints model. Compare and contrast the assertions in Listings 7–3 and 7–4. (Assertions will be covered in the next section.)

Listing 7–3. *Visual Studio's Vanilla Assertion*

```
Assert.Equals(myString, "Hello");
```

Listing 7–4. *NUnit's Constraint-based Assertion*

```
Assert.That(myString, Is.EqualTo("Hello"));
```

This is largely a syntactic difference with the latter more closely matching the English language sentence "Assert that myString is equal to 'Hello'." It is largely a personal preference as to which should be used.

RhinoMocks

Back in Listing 7–1, the Customer implementation of the IActiveRecord interface had an embedded dependency on the DataAccessLayer static class. The problem is that testing the Customer class in isolation is extremely difficult because the DataAccessLayer, in turn, has a dependency on the database itself. If the database is unavailable, the DataAccessLayer will eventually time out in its attempt to save to the Customer data and the test will fail. This situation is certainly not desirable: the Customer class should be testable with the database unavailable and, even if the database *were* available, it should not save the data in the context of a unit test.

Listing 7–5 refactors the Customer class so that the DataAccessLayer is injected as a dependency on construction.

Listing 7–5. *The Refactored Customer Class, which Accepts an IDataAccessLayer as an Explicit Dependency*

```
public class Customer : IActiveRecord
{
    #region Constructors

    public Customer(IDataAccessLayer dataAccessLayer, Name name, Address address,↵
EmailAddress emailAddress)
    {
        _dataAccessLayer = dataAccessLayer;
        _name = name;
        _address = address;
        _emailAddress = emailAddress;
    }

    #endregion

    #region IActiveRecord Implementation

    public int? Save()
```

```
    {
        return _dataAccessLayer.SaveCustomer(_name.Title, _name.FirstName, _name.Surname, ↵
_address.Street, _address.City, _address.State, _address.ZipCode, _emailAddress);
    }

    public bool Update()
    {
        // ...
    }

    public bool Delete()
    {
        // ...
    }

    #endregion

    #region Fields

    private IDataAccessLayer _dataAccessLayer;
    private int _ID;
    private Name _name;
    private Address _address;
    private EmailAddress _emailAddress;

    #endregion
}
```

Notice that the DataAccessLayer has been refactored and is no longer a static class. It now has two parts, an interface (IDataAccessLayer) and the implementation that is provided to the Customer class. One of these implementations is likely to be something along the lines of SQLServerDatabase, which provides an implementation that saves Customer objects to a SQL Server database. Now the tests can be rewritten to provide their own minimal IDataAccessLayer implementation that does not access a database. All such dependencies should be *mocked*.

Listing 7–6. The Unit Test that uses a Mocked Version of the IDataAccessLayer

```
[Test]
public void Customer_Can_Be_Saved()
{
    MockRepository mocks = new MockRepository();
    IDataAccessLayer dataAccessLayer = mocks.StrictMock<IDataAccessLayer>();
    Customer customer = new Customer(dataAccessLayer, /* . . . */);
    Expect.Call(dataAccessLayer.SaveCustomer(/* . . . */).Return(1);
    mocks.ReplayAll();
    Assert.Equals(customer.Save(), 1);
    mocks.VerifyAll();
}
```

Listing 7–6 shows a unit test that asserts that the Customer class' Save method calls the IDataAccessLayer's SaveCustomer method and passes in the correct parameters. This is achieved using RhinoMocks' StrictMock, which disallows calls to any methods other than those that have been explicitly expected. The SaveCustomer method is then mocked so that, regardless of the parameters passed in, it will return the integer value '1'.

■ **Tip** The creation of the `MockRepository` is a candidate for putting in module or assembly initialization.

If the initial version of the `Customer` class was written using a test-first approach, it is likely that the `DataAccessLayer` would have been refactored from a static class to an instance of an `IDataAccessLayer` implementation. The dependency would, therefore, always have been injected because the Customer's interface, testability, and subsequent usability becomes more important than the implementation, which is often given much more credence.

NCover

NCover (`www.ncover.com`) is a code coverage tool that will examine an assembly or executable and determine which parts of the code have been executed. When run against unit tests, the code coverage metrics that are important are those of the underlying tested, code. If unit tests are executing a piece of code, then that code is untested. The aim is not necessarily to achieve 100% coverage, but to hit an achievably high level of coverage without significantly degrading productivity.

NBehave

Behavior Driven Development (BDD) is another popular programming paradigm whereby Test Driven Development (TDD) and Domain Driven Design (DDD) are unified. It is more of a catch-all term for established best-practices that, when implemented concurrently in the one project, result in BDD.

NBehave encourages the use of ubiquitous language that should be shared between developers, designers, the client, and all other stakeholders in a project. It also allows the specification of scenarios that the software must fulfill and then tracks which scenarios have been implemented and which are still part of the product backlog.

Writing Tests

As with all programming tasks, writing tests gets easier with practice. It may feel, at first, that there has been a drop in productivity, but remember to take into account that all tests are saving valuable time in the future. Recall a time—and almost every programmer has had this experience—when you lost hours debugging the most infuriating defect that seemed to confound all the established logic of the universe, only to discover that the cause was mind-meltingly trivial. This is exactly the sort of situation that unit testing aims to prevent at the cost of a little bit of overhead throughout development.

Assertions

An assertion is the basic building block of the unit test. In general coding scenarios, assertions verify that a predicate evaluates to true. If they evaluate to false, an error has occurred. In unit testing, a failed assertion corresponds to a failed test. Each test will likely contain multiple assertions, but it will certainly utilize at least one.

Listing 7–7. A Minimal Unit Test that Makes an Assertion that Fails

```
[TestMethod]
public void TestMethod()
{
    Assert.Equals(3, 2);
}
```

The assertion in Listing 7–7 tests the integer values 3 and 2 for equality, which returns false, so this test method would then fail.

All sorts of predicated expressions on many different types can be tested in an assertion: string equality, integer inequality, custom object equality, etc. Always remember the difference between reference equality and logical equality, as exemplified by the assertions in Listing 7–8.

Listing 7–8. The Difference Between Reference Equality and Logical Equality Is a Common "Gotcha"

```
[TestMethod]
public void TestMethod()
{
    MyClass a = new MyClass();
    MyClass b = new MyClass();
    Assert.AreEquals(a, b);      // Logical equality
    Assert.Equals(a, b);         // Reference equality
}
```

Handling Exceptions

The desired behavior of a test is often to throw an exception. Most unit testing frameworks have simple provisions for this, including Visual Studio tests and NUnit. Marking a method with the ExpectedException attribute, which requires the exception type as a parameter, will ensure that the test passes if, and only if, the method body throws the exception.

Listing 7–9. Handling a Test that Expects an Exception to Be Thrown

```
[TestMethod]
[ExpectedException(typeof(DivideByZeroException)]
public void DivideByZeroTest()
{
    int x = testedClass.IntegerDivision(1, 0);
}

// Code to be tested
public int IntegerDivision(int a, int b)
{
    if(b == 0)
    {
        throw new DivideByZeroException();
    }
    return a / b;
}
```

There is a problem with the code in Listing 7–9. The last line of the method where the current execution context falls out of the method scope is never called. The exception thrown on the previous line unwinds the stack from that point and results in a passed test. The test runner catches this exception, passes the test because that exception was supposed to be thrown, and then moves on to the next test. If you are operating a code coverage framework and including your tests coverage in the metrics, this last line will not be included. To circumvent this in NCover, you can add the //ea (exclude attribute) command-line switch to omit methods with the ExpectedException attribute from code coverage. It's not ideal, but it's a suitable workaround.

If you are using NUnit, there's another option available, shown in Listing 7–10, that fits in better with the normal style of asserting expected behavior.

Listing 7–10. Asserting that a Piece of Code Throws an Expected Exception in NUnit

```
[Test]
public void DivideByZeroTest()
{
    Assert.Throws(typeof(DivideByZeroException), () => testedClass.IntegerDivision(1, 0));
}
```

The first argument is the type of exception that should be thrown by the second argument, which is a delegate that expects no parameters. This code will be fully covered by NCover.

AAA: Arrange, Act, Assert

A popular way to organize unit tests is called 'Arrange, Act, Assert' or 'AAA'. The steps involved are:

1. Arrange: set up the state that is required for the test.

2. Act: execute the code that is to be tested.

3. Assert: use assertions to test that the expected state change occurred.

Listing 7–11 shows an example of the AAA system in practice.

Listing 7–11. Using the Arrange, Act, Assert System of Organizing Tests

```
[TestMethod]
public void Test()
{
    // Arrange

    // Act

    // Assert
}
```

Most of the time, the Arrange and Act steps are common to a number of separate assertions that can be taken individually so that each test corresponds to a single, atomic expectation. When the test runner fails a test, it's subsequently easier to find the specific failing assertion. In this scenario, each test can correspond to a subclass of the AAA base class (see Listing 7–12).

■ **Tip** Naming tests is incredibly important. Imagine that you have just coded a new feature and run all of the existing tests. Sadly, you have broken a regression test and need to determine what change you made that went wrong. If the tests are all named badly—like `Test()` and `Test1()`–then you are in trouble. Your debugging time has just increased while you decipher the intent of the testing code.

The moral of the story is that you need to empathize with your fellow programmer and name your tests properly. It is better to be extremely verbose than vague or ambiguous. This is also a good place to name_your_methods_with_underscores_separating_each_word. When the test fails, at least you have a neat, natural language sentence that explains exactly what went wrong.

Listing 7–12. Abstracting the AAA Into a Subclass

```
public abstract class TestBase
{
    [TestInitialize]
    public void Initialization()
    {
        Arrange();
        Act();
    }

    protected virtual void Arrange() {}
    protected abstract void Act();
}

public MyTestCases : TestBase
{
    private IDivider _divisionImplementation;
    private int _divisionResult;

    protected override void Arrange()
    {
        _divisionImplementation = new IntegerDivider();
    }

    protected override void Act()
    {
        _divisionResult = _divisionImplementation.Divide(5, 5);
    }

    [TestMethod]
    public void Division_By_Self_Should_Return_1()
    {
        Assert.Equals(_divisionResult, 1);
    }
}
```

161

Remember that the entry point for each test is the `TestMethod` but that, before each test is executed, the `TestInitialize` method is executed. Intialization is split into two parts: arranging the state, which is virtual and empty by default so it can be ignored, then executing the code to be tested, which is abstract and therefore *must* be implemented.

Public Methods Only

There is some confusion over whether private methods should be tested. On the one hand, each unit test should test the minimal functionality in isolation: testing a method that calls another method is more like an integration test and increases the possible fault paths. However, testing private methods breaks encapsulation and is only achievable by circumventing privatization of a method. It is probably best just to test public methods. If you are testing your public methods and a private method is never covered, then the private method is obsolete and serves no purpose. Testing public methods only keeps the implementation of the method private, which protects the tests from any fluctuations in implementation. This can only be a good thing.

It is possible to open up internal methods to other assemblies using the `InternalsVisibleTo` attribute in the `AssemblyInfo`. The difference here is that the methods are considered public to the other classes contained in the same assembly.

Summary

Unit testing is very much a recommended practice. Although there will be many readers who have already been converted and thus unit test as a matter of course, there are still many development teams who have shifted unit testing to the back-burner indefinitely.

It's not easy to switch to unit testing, but that is no reason not to do so. The effort expended up front will be recouped manifold in future savings. It's finally time to bring unit testing to the fore and implement this practice as part of your daily work. If you are "merely" a grunt programmer in your team, keep pressing for unit testing. When the benefits are reaped, you can be the first to say, "I told you so" and associate yourself with a resounding success.

However, bear in mind that your product is only as good as its tests. While this correctly implies that having no tests will likely result in a defect-ridden product, having *some* tests does not instantly yield a defect-free product. You need the *right* tests, which differ from method to method and class to class.

CHAPTER 8

■■■

Data Access Layer

Silverlight and some WPF applications do not use offline storage for persisting data. Instead, they use a relational database to store the object data in a structured format. Rather than employing serialization, applications that use a relational database for storage will have a dedicated Data Access Layer (DAL) that serves to insulate the model from additional responsibility while allowing clients to load and save the model state.

There are four typical operations that the DAL should provide for each object in the model: create, read, update, and delete (often given the unfortunate acronym CRUD). These operations correspond to inserting new records in the database, retrieving records from the database, editing existing records, and removing records entirely from the database, respectively. Clients can combine these simple operations to fulfill all of the requirements necessary to interact with application data.

DALs can be implemented in many different ways, from simplistic wrappers around SQL statements to complex modules that require maintenance in their own right. Explaining how to fit the latter into an MVVM application is the focus of this chapter.

Object-Relational Dichotomy

At a coarse-grained level, the .NET Framework uses classes that interact with each other in order to solve a particular problem. These classes are a mixture of data, which comprise the state of an object, and method implementations, which transform the data in some meaningful way. Relational database management systems (RDBMS), on the other hand, consist solely of data that has no associated behavior—absent stored procedures, of course. An RDBMS solves a very specific problem that does not concern objects. That is, it does not concern them until one tries to convert from one to the other (from objects to database tables or vice versa).

DATABASE KEYS

Database tables should always have some sort of key that uniquely identifies each record and distinguishes it from other records in the same table. There are also different kinds of keys. Natural keys are composed of data that is a real-world property of the entity being mapped. The natural key for a person could be his name, but this precludes multiple people being stored who share the same name. Natural keys can be hard to determine without resorting to a composite key, which is a key made up of more than one property that, when combined, uniquely identifies an entity. For a person, his name and date of birth could be combined to form a natural composite key, but even this is dissatisfying because it prevents the—rare but plausible—case of two people sharing both name and birth date. For this reason, rather than struggling to force a natural key on an entity, a surrogate key is often used. This is a value that does not relate to the entity directly and is contrived to satisfy the requirement for uniqueness. Typically, the surrogate key is an integer that auto-increments with each additional record added to the table, or a Universally Unique Identifier (UUID), which is a 32-byte (128–bit) value that is virtually guaranteed to be unique (there are roughly 3.4×10^{38} possible values). Object-Relational Mapping (ORM) libraries, as discussed in this chapter, typically recommend surrogate keys for simplicity.

In an RDBMS, data is stored in tables, which are two-dimensional data structures where each column applies to an atomic datum and each row is a full record of a single entry in the table. Table 8–1 shows a trivial database design that contains products, customers, and orders aggregated into one monolithic table.

Table 8–1. A Monolithic—Unnormalized—Database Table

Product Name	Product Price	Customer Name	Customer Address	Order Number	Order Date
XBox 360	100.00	Gary Hall	Sommershire, England	XX217P11D	08/02/2010
HP Probook	500.00	Gary Hall	Sommershire, England	XX217P11D	08/02/2010
Pro WPF and Silverlight MVVM	40.00	A. Reader	Yorton, Sumplace	IJ094A73N	11/10/2010
Pro WPF and Silverlight MVVM	40.00	A. Reader	Theirton, Utherplace	IJ876Q98X	10/02/2010

This table poses a number of problems that render it so difficult and potentially problematic to use that it is almost useless. The most egregious problem is that there is so much repeated data. If the name of this book or its price were to change, the database would require changes in two different places. Similarly, if I changed my name or address, the database would have to be changed wherever this data occurred. The repetition is unnecessary and causes a maintenance headache, at best. Also, how is the correct "A. Reader" found without using both their name and address? As it stands, there is no single distinguishing column that allows differentiation between the two customers, so their whole data record must be used to ensure uniqueness.

Normalization is the process of refactoring a database so that it conforms to a structure more suitable for querying. It frees the database of anomalies that negatively affect the integrity of the data.

There are many different levels of normalization, called normal forms (or NF), which are assigned an ascending index to indicate the rigor of the normalization. Although normalization can progress to 6th Normal Form (6NF), 3rd Normal Form is usually considered sufficient because, by this point, the tables are quite likely to be free of anomalies. When the database table from Table 8–1 is normalized, the result is what is shown in Table 8–2.

Table 8–2. Table 8–1 Normalized to 3NF

Product Code	Product Name	Product Price
X360	XBox 360	100.00
HPP	HP Probook	500.00
WPFMVVM	Pro WPF and Silverlight MVVM	40.00

Customer ID	Customer Name	Customer Address
1	Gary Hall	Sommershire, England
2	A. Reader	Yorton, Sumplace
3	A. Reader	Theirton, Utherplace

Order Number	Order Date	Customer ID
XX217P11D	08/02/2010	1
IJ094A73N	11/10/2010	2
IJ876Q98X	10/02/2010	3

There are now three tables: Products, Customers, and Orders. The products and customers have been assigned identity columns that uniquely differentiate each record as being distinct. However, there is a table missing that links each order to the products that the customer purchased. For this, an OrderLine table is required, as shown in Table 8–3.

Table 8–3. The OrderLine table

Order Number	Product Code
XX217P11D	X360
XX217P11D	HPP
IJ094A73N	WPFMVVM
IJ876Q98X	WPFMVVM

This table allows an order to contain multiple products while simultaneously allowing each product to be used in different orders. It is an example of a many-to-many relationship and contrasts to the one-to-many relationship between orders and customers (an order belongs to a single customer, but a customer can create multiple orders).

Now, imagine that there are corresponding Product, Order, and Customer classes, each of which contains the same data as is here in the database tables. However, there are also operations on the classes that allow collaborations between the object instances. Listing 8–1 is an example implementation of such classes.

Listing 8–1. A Sample Implementation of the Product, Order, and Customer Classes

```
public class Product
{
    public Product(string name, decimal price)
    {
        Name = name;
        Price = price;
    }

    public string Name
    {
        get;
        private set;
    }

    public decimal Price
    {
        get;
        private set;
    }
}

public class Customer
{
    public Customer(int id, string name)
    {
        ID = id;
        Name = name;
        _orders = new List<Order>();
    }

    public int ID
    {
        get;
        private set;
    }

    public string Name
    {
        get;
        private set;
    }

    public IEnumerable<Order> Orders
```

```
    {
        get { return _orders; }
    }

    public void AddOrder(Order order)
    {
        _orders.Add(order);
    }

    private ICollection<Order> _orders;
}

public class Order
{
    public Order(string code, Customer customer)
    {
        Code = code;
        Customer = customer;
        OrderLines = new List<Product>();
    }

    public string Code
    {
        get;
        private set;
    }

    public Customer Customer
    {
        get;
        private set;
    }

    public IEnumerable<Product> OrderLines
    {
        get;
        private set;
    }

    public void AddOrderLine(Product product)
    {
        _orderLines.Add(product);
    }

    private ICollection<Product> _orderLines;
}
```

Notice that there is no OrderLine class; it is simply implied in the relationship between Order and Product. This is a key signifier for how different the two paradigms are and the difficulty that is inherent in reconciling the object-relational dichotomy.

Mapping Object Relationships

There are many different relationship types that can exist between objects. Objects can be compositions of other objects, whereby the container and the contents are both intrinsically linked. If the containing class is destroyed, then all of the contained objects are also destroyed. The UML diagram in Figure 8–1 shows the Customer class is composed of Orders.

Figure 8–1. *The Customer class has a composition relationship with the Order class.*

If a specific Customer instance is destroyed, all of the Order instances that it contains should also be destroyed. The relationship between Order and Product is one of aggregation, which does not link the lifetimes of the two objects so strictly. Instead, the two can be created and destroyed independently, as shown in Figure 8–2.

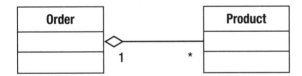

Figure 8–2. *The Order class has an aggregation relationship with the Product class.*

This makes sense because each Product is not wedded to a specific Order. If the relationship was composition, deleting an Order would consequently delete all of the Products in that Order, so no-one could subsequently purchase any more of that Product!

In the RDBMS, both of these relationships would be one-to-many, with the primary key of the Customer table referenced as a foreign key within the Order table. The difference would be that the composition relationship would require the ON CASCADE DELETE option when creating the Order table.

The contained objects in composition and aggregation need not be collections. Suppose the Customer class was refactored so that the customer's address was placed into its own Address class. The Address would only ever be referenced by the one Customer object, and the Customer object would only have one address. This, then, is a one-to-one composition relationship, as shown in Figure 8–3.

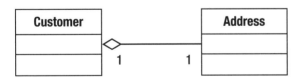

Figure 8–3. *The Customer class has a composition relationship with the Address class, but it is one-to-one.*

There are two ways to handle this relationship in the RDBMS. The first option is to ignore that it is one-to-one and decide which side seems most reasonable for multiplicity. In this instance, it makes more sense for customers to be allowed to store multiple addresses—in case the shipping address differs from the billing address, for example—rather than pander to the small demographic of customers who live at the same address. From this point, the tables can have a foreign key relationship to satisfy the new multiplicity: Address would be handed the Customer ID field as a foreign key. The other option would be to flatten the relationship out on the RDBMS side because it serves no purpose, leaving all of the address data in the Customer table. The objects may be retrieved with a composition relationship, but the database itself ignores that and stores the data in a single table.

The final object relationship occurs when two objects have a many-to-many relationship, as shown in Figure 8–4.

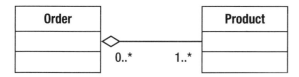

Figure 8–4. *The Product and Order classes have a many-to-many relationship.*

Orders can contain many Products, and Products can belong to many Orders. In fact, the multiplicity 1..* indicates that an Order *must* have at least one Product, whereas 0..* implies that Products can exist wholly independent of Orders. In this scenario, an *association table* is required, which links the Order and Product tables together. This is necessary, because a many-to-many relationship cannot exist in an RDBMS and must be factored out into two one-to-many relationships instead. The OrderLine table from Table 8–3 is exactly the association table that is required in this case.

Mapping Class Hierarchies

Although it is advisable to look first at the possibility of composing objects through a "has-a" relationship, object-oriented programming provides the facility for deriving one class from another to form an "is-a" relationship. With a sufficiently complex domain model, class hierarchies can form that succinctly solve the problem at hand. Mapping this to a relational model is certainly achievable, but there are three options to choose from that each present themselves as appropriate under varying circumstances.

To make these examples clearer, I am going to alter the design of the e-commerce system to include a class hierarchy. Customer seems like a good option with two subclasses inheriting from a base class (see Figure 8–5).

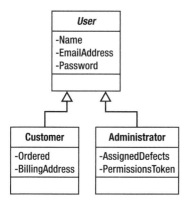

Figure 8–5. *The Customer class refactored to distinguish between different types of User*

The common data (the Customer's Name, EmailAddress, and Password) have been extracted and placed into a superclass called User, which is marked as abstract and cannot be instantiated in its own right. The Customer class now only contains the Orders list and inherits the other data from the User. A second subclass has been created to represent administrators for the application. Administrators also have a Name, EmailAddress, and Password, but they have a PermissionsToken, which would determine what level of administrative privileges the administrator possesses, and a list of AssignedDefects, which are bugs that have been handed to them for investigation and fixing. Now that the inheritance hierarchy is in place, the mapping options can be examined.

Table-Per-Class-Hierarchy

The easiest option, from an implementation standpoint, is to flatten the whole hierarchy down and create a single table that incorporates all of the data (see Table 8–4). While the User data will undoubtedly be shared and not repeated, each record will contain redundant data depending on whether it applies to a Customer or an Administrator. This can affect data integrity, too, because the AssignedDefects and Orders fields are collections that hold a one-to-many relationship with their respective object types. The tables that contain the data for these fields are not prevented from referencing a row in the User table of either Customer or Administrator type. This could leave Customers with AssignedDefects and Administrators with Orders, which is clearly erroneous.

Table 8–4. *The User Class Hierarchy Implemented as a Single Table*

UserID	Name	EmailAddress	Password	BillingAddressID	PermissionsToken
1	Gary Hall	gary.hall@apress.com	112ADP33X	NULL	76
2	Joe Bloggs	Joe.Bloggs@hotmail.co.uk	938BCX82L	45	NULL
3	John Doe	John_Doe@hotmail.com	364PZI32H	33	NULL

Table-Per-Concrete-Class

Each concrete class—that is, each non-abstract class—has its own corresponding table. The database does not recognize that there is shared data between the different subclasses. In Table 8–5, the User abstract class is ignored, and the two tables replicate the Name, EmailAddress, and Password fields, which is somewhat redundant. However, the Order and Defect tables will correctly reference the separated Customer and Administrator, respectively, with no possibility of a mix-up. As long as a user cannot be both a Customer and an Administrator, the redundancy is not too much of a problem.

Table 8–5. *The User Class Hierarchy Implemented with a Table for Each Subclass*

CustomerID	Name	EmailAddress	Password	BillingAddressID
1	Joe Bloggs	Joe.Bloggs@hotmail.co.uk	938BCX82L	45
2	John Doe	John_Doe@hotmail.com	364PZI32H	33

AdministratorID	Name	EmailAddress	Password	PermissionsToken
1	Gary Hall	gary.hall@apress.com	112ADP33X	76

Table-Per-Class

The final alternative is to include the abstract base class and allow it a table of its own. The subclass tables then hold a foreign key reference to the appropriate User, so the shared data is given one single schema in the database (see Table 8–6). While the implementation of this method is a little more complicated, the database is properly normalized. The application could be extended to allow a User to be simultaneously a Customer and an Administrator without any alterations to the database structure.

Table 8–6. *The User Class Hierarchy Implemented with a Table for Each Concrete Class*

UserID	Name	EmailAddress	Password
1	Gary Hall	gary.hall@apress.com	112ADP33X
2	Joe Bloggs	Joe.Bloggs@hotmail.co.uk	938BCX82L
3	John Doe	John_Doe@hotmail.com	364PZI32H

CustomerID	UserID	BillingAddressID
1	2	45
2	3	33

AdministratorID	UserID	PermissionsToken
1	1	76

DAL Implementations

So far, there is a domain model of a simple e-commerce system and a corresponding database structure. What is left is to bridge the gap with the code that will perform the CRUD operations required by the clients of the model—most likely to be the ViewModel. The objective of the DAL code is to protect the object schema from changes to the database schema. This requires a type of mediator that will isolate the object model from the domain model while allowing clients to transfer data to and from each schema.

The DataMapper pattern [PoEAA ,Fowler] is employed throughout the DAL to keep model classes and the database independent of each other and, more important, independent of the DataMapper itself (see Figure 8–6). Only the clients of the DataMapper are aware of its existence and use it to interact with the RDBMS.

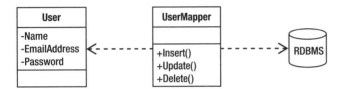

Figure 8–6. *The DataMapper pattern: A UserMapper acts as the mediator between the RDBMS and User*

class

A big decision must be made whether to implement the DAL manually, which allows a greater degree of control over the code, or whether to integrate a third-party library, which will generate the mapping layer automatically. Although the latter will undoubtedly be quicker to implement, assimilating a library into a project remains a non-trivial task that requires significant developer resource. There are enough Object Relational Mapping (ORM) libraries available—at no cost—that using an existing solution should be the default position. However, guidance for manually implementing the DAL is provided to give background on the internal workings of an ORM. Then, the current most popular third-party ORM libraries are briefly compared and contrasted.

Manual Implementation

Before undertaking the monumental task of manually implementing a mapping layer, consider whether the resources required are worth the gains in control. Reinvention of the wheel should be avoided if possible, especially when there are so many compelling ORM libraries available. The DAL fits into the category of application infrastructure—any effort expended building infrastructure is effort diverted from adding true value to a project. Caveats aside, it is still beneficial to understand what goes into a mapping layer because there is a lot of noise generated by third-party components that must remain domain agnostic so that it remains all things to all people, which is not an easy task.

Listing 8–2 shows the interface of the UserMapper class that will be used by the ViewModel to interact with the underlying data storage mechanism. The implementation will follow: method-by-method. For now, notice that there are four methods for finding Users, two of which return a unique User when given their ID and EmailAddress fields, respectively, two of which return lists of Users. The FindByName method accepts a partial name and, because User Names are not unique, multiple User instances may be returned. The FindAll method, on the other hand, returns every user in the database without discrimination.

There is also a single method each for the remaining create, update, and delete aspects of the CRUD acronym, each accepting an existing User instance to act upon.

Listing 8–2. The Interface for the UserMapper Class

```
public class UserMapper
{
    public User FindByID(int id)

    public User FindByEmailAddress(string emailAddress)

    public IEnumerable<User> FindByName(string name)

    public IEnumerable<User> FindAll()

    public void Update(User user)

    public int Insert(User user)

    public void Delete(User user)
}
```

To implement this class succinctly, some helper methods will be required to avoid needless repetition of database access code (see Listing 8–3). The .NET Framework provides the ADO.NET services for accessing databases without tying code to a specific vendor. The class will require a database Connection, which (for now) will be opened and closed inside each method, making each action atomic. A Command will be executed on the Connection, instructing the data store to return the requested data, insert new records, and update or remove existing records. The DataReader class will be examined to retrieve the correct data into newly instantiated User objects in each of the Find* methods.

Listing 8–3. Database Interaction Helper Methods

```
public UserMapper(string connectionString)
{
    _connectionString = connectionString;
}

private string _connectionString;
private IDbConnection _databaseConnection;

private bool ConnectToDatabase(string connectionString)
{
    bool success = false;
    _databaseConnection = new SqlConnection(connectionString);
    try
    {
        _databaseConnection.Open();
        success = true;
    }
    catch (Exception)
    {
        success = false;
    }
    return success;
}
```

```
    private void DisconnectFromDatabase()
    {
        if (_databaseConnection.State != ConnectionState.Open)
        {
            _databaseConnection.Close();
        }
    }

    private IDataReader ExecuteReadCommand(IDbCommand command)
    {
        IDataReader dataReader = null;
        if (_databaseConnection.State == ConnectionState.Open)
        {
            dataReader = command.ExecuteReader();
        }
        return dataReader;
    }

    private User CreateUserFromReader(IDataReader dataReader)
    {
        int id = dataReader.GetInt32(0);
        string name = dataReader.GetString(1);
        string emailAddress = dataReader.GetString(2);
        string password = dataReader.GetString(2);

        return new User(id, name, emailAddress, password);
    }

    private IEnumerable<User> Find(string sqlCommand)
    {
        ConnectToDatabase(_connectionString);

        IDbCommand findByIDCommandCommand = new SqlCommand(sqlCommand, ↩
    (SqlConnection)_databaseConnection);

        IDataReader userReader = ExecuteReadCommand(findByIDCommandCommand);

        ICollection<User> users = new List<User>();
        while (userReader.Read())
        {
            users.Add(CreateUserFromReader(userReader));
        }

        DisconnectFromDatabase();

        return users;
    }
```

ViewModels must construct this mapper and furnish it with a relevant connection string into the database. ConnectToDatabase/DisconnectFromDatabase methods are self-explanatory and will be called at the start and end of each method. Alternatively, the connection could be kept alive for the lifetime of the class or maintained manually by the client code, which will group retrieving, editing, and deleting code into an atomic unit that can share a connection. In an online application that operates over a stateless protocol—such as HTTP—it is recommended that the connection is initiated when the request commences and is closed as the request is terminated.

The Find method is parameterized to accept a specific SQL statement that will return records from the User table. Each public Find* method will utilize this to avoid code repetition. The ADO.NET calls return IDataReader implementations, which can be interrogated to iterate over and retrieve data from a table. The CreateUserFromReader method accepts an IDataReader, extracts the data from each field in the current row, and constructs a new User object from this data.

■ **Tip** All of this helper code could be factored out into a low-level data access interface, which could be injected into each mapper. As it stands, this code is dependent on the SQL implementations of the generic ADO.NET interfaces. This is acceptable for an example, but further refactoring would be advised for production code. It is also worth noting the lack of acceptable error handling in the examples.

The public interface is implemented in Listing 8–4, and this mapper is now ready to be used by a ViewModel or other client code.

Listing 8–4. The Implementation of the UserMapper's Public Interface

```
public User FindByID(int id)
{
    IEnumerable<User> users = Find(string.Format("SELECT * FROM User WHERE ID = {0}", id));
    return users.SingleOrDefault();
}

public User FindByEmailAddress(string emailAddress)
{
    IEnumerable<User> users = Find(string.Format("SELECT * FROM User WHERE EmailAddress =
 {0}", emailAddress));
    return users.SingleOrDefault();
}

public IEnumerable<User> FindByName(string name)
{
    return Find(string.Format("SELECT * FROM User WHERE Name LIKE '%{0}%'", name));
}

public IEnumerable<User> FindAll()
{
    return Find("SELECT * FROM User");
}

public void Update(User user)
{
    string updateUserCommandText = string.Format("UPDATE User SET Name='{0}',
 EmailAddress='{1}', Password='{2}' WHERE ID={3}", user.Name, user.EmailAddress,
 user.Password, user.ID);

    IDbCommand updateCommand = new SqlCommand(updateUserCommandText,
```

```
    (SqlConnection)_databaseConnection);

    updateCommand.ExecuteNonQuery();
}

public int Insert(User user)
{
    string insertUserCommandText = string.Format("INSERT INTO User(Name, EmailAddress,↵
Password) VALUES('{0}', '{1}', '{2}')", user.Name, user.EmailAddress, user.Password);

    IDbCommand insertCommand = new SqlCommand(insertUserCommandText,↵
(SqlConnection)_databaseConnection);

    int userID = (int)insertCommand.ExecuteScalar();

    return userID;
}

public void Delete(User user)
{
    string deleteUserCommandText = string.Format("DELETE FROM User WHERE ID={0}", user.ID);

    IDbCommand deleteCommand = new SqlCommand(deleteUserCommandText,↵
(SqlConnection)_databaseConnection);

    deleteCommand.ExecuteNonQuery();
}
```

It is clear even from this trivial example—which has not even considered the class hierarchy that could inherit from the User class—that manually implementing a data mapping layer is time consuming. All newly written code is prone to errors, and the only guaranteed way to avoid introducing new defects is *not to write code at all*. Ordinarily, this is impractical, but with such a rich array of ORM libraries available, it is perhaps the sensible choice.

Third-Party Implementations

The following third-party components share some similarities and have some important differences that may influence whether or not they are appropriate for a certain project. Perhaps it may be pertinent to develop a miniature prototype to find which ORM library best fits the requirements at hand. At least if things go awry, no harm will be caused to production code and minimal time will be diverted from more pressing tasks.

For all of these explanations, the simplistic e-commerce system's tables that have been created thus far will be used to automatically generate a mapping layer.

LINQ to SQL

LINQ to SQL (L2S) goes further than merely generating mapping code: it creates domain objects whose schema is inferred from an existing database. Its learning curve is low relative to the alternatives, and it is seamlessly integrated into Visual Studio 2010. A mapping file (.dbml) can be generated automatically from an existing database schema within seconds and then used immediately in an application (see Figure 8–7). This makes L2S a compelling choice, even though it omits a few features that the alternatives boast.

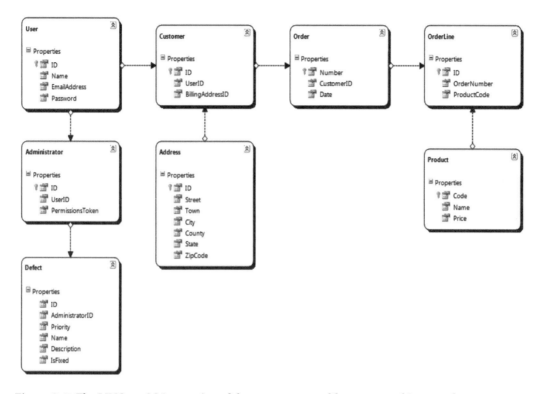

Figure 8–7. The LINQ-to-SQL mapping of the e-commerce tables, generated in seconds

The graphical designer generates a class for the User table and a `DataContext` that is used to interact with the database. For security purposes, it is advisable to construct the `DataContext` with an existing database connection that has been created without exposing the connection string details. The `DataContext.Users` property is a `System.Data.Linq.Table<User>` type and can be queried using either the LINQ query syntax or the built-in `IEnumerable` extension methods (see Listing 8–5).

Listing 8–5. Access a User by Name Using Both Syntaxes

```
DataContext dataContext = new DataContext(connection);

// LINQ style
var matchingUsers = from user in dataContext.Users
                    where user.Name.Contains("Hall")
                    select user;

// IEnumerable extensions style
IEnumerable<User> matchingUsers = dataContext.Users.Where(u => u.Name.Contains("Hall"));
```

LINQ to SQL will automatically generate relationships between classes that map to their equivalent database structure, analyzing foreign key constraints and association tables to approximate a domain model as closely as possible. The classes are all declared partial, so methods can be added directly without the need to subclass or wrap the generated model. Furthermore, bespoke stored procedures can also be attached to the `DataContext` and executed like normal methods. Of course, there is the implicit overhead of querying the database, so this should be used sparingly like all database access. However, being automatic, L2S does not allow a great deal of control of the generation of the model classes. There are a few parameters that can be tweaked, but, for fine-grained control of the process, another library may suffice.

L2S also implements the Unit of Work pattern (see the section "Unit of Work" later in this chapter) so that all changes to the model are committed in a single, atomic transaction.

Entity Framework

Entity Framework is a more fully rounded ORM framework than LINQ to SQL, allowing more complex relationships between model classes, which it calls entities (see Figure 8–8).

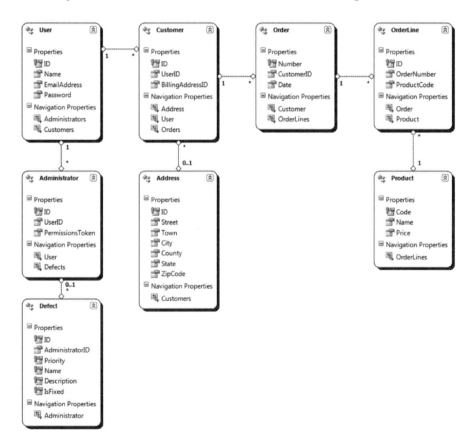

Figure 8–8. The E-commerce database mapped using Entity Framework

Entity Framework is, conceptually, the older brother of LINQ to SQL. Whereas L2S can only manage a 1–1 mapping of domain objects to database tables, EF allows for more complex object relationships.

With the advent of .NET Framework 4, LINQ to Entities is recommended for all but trivial applications or prototyping, which form the target audience of LINQ to SQL.

NHibernate

NHibernate is a popular third-party ORM framework that is not integrated into Visual Studio. It uses XML files for declarative definition of objects and how they map to a database table. Listing 8–6 shows a mapping file that covers part of the e-commerce model.

Listing 8–6. NHibernate Mapping XML File Showing the Definitions of Some Mappings

```xml
<?xml version="1.0" encoding="utf-8" ?>
<hibernate-mapping xmlns="urn:nhibernate-mapping-2.2"
                   assembly="ECommerce.Model"
                   namespace="ECommerce.Model">

  <class name="Product">
    <id name="Code">
      <generator class="assigned" />
    </id>
    <property name="Name" />
    <property name="Price" />
  </class>

  <class name="User">
    <id name="ID">
      <generator class="identity" />
    </id>
    <property name="Name" />
    <property name="EmailAddres" />
    <property name="Password" />
    <union-subclass name="Customer">
      <component name="BillingAddress" class="ECommerce.Model.Address, ECommerce.Model" />
      <bag name="Orders" table="OrderLine" cascade="all">
        <key column="CustomerID"/>
        <many-to-many column="OrderID" class="ECommerce.Model.Order, ECommerce.Model"/>
      </bag>
    </union-subclass>
    <union-subclass name="Administrator">
      <property name="PermissionsToken" />
    </union-subclass>
  </class>

  <class name="Order">
    <id name="Number">
      <generator class="assigned" />
    </id>
    <component name="Customer" class="ECommerce.Mode.Customer, ECommerce.Model" />
    <property name="Date" />
  </class>

</hibernate-mapping>
```

There are many different options available with NHibernate, and a very rich and complex mapping can be generated. However, as the XML shows, there is a steep learning curve that must be overcome when working with NHibernate. Whereas Linq-to-SQL and Entity Framework both integrate seamlessly with Visual Studio and have their own graphical editor to ease configuration, there is no equivalent available for NHibernate. This can negatively impact development velocity for a while until each developer becomes more familiar with the configuration.

■ **Note** This does not apply specifically to NHibernate, but to development in general. Try not to let particular skills amalgamate in a single developer silo. Try to spread the requisite skillset throughout the team's members so as to minimize the impact of a single developer leaving the project. Try, for example, to implement some pair programming when investigating new technologies or libraries, such as NHibernate, so that multiple developers accrue knowledge together.

Supporting Patterns

All of the previous examples of data mapping implementations may have solved the impedance mismatch between relational and object data models, but they introduced a highly undesirable side effect. They all placed a heavy burden on the client code—which will most often be ViewModel code—that detracts from its intended responsibility. A sufficiently complex collaboration of multiple domain objects will result in a ViewModel developer writing querying code that efficiently retrieves the required objects from storage. To alleviate this burden, a further level of abstraction is required that will contain the guts of the database interaction and expose a high-level interface that is simple for the ViewModels to use.

The Repository Pattern

The Repository pattern [PoEAA ,Fowler] fulfills this remit, mediating between the domain and data mapping layers.

Collaboration

As shown in Figure 8–9, the ViewModel does not use the data mapper directly. In fact, the data mapper becomes one of many possible strategy implementations that the repository can use; another being an in-memory or mocked mapper that can be used for unit testing purposes.

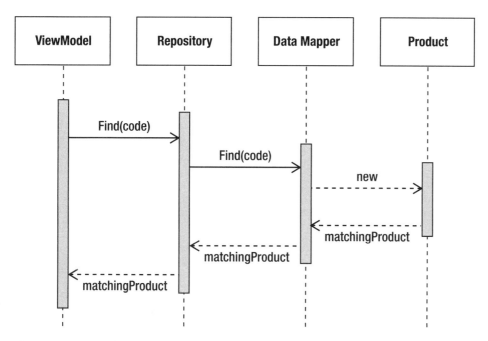

Figure 8–9. *Using the repository to retrieve a Product instance when given its Code*

The repository need not wrap the data mapper as closely as implied in Figure 8–9 and can provide a more coarse-grained interface to accessing domain objects. However, its main purpose is to make the ViewModel's job easier and to reduce the effort of object retrieval to free up development time for focusing on the ViewModel's main responsibilities.

Unit of Work

Even with a repository in place, one area still remains that clouds the responsibilities of the ViewModel code: tracking domain object changes. Other than operating to different data representation paradigms, the object-relational dichotomy also reveals itself in how they both handle messaging. In an object model, messages passed between objects are supposed to be atomic, fine-grained, and strictly serving a single purpose. However, when communicating with a database—which will involve crossing a process or, more commonly, a network boundary—these small-but-frequent messages become a wasteful bottleneck. It is better to roll together all of the interaction that should occur into one large chunk and limit communication to as few messages as possible.

The Unit of Work [PoEAA, Fowler] pattern tracks changes to a domain model and, when requested to commit, will send all of the necessary updates in a single database query. It may be worthwhile bearing in mind that there should be a business case for implementing the unit of work—the extra hits to the database may not prove problematic to your application. Adding the Unit of Work pattern indiscriminately is akin to premature optimization, which, without proving that a bottleneck exists, is a waste of resources. Remember: you ain't gonna need it.

Collaboration

Figure 8–10 shows the collaboration between the classes involved in the Unit of Work pattern.

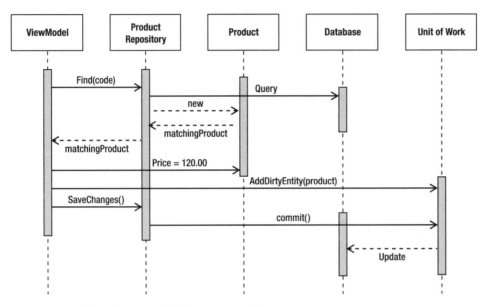

Figure 8–10. *The Unit of Work UML sequence diagram*

The ViewModel holds a reference to a Repository as well as UnitOfWork. When a new entity is created, the UnitOfWork is informed so that it can persist all of the changes made to in-memory objects all in one atomic transaction.

Creating the Data Schema

The data schema that the RDBMS eventually contains is all too often written early in a project's lifetime, and any subsequent changes to it are considered expensive. Once written, the object model is then built on top of the data schema with little room to maneuver if requirements change. In an agile project, the data schema will be constructed in a very different fashion, which may seem alien at first but presents some compelling benefits.

Generate, Not Create

The main difference is that the data schema is not written at all; it is generated. The object model already contains a mixture of data and behavior, so the data schema can be seen as a subset of the object model anyway. The object model is also likely to be quite volatile and will require changing frequently in its early stages. By generating the data schema, change becomes just as acceptable here as it is in the object model. A final difference is that the data schema should not be subject to a big, up-front design. At any one time in the project, only the parts of the database that are in use by the object model should have been generated.

Summary

This chapter covered how to integrate an RDBMS into a modern WPF or Silverlight application. A brief overview of how an RDBMS organizes data into structures was presented, along with the different data schemas that can be created from the same basic object types.

We examined the impedance mismatch between the object model and the data schema and investigated different avenues that can be taken to overcome this obstacle. Although implementing your own ORM is certainly possible, such infrastructure is best left to third-party components that can be used for free even in commercial projects. The time spent integrating such libraries is time saved by not reinventing the wheel.

Finally, it was recommended that the data schema be generated from the object model, rather than trying to infer a suitable object model from the data schema. This will ensure that the data schema is as flexible and open to change as the object model should be by default.

CHAPTER 9

■ ■ ■

Application Support

So far, this book has covered the individual layers of the MVVM architecture—model, view, and ViewModel—in sufficient detail to create an application employing this pattern. There are some remaining modules of important functionality that have been omitted thus far.

This chapter will plug those holes with the glue that binds together the three aforementioned layers. This is the application support (henceforth app support) that covers a whole gamut of extra functionality that does not sit comfortably in any of the established layers of MVVM. This chapter will deal with four of these modules that are most commonly required in a modern WPF or Silverlight application.

Topics covered in this chapter are: the serialization of the object graph, implementing a data access layer, allowing users to configure the behavior, and settings of the application, and adding extensibility via plug-ins.

The diagram in Figure 9–1 shows how the layers are organized when app support layers are added to the architecture. The arrows indicate the direction of the dependencies.

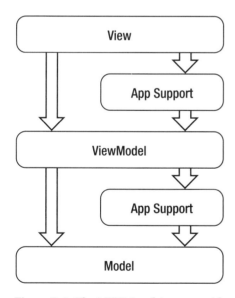

Figure 9–1. The MVVM architecture with app support layers in place

It is more common for app support functionality to sit between the ViewMmodel and model than between the view and ViewModel! This is because there are more areas that require wrapping in view-model classes for consumption by the view, yet are not strictly part of the model itself.

Another pertinent point of notice is that each of these layers need not be implemented as single assemblies. On the contrary, it makes more organizational sense to split app support functionality into separate modules both to facilitate reuse and to maintain a strict focus on the single responsibility principle. Furthermore, if a plug-in architecture is implemented early, it can be leveraged to include functionality that would otherwise be built in to the core of the application. Of course, caution must be taken with a plug-in architecture as it is no trivial task. Its implementation must be fully planned, estimated, and—most importantly—*justified* with a business case.

Serialization

Serialization is the term applied to the process of storing the state of an object. Deserialization is the opposite: restoring an object's state from its stored format. Objects can be serialized into binary format, an XML format, or some tertiary, purpose-built format if required. This section deals primarily with binary serialization that can be used to save the object to persistent storage, such as a hard drive, to enable the object to be deserialized at a later date. Binary serialization is also used for transmitting objects over a process or network boundary so that the object's state can be faithfully recreated on the receiving end.

An object graph is a directed graph that may be cyclic. Here, the term *graph* is intended in its mathematical definition: *a set of vertices connected by edges*. It is not to be confused with the more common use of the word *graph* which is shorthand for *the graph of a function*. In an object graph, the vertices are instances of classes and the edges represent the relationships between the classes, typically an ownership reference.

Serialization operates on a top-level object and navigates each object, saving the state of value types such as string, int, or bool, and then proceeding down through the other contained objects where the process continues. This process continues until the entire graph has been saved. The result is a replica of the graph that can be used to recreate each object and their relationships at a later date.

In an MVVM application, the model will be serialized, most commonly to save its current state to disk to be loaded again later. This allows the user to stop what they are currently doing and return to the application whenever it is next convenient to them, yet have their current work available on demand.

Serializing POCOs

There are a number of options for serializing the model, and each has its respective strengths and weaknesses. All of these methods are part of the .NET Framework, which performs all of the heavy-lifting. Client applications need to provide some hints to the serialization classes so that they can properly create a replica of the object graph.

These hints come in three forms: implicit, explicit, and external. Implicit and explicit serialization both require alterations to be made directly on the model classes. They differ in how much control they afford the classes in describing themselves and their structure to the serialization framework. External serialization can be performed on any class, even those that are marked as sealed and have no avenues for extension or alteration. Although external serialization may require intimate knowledge of the internal implementation of a class, its benefits may outweigh this cost.

Invasive Serialization

There are two ways of enabling serialization on an object. Firstly, the SerializableAttribute can be applied to the class, as exemplified in Listing 9–1.

Listing 9–1. Marking a Class as Serializable

```
[Serializable]
public class Product
{
    public Product(string name, decimal price, int stockLevel)
    {
        Name = name;
        Price = price;
        StockLevel = stockLevel;
    }

    public string Name
    {
        get;
        private set;
    }

    public decimal Price
    {
        get;
        private set;
    }

    public int StockLevel
    {
        get;
        private set;
    }
}
```

This is extremely trivial and, although technically invasive, does not require a great deal of alteration to the class. As might be expected, this is a semantic addition to the class and does not really add any extra functionality; it just *allows* the class to be serialized by the framework. Omitting this attribute yields a SerializationException when an attempt is made to serialize the class, so it is akin to a serialization opt-in mechanism.

■ **Note** Be aware that the Serializable attribute is a requirement for *every* object in the graph that is to be serialized. If a single class is not marked as Serializable, the whole process will fail, throwing a SerializationException.

There is more work required to actually perform the serialization, as shown in Listing 9–2.

Listing 9–2. Serializing the Product Class

```
public void SerializeProduct()
{
    Product product = new Product("XBox 360", 100.00, 12);
```

187

```
    IFormatter formatter = new BinaryFormatter();
    Stream stream = new FileStream("Product.dat", FileMode.Create, FileAccess.Write, ↵
FileShare.None);
    formatter.Serialize(stream, product);
    stream.Close();
}
```

First of all, the product instance is created. An IFormatter implementation, here the BinaryFormatter, is also instantiated. The IFormatter knows how to take data from the objects and transform them into another format for transmission or storing. It also knows how to perform deserialization, ie: loading the objects back to their former state from the storage format. The BinaryFormatter is one implementation of this interface, outputting binary representations of the underlying data types.

■ **Tip** There is also the SoapFormatter implementation that serializes and deserializes to and from the SOAP format. The IFormatter can be implemented to provide a custom format if it is required, but it may help to subclass from the abstract Formatter class, which can ease the process of developing customer serialization formatters.

Formatters write the output data to streams, which allows the flexibility to serialize to files with the FileStream, in-process memory using the MemoryStream or across network boundaries via the NetworkStream. For this example, a FileStream is used to save the product data to the *Product.dat* file. The serialization magic happens in the Serialize method of the chosen IFormatter implementation, but don't forget to close all streams when the process is finished.

Deserialization is trivially analogous, as shown in Listing 9–3.

Listing 9–3. Deserializing the Product Class

```
public void DeserializeProduct()
{
    IFormatter formatter = new BinaryFormatter();
    Stream stream = new FileStream("Product.dat", FileMode.Open, FileAccess.Read, ↵
FileShare.Read);
    Product product = (Product) formatter.Deserialize(stream);
    stream.Close();
}
```

Note that the IFormatter.Deserialize method returns a vanilla System.Object that must be cast to the correct type.

Hold on, though. The Product class definition indicated that the three properties had private setters, so how can the deserialization process inject the correct values into the Product? Note also that there is no default constructor because it was overridden to provide initial values for the immutable properties. The serialization mechanism circumvents these problems using reflection, so this example will work as-is without any further scaffolding. Similarly, private fields are serialized by default.

More control over the process of serializing or deserializing may be required, and this is provided for by the ISerializable interface. There is only one method that requires implementing, but a special constructor is also necessary to allow deserializing (see Listing 9–4). The fact that constructors cannot be contracted in interfaces is a shortcoming of the .NET Framework, so be aware of this pitfall.

Listing 9–4. Customizing the Serialization Process

```
[Serializable]
public class Product : ISerializable
{
    public Product(string name, decimal price, int stockLevel)
    {
        Name = name;
        Price = price;
        StockLevel = stockLevel;
    }

    protected Product(SerializationInfo info, StreamingContext context)
    {
        Name = info.GetString("Name");
        Price = info.GetDecimal("Price");
        StockLevel = info.GetInt32("StockLevel");
    }

    [SecurityPermissionAttribute(SecurityAction.Demand, SerializationFormatter = true)]
    public void GetObjectData(SerializationInfo info, StreamingContext context)
    {
        info.AddValue("Name", Name);
        info.AddValue("Price", Price);
        info.AddValue("StockLevel", StockLevel);
    }

    public string Name
    {
        get;
        private set;
    }

    public decimal Price
    {
        get;
        private set;
    }

    public int StockLevel
    {
        get;
        private set;
    }
}
```

The class describes its structure to the SerializationInfo class in the GetObjectData method and is then serialized. The labels that were used to name each datum are then used in the custom constructor to retrieve the relevant value during deserialization. The deserialization constructor is marked as protected because the framework finds it via reflection yet it is otherwise hidden from consumers of the class. The GetObjectData method is marked with the SecurityPermission attribute because serialization is a trusted operation that could be open to abuse.

The problem with this custom serialization is that the class is no longer a POCO: it is a class that is clearly intended to be serialized and has that requirement built-in. Happily, there's a way to implement serialization with being so invasive.

External Serialization

The benefits and drawbacks of invasive serialization versus external serialization are a choice between which is most important to enforce: encapsulation or single responsibility. Invasive serialization sacrifices the focus of the class in favor of maintaining encapsulation; external serialization allows a second class to know about the internal structure of the model class in order to let the model perform its duties undistracted.

Externalizing serialization is achieved by implementing the ISerializationSurrogate interface on a class dedicated to serializing and deserializing another (see Listing 9–5). For each model class that requires external serialization, there will exist a corresponding serialization surrogate class.

***Listing 9–5.** Implementing External Serialization for the Product Class*

```
public class ProductSurrogate : ISerializationSurrogate
{
    [SecurityPermission(SecurityAction.Demand, SerializationFormatter = true)]
    public void GetObjectData(object obj, SerializationInfo info, StreamingContext context)
    {
        Product product = obj as Product;
        if (product != null)
        {
            info.AddValue("Name", product.Name);
            info.AddValue("Price", product.Price);
            info.AddValue("StockLevel", product.StockLevel);
        }
    }

    [SecurityPermission(SecurityAction.Demand, SerializationFormatter = true)]
    public object SetObjectData(object obj, SerializationInfo info, StreamingContext↵
context, ISurrogateSelector selector)
    {
        Type productType = typeof(Product);
        ConstructorInfo productConstructor = productType.GetConstructor(new Type[] {↵
typeof(string), typeof(decimal), typeof(int) });
        if (productConstructor != null)
        {
            productConstructor.Invoke(obj, new object[] { info.GetString("Name"),↵
info.GetDecimal("Price"), info.GetInt32("StockLevel") });
        }

        return null;
    }
}
```

The interface requires two methods to be fulfilled: GetObjectData for serializing and SetObjectData for deserializing. Both must be granted security permissions in order to execute, just as with the ISerializable interface. The object parameter in both cases is the model object that is the target of this serialization surrogate. A SerializationInfo instance is also provided to describe the object's state and to retrieve it on deserialization. SetObjecData, in this example, uses reflection to discover the constructor of the Product class that accepts a string, decimal, and int as parameters. If found, this constructor is then invoked and passed the data retrieved by the serialization framework. Note that the return value for the SetObjectData method is null: the object should not be returned as it is altered through the constructor invocation.

The reflection framework allows the serialization code to deal with very defensive classes that, rightly, give away very little public data. As long as the fields are known by name and type, they can be retrieved, as shown in Listing 9–6.

Listing 9–6. Retrieving a Private Field Using Reflection

```
[SecurityPermission(SecurityAction.Demand, SerializationFormatter = true)]
public void GetObjectData(object obj, SerializationInfo info, StreamingContext context)
{
    Product product = obj as Product;
    if (product != null)
    {
        // ...
        // find the private float field '_shippingWeight'
        Type productType = typeof(Product);
        FieldInfo shippingWeightFieldInfo = productType.GetField("_shippingWeight",↵
BindingFlags.Instance | BindingFlags.GetField | BindingFlags.NonPublic);
        float shippingWeight = (float)shippingWeightFieldInfo.GetValue(product);
        info.AddValue("ShippingWeight", shippingWeight);
    }
}
```

The BindingFlags specify what sort of data the reflection framework is looking for, which in this case is a private instance field.

In order to serialize the product with this external serializer, the formatter that is used must be furnished with the surrogate, as shown in Listing 9–7.

Listing 9–7. Serializing Using a SurrogateSelector

```
public void SerializeProduct()
{
    Product product = new Product("XBox 360", 100.00M, 12);
    IFormatter formatter = new BinaryFormatter();
    SurrogateSelector surrogateSelector = new SurrogateSelector();
        surrogateSelector.AddSurrogate(typeof(Product), new↵
StreamingContext(StreamingContextStates.All), new ProductSurrogate());
        formatter.SurrogateSelector = surrogateSelector;
        Stream stream = new FileStream("Product.dat", FileMode.Open, FileAccess.Read,↵
FileShare.None);
        Product product = (Product)formatter.Deserialize(stream);
}
```

The addition is linking the Product type with the ISerializationSurrogate implementation that will be used to serialize and deserialize each instance that occurs in the object graph. The StreamingContext class is used throughout the serialization framework to describe the source or destination of the deserialization or serialization process, respectively. It is used here to allow linking multiple surrogates that target different sources or destinations, so the Product could, in theory, be serialized by two different surrogates, one for remoting the object and one for saving the object to a file. The StreamingContext.Context property can also be set in the serialization code and read from within the GetObjectData or SetObjectData methods of the ISerializationSurrogate implementation to inject a dependency or to provide extra settings, for example.

Note that the serialization code has now been fully separated from the Product class. In fact, it need not even be marked with the Serializable attribute. This allows the serialization code to live in a separate assembly that depends up the Model assembly (or assemblies) and is, in turn, depended upon by the ViewModel assembly.

Extensibility

As discussed earlier in this book, application code is typically separated into assemblies that each deal with specific functionality that the application requires. It is possible to take this one step further: avoid linking the assemblies statically and, instead, have some of the assemblies loaded dynamically at run-time. The application is then split conceptually into a "host" and a number of "extensions." Each extension can provide additional functionality to the host and can be changed and redeployed independently of the host.

■ **Note** As of version 4, Silverlight now has access to the Managed Extensibility Framework that is covered in this section. Silverlight applications can now benefit from extensibility just as much as their WPF brethren.

Why Extend?

There are many compelling reasons to allow your application to be extended, and a few of these will be covered here. First, though, a short warning: enabling the ability to extend an application should not be taken lightly. Although the framework covered in this section that allows extensions to be loaded is very simple, thought must still be given to where extensions can occur in the application, and this diverts resources from adding direct value to the product. Unless there is a strong case for supporting extensibility, it is more than likely that it should not be undertaken.

Natural Team Boundaries

Software development teams are increasingly spread across geographically disparate locations. It is not uncommon to have teams in Europe, Asia, and North America all working on different parts of the same application. One way to separate the responsibilities of each team is to allocate one team to be the host developers and split the rest of the application's functionality into extensions that teams can work on almost in isolation.

Good communication lines and a high level of visibility are required to ensure that such intercontinental development succeeds. If the host application developers can expose the right extension points for other teams, then they can diligently work on their section of the application without constantly seeking approval or answers from a central authority. Each team becomes accountable for their extension and claims ownership of it, taking praise and criticism for its good and bad parts, respectively.

Community

Modern applications do not always perform the exact functions that users require, but instead fulfill a default requirement that make them useful. To avoid the gaps that are being filled by your competitors, you could try to cram every feature that everyone wants into the product. This would probably delay the project, if not paralyze it outright. Even if such a product was eventually released, it is likely that the features would be diluted in some way so that the deadlines could be hit.

An alternative would be to allow people to extend the application themselves, independent of the main development team. Communities can spring up around even the most unlikely application; these communities are often as passionate as you are about your product, because it solves their problems in some way. Community extensibility is the greatest form of consumer empowerment and you can benefit by embracing this. By providing end-users with an API and allowing them to extend your core product, functionality that was previously demoted in priority or scrapped altogether can be implemented by third-parties with little development cost to your business. Your customers will benefit whether or not they participate in development, and your sales will be boosted by selling to a demographic that was otherwise not catered to.

Using Managed Extensibility Framework

Extensibility of an application can be facilitated in many ways. The simplest and quickest method currently available is by leveraging the Managed Extensibility Framework (MEF). Previously, MEF was a project on Microsoft's open source project community, CodePlex. However, it has now been integrated into the .NET Framework and resides in the `System.ComponentModel.Composition` namespace. MEF allows the developer to specify import and export points within the code through the use of attributes.

Import

The `ImportAttribute` can be applied to properties, fields and even constructor parameters to signify a dependency that will be fulfilled by a corresponding MEF Export. Listing 9–8 shows an example of all three places that the `ImportAttribute` can be used.

Listing 9–8. Using the ImportAttribute on a Class

```
using System.ComponentModel.Composition
…
public class DependentClass
{
    [ImportingConstructor]
    public DependentClass(IDependency constructorDependency)
    {
    }

    [Import]
    public string StringProperty
    {
        get;
        set;
    }

    [Import]
    private int _privateIntField;
}
```

This shows how easy it is to indicate extension points in a class: simply add the Import attribute and the dependency will be injected at runtime. How this works is covered a little later. Note that the constructor has the ImportingConstructor attribute applied. At runtime, MEF will implicitly indicate that all of the parameters must be imported. This is very useful outside of extensibility scenarios and indicates that MEF would be a good fit for a simple dependency injection framework. If only a subset of the constructor's parameters should be imported, the applicable arguments can be individually marked with the Import attribute.

All types can be imported and exported using MEF, including built-in CLR types and complex user-defined classes. In the example, the string property is marked for importing and will have its value set by an exported string. It is not just public members that can be imported; private constructors, properties, and fields can also be imported. This allows dependencies to be placed directly into the object without having to compromise encapsulation.

■ **Note** Importing a private member requires FullTrust to be specified on the caller due to the use of reflection to discover and set the value. It will fail if the correct permissions are not set.

Importing single values is certainly useful, but it is also possible to import collections, as shown in Listing 9–9.

Listing 9–9. Importing a Collection

```
[ImportMany]
public IEnumerable<string> Messages
{
    get;
    private set;
}
```

The collection is a merely a generic IEnumerable typed to hold strings with the ImportMany attribute added to indicate that more than one value should be imported into this property.

Before moving on to exporting values, there are a few parameters that can be set on these attributes which are worth examining.

AllowDefault

If set to true, this parameter allows the imported member to be set to default(T) if there is no matching export in the container where T is the type of the member. So, reference types will default to null and numeric value types will default to 0.

AllowRecomposition

If true, AllowRecomposition will set the imported value every time the matching exports change. This is especially useful for importing collections whose values may be exported in more than one location.

ContractName

When exporting and importing values, it is very possible that you will wish to export and import the same type in multiple places. To avoid confusing which import corresponds to which export, the ContractName string can be set so that each contract is uniquely identifiable. Without this, only the ContractType is matched between Export and Import attributes.

ContractType

Although the type is inferred by default, you may wish to import or export a specific type. For example, it is common to import an interface while exporting concrete implementations of that interface. In order to export the correct type, the ContractType value can be overridden.

IPartImportsSatisfiedNotification Interface

This interface can be implemented by any class that specifies at least one Import attribute. It contains only one method which is parameterless and void, as shown in Listing 9–10.

Listing 9–10. *The IPartImportsSatisfiedNotification*

```
public interface IPartImportsSatisfiedNotification
{
    void OnImportsSatisfied();
}
```

Due to the fact that importing is intrinsically linked with a class' construction, this method acts as notification that the class is now ready to use. Any extra initialization code should be performed here because you cannot guarantee that all of the import contracts have been fulfilled while inside the constructor.

Export

Exporting values is even more trivial than importing, as Listing 9–11 shows.

Listing 9–11. *Exporting Members*

```
public class ExportingClass
{
    [Export]
    public string StringProperty
    {
        get;
        get;
    }

    [Export]
    private int _privateIntField;
}

[Export(ContractType = typeof(IDependency))]
public class ConcreteDependency : IDependency
{
}
```

All of the exports in this example correspond to the imports in Listing 10-8. Note, however, that there is no requirement that a private field import be fulfilled by a private field export.

Catalogs

The whole point of MEF is to allow the exported members to live in separate assemblies from the imported members. Somehow, the assemblies that they each reside in must be discovered. MEF uses the concept of catalogs to achieve this. There are a number of different catalog types that each search for extensions in slightly different ways. At base, each of the catalogs present the types that contain either import or export attributes to a container that will organize the next step of the process.

TypeCatalog

The TypeCatalog accepts a collection of Type instances which are examined for attributed parts that are either marked for export or import (see Listing 9–12).

Listing 9–12. Composing Parts by Type

```
Type[] types = {typeof(ComposableClassA), typeof(ClassB), typeof(ImportingClass),
  typeof(ExportingClass)};
TypeCatalog typeCatalog = new TypeCatalog(types);
```

AssemblyCatalog

The AssemblyCatalog takes the TypeCatalog a step further by examining all of the types within an assembly. The catalog accepts either an instance of an Assembly or a string path to an assembly file.

DirectoryCatalog

The logical next step is for all of the assemblies contained within a directory to be examined. The DirectoryCatalog searches a specified directory for DLL files to explore. The DLL extension filter can also be changed if required.

AggregateCatalog

As you will see in the next section, the container that uses the catalogs to discover the importing and exporting types only accepts a single catalog instance, rather than a collection of them. Instead, the Composite Pattern [GoF] is used to allow a number of disparate ComposablePartCatalog subclasses to be used as a single instance. The AggregateCatalog accepts a number of ComposablePartCatalog objects as constructor parameters and presents the aggregated parts to the container. It is more than likely that one or more of the previous catalog types will be used and packaged together using the AggregateCatalog.

Container

The System.ComponentModel.Composition.Hosting namespace is home to the classes that collaborate to fulfill the imported members by looking for exported members. The CompositionContainer is responsible for orchestrating this process and at least one instance of this class will be required to fulfill all of the contracts.

The container must be furnished with a `ComposablePartCatalog` so that the `Export` and `Import` attributed classes can be discovered (see Listing 9–13). The container can then be asked to resolve all of the dependencies given the found inputs.

Listing 9–13. *Initializing the MEF Container*

```
DirectoryCatalog  directoryCatalog = new DirectoryCatalog
(Properties.Settings.Default.ExtensionsDirectory);

CompositionContainer container = new CompositionContainer(new AggregateCatalog(new
 AssemblyCatalog(Assembly.GetEntryAssembly()), directoryCatalog));

container.ComposeParts(this);
```

In Listing 10-13, a `DirectoryCatalog` is initialized to a directory set in the application's settings file. It is then added to an `AggregateCatalog` along with an `AssemblyCatalog` that will search the initiating executable file. From this, a `CompositionContainer` is created and the extension method `ComposeParts` is called, with the current class instance passed in to resolve its imports.

From here, the possibilities are limited primarily by imagination. MEF can be used as a dependency injection framework or to provide functionality to an application. However, specific to WPF and Silverlight, it is pertinent to show how visual components can be shared between a host and its extensions.

Extending A WPF Application

Extending any application requires prior knowledge of the parts that will allow extensions. At compile time, the developers must know about the interfaces that will be shared between the host and its extensions. There will be interfaces outlining contracts for the context that the host will make available to extensions as well as interfaces outlining the extra behavior or data the extensions may provide.

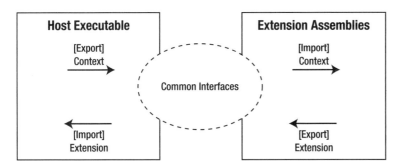

Figure 9–2. *The host process shares common interfaces with the extensions*

As Figure 9–2 shows, the host executable will export some data or behavior that the extensions will be able to import and act upon. In turn, the extensions will export data and behavior that the host will import. Tying this together will be a common library of interfaces that are used on the import side and implemented on the export side. These interfaces must be specific enough to be useful but generic enough that many possible extensions could be created from the same interface.

Defining An Extension Contract

The extension contract forms a separate assembly that is referenced by both the host project and each extension project. A trivial example of an extension contract would provide no contextual state information to the extension and merely allow the extension to be identified and executed, as if it were a stand-alone application (see Listing 9–14).

Listing 9–14. *Defining a Minimal Extension Contract*

```
public interface IExtension
{
    public string Name { get; }

    public void Execute();
}
```

In order to use this, the host application would have to import it into a class. Having a string name and an execute action fits with a typical user interface button. However, what if there are many IExtension implementations imported, not just one? Rather than try to dynamically create a new button for each extension, this sort of user interface has already been created in the form of menus. Listings 9–15 and 9–16 show importing the extensions into a ViewModel class and the XAML binding the WPF Menu control to show the IExtension.Name property as the Menu's Header value and the IExtension.Execute() method is wrapped in a RelayCommand so that it can be databound, too.

Listing 9–15. *The ExtensionViewModel that Wraps the IExtension for Databinding*

```
public class ExtensionViewModel
{
    public ExtensionViewModel(IExtension extension)
    {
        _extension = extension;
    }

    public string Name
    {
        get { return _extension.Name; }
    }

    private RelayCommand _executeCommand;
    public ICommand ExecuteCommand
    {
        if(_executeCommand != null)
        {
            _executeCommand = new RelayCommand(param => _extension.Execute(), param =>↵
_extension != null);
        }
        return _executeCommand;
    }

    private IExtension _extension;
}
```

This is a typical model-wrapping ViewModel class. It is a mediating adaptor that exposes model (IExtension instances, in this case) properties for data binding and creates commands that fire model methods.

Listing 9–16. The MainViewModel Imports IExtensions Privately and Exposes ExtensionViewModel Instances

```
public class MainViewModel : IPartImportsSatisfiedNotification
{
    public MainViewModel()
    {
        Extensions = new ObservableCollection<ExtensionViewModel>();
        _directoryCatalog = new DirectoryCatalog(@"C:\Extensions\");
        _container = new CompositionContainer(new AggregateCatalog(new↵
AssemblyCatalog(Assembly.GetEntryAssembly()), _directoryCatalog));
        _container.ComposeParts(this);
    }

    public ObservableCollection<ExtensionViewModel> Extensions
    {
        get;
        private set;
    }

    void IPartImportsSatisfiedNotification.OnImportsSatisfied()
    {
        Extensions.Clear();
        foreach(IExtension extension in _extensions)
        {
            Extensions.Add(new ExtensionViewModel(extension));
        }
    }

    private CompositionContainer _container;
    private DirectoryCatalog _directoryCatalog;

    [ImportMany(typeof(IExtension), AllowRecomposition = true)]
    private IEnumerable<IExtension> _extensions;
}
```

This code combines loading the container, furnishing it with some catalogs to look for imports and exports, and detecting when the composition is complete so that the extensions can be wrapped in preparation for user interface consumption. Note that extension assemblies should be deployed to the C:\Extensions to be found by this example. There is a strong case for declaring that this code is doing too much, but it is only demo-ware intended to convey a point—certainly not production quality code.

Listing 9–17. The XAML Is Quite Trivial, Serving Only to Bind to the View-Model Classes

```
<MenuItem ItemsSource="{Binding Extensions}" Header="Extensions">
    <MenuItem.ItemContainerStyle>
        <Style TargetType="MenuItem">
            <Setter Property="Header" Value="{Binding Header}" />
            <Setter Property="Command" Value="{Binding ExtensionSelectedCommand}" />
        </Style>
    </MenuItem.ItemContainerStyle>
</MenuItem>
```

The XAML in Listing 9–17 can be added to a Menu control and will list the loaded extensions as individual MenuItem children. A task to practice your MVVM skills would be to add the feature where, if no extensions are available, the "Extensions" menu option should disappear altogether (otherwise, it would be empty and this provides for a poor user experience).

The utility of this extension is, admittedly, quite limited, but it lays the necessary foundations on which more complex interactions can be built.

Sharing User Interface Components

In a MVVM scenario, extensions are likely to contain new model data and behavior. However, unless these new classes are new implementations of existing interfaces that the host knows how to present in the user interface, it will be necessary to expose custom views that the host can import. As reiterated throughout this book, when a view needs to present model data and execute behavior upon a model, a ViewMmodel intermediary is recommended so that the model and view are insulated from changes to one another.

Whereas the host may have its three MVVM layer implemented in three separated assemblies, the extension may host the entire MVVM vertical-slice in one assembly for simplicity. The developers are trusted not to circumvent the ViewMmodel layer merely because they can. Figure 9–3 shows the assemblies and dependencies involved when extending a user interface.

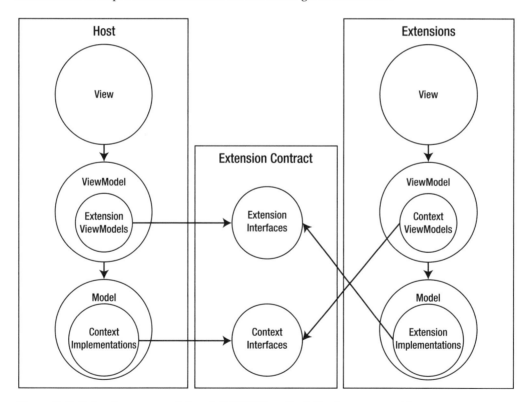

Figure 9–3. Extensions can contain a full MVVM vertical slice in one assembly.

Both the host and extension assembly contain a full MVVM implementation in this example. The intermediate extension contract assembly contains only interfaces that define the shared context and extensions.

To exemplify this in code, a meaningful scenario is required. Imagine a Customer Relationship Management (CRM) application whose host is little more than a database of customer data with the ability to add, edit, and delete customer records. One possible extension to this minimal contact management application could be the ability to track the customer's credit account. As the user cycles through the customer records, they would be able to select a custom function from a menu that would fire the account extension, passing in the current customer record as context. The extension would be a separate dialog window displaying the customer's past transactions with the business.

Listing 9–18. The AccountsExtension Implementation

```
public class AccountsExtension : ICRMExtension
{
    public void StartExtension(ICustomer customerContext)
    {
        AccountsView accountsView = new AccountsView();
        accountsView.DataContext = new AccountsViewModel(customerContext, new↩
 Accounts(customerContext));
    }
}
```

Listing 9–18 shows the implementation of a possible ICRMExtension interface. When the StartExtension method is called with an ICustomer passed in as context, the extension manually creates a view and sets its DataContext to the applicable ViewModel implementation, which accepts the ICustomer as a model to expose and extend.

In a real scenario, it is likely that a data access layer interface may be passed in so that the extension could also load and save data to persistent storage.

Attaching a DataTemplate

The previous example covered hosting a new dialog window inside a host application. However, this is a great user experience; it can be improved by integrating the extension's user interface into the host's user interface. One option for doing this is to maintain a list of tabs that each show a different facet of the customer's data. The default tab would show the customer's contact information while extensions could be added for sales, order tracking, technical support, etc. Each Tab control's content can be set to a ViewModel instance and automatically displayed by linking the ViewModel and its corresponding view with a DataTemplate.

Declaring a DataTemplate inside the extension's XAML will not work because the host application will not respect it unless it is part of the host's resources. To solve this problem, when each extension is loaded, a new DataTemplate association can be created programmatically in the host so that the link occurs automatically. Each subsequent request to display the extension's ViewMmodel will implicitly replace it with the specified view (see Listing 9–19).

Listing 9–19. Methods to Register and Unregister a New DataTemplate

```
private void RegisterDataTemplate(Type dataType, Type visualType)
{
    DataTemplate dataTemplate = new DataTemplate();
    dataTemplate.VisualTree = new FrameworkElementFactory(visualType);

    Resources.Add(new DataTemplateKey(dataType), dataTemplate);
```

```
}

private void UnregisterDataTemplate(Type dataType)
{
    Resources.Remove(new DataTemplateKey(dataType));
}
```

The two methods shown in Listing 9–19 should be part of the App.xaml.cs file in the view, or in some other way have access to the application's Resources property. RegisterDataTemplate requires two types as arguments, the first is the ViewModel type to which controls will be bound and the second is the view type that will be displayed. The view type must be wrapped in a FrameworkElementFactory that is subsequently set to the VisualTree property of a DataTemplate instance, while the ViewModel type is wrapped in a DataTemplateKey in order to add it to the application's Resources dictionary. Whenever an extension—or any other code, in fact—requires linking a data type to a visual type with a DataTemplate, RegisterDataTemplate should be called with the applicable types.

Limitations

While undeniably useful, MEF is far from a panacea. In fact, it has a number of caveats that could preclude it as a viable choice for an extensibility framework. A couple of these limitations are covered here, and a potential alternative to MEF is posited.

Decorating POCOs

Similar to the problem with invasive serialization, MEF requires that objects are decorated with attributes. Depending on how zealously you defend your domain model's purity, this adulteration may be a minor annoyance or a major roadblock. However, it need not be an insurmountable problem as wrappers could be fashioned to retain the agnosticism of the domain model while leveraging MEF for extensibility.

Single Process, Single AppDomain

MEF has complete control over how the extension points are discovered and integrated within your application. As a result, you must accept whatever MEF dictates and, sadly, this is sometimes not desirable. MEF loads all of the extension assemblies in the same process and AppDomain as the host.

Loading extensions into the same process implies that a crash in an extension will concomitantly crash the host process. If an exception goes uncaught in an extension module, it will leak into the host process and cause a crash there, which could pose a problem for your particular project needs.

By loading the extensions into the same AppDomain, the extensions cannot be given any settings which vary by AppDomain. This means, for example, that the extensions cannot be given a different security level setting; they all inherit the host's trust level.

The similarly acronymed Managed Add-in Framework (MAF) solves both of these problems and allows every different extension to be loaded into its own process, protecting the host process from crashes. However, there is a lot more integration required before the framework is usable. The trade-off between development speed and configurability is definitely worth considering when choosing which framework to integrate into your project.

Summary

In this chapter, you have covered a layer of architecture that often is assumed as trivial during planning and estimation. Application support can provide a number of different facilities that are no less necessary than the main features. In fact, these facilities often underpin the main features, so equal care and diligence should be shown in integrating such important foundations.

Serialization is typically associated with off-line storage and paired with WPF, in contrast to Silverlight's common reliance on an RDBMS for persistent storage. The ability to serialize a domain model is a very important part of an application's support structure. This chapter covered some of the options available to developers.

Many modern applications also allow third-parties to create extensions that can add features to the core functionality. In a similar vein, an application could be split into functional components, each of which is assigned to a different geographically distributed team. This would help alleviate many of the problems that are common to distributed development. Extensibility can be built into an application with relatively little integration work required thanks to the Managed Extensibility Framework, which has been integrated into the .NET Framework as of version 4.0. Even visual WPF and Silverlight controls can be shared between the extensions and the host with minimal effort.

CHAPTER 10

Sample Application

This chapter is the apex of this book: the sample application will aggregate all of the details covered in previous chapters. The application will be developed using an iterative approach, with the first three iterations covered.

Requirements

As with all agile projects, the requirements will not be set in stone at any point during the application's lifetime. There will be a limited amount of up-front design: enough to comfortably fill the first iteration, which should result in a working—albeit unsellable—product. That means, limited functionality but without crashing bugs or unhandled exceptions.

The Application

The application itself will be personal financial software intended to track a single user's physical accounts—checking accounts, current accounts, credit cards, loans, and so forth.

Figure 10–1 features just enough documentation to start implementing the application.

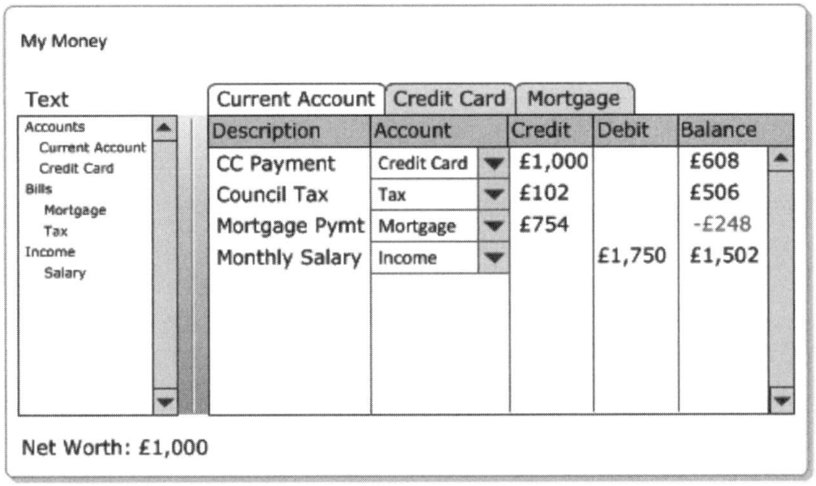

Figure 10–1. The main screen design of the My Money application

The expected behavior is that double-clicking an account from the list on the left should open the account in a new tab on the right. Each tab's content should be a DataGrid control listing the transactions that pertain to this account. Figure 10–2 is a diagram that illustrates the My Money class.

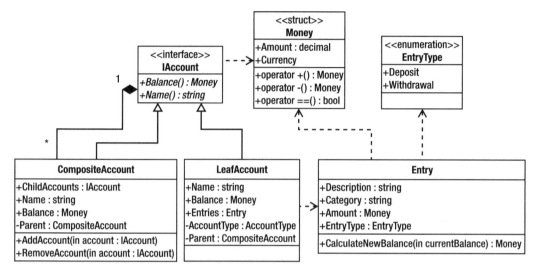

Figure 10–2. The initial My Money class diagram

Model and Tests

As far as is possible, it is recommended that the tests for any class are written first. Ideally, this code should not even compile in the first instance, as it will contain type names that have not yet been defined. This forces you to think in advance about the public interface expected of a type, which results in more useable and understandable classes. Similarly, do not be afraid to refactor aggressively. With unit tests in place, you can be assured that changes do not break previously working code.

■ **Tip** Although all of the tests written in this book are very simplistic and, consequently, somewhat repetitive, there is often a need to structure tests in a more logical and reusable fashion. The Assembly-Action-Assert paradigm is a very useful way of organizing unit tests and holds a number of benefits over the plain tests exemplified here.

Money

A good starting point for the tests is the Money value type, which neatly encapsulates the concept of a monetary value. The requirements indicate that multiple currencies will need to be supported in the future, and so it is best to deal with this now because it will save much more effort in the future. A monetary value consists of a decimal amount and a currency. In .NET, currency data is stored in the `System.Globalization.RegionInfo` class, so each `Money` instance will hold a reference to a `RegionInfo` class. Mathematical operations on the `Money` class will also require implementation, as there will be a lot of addition and subtraction of `Money` instances.

There are two types of arithmetic that will be implemented in the `Money` type: addition and subtraction of other `Money` instances and addition, subtraction, multiplication, and division of decimals. This is best exemplified using a unit test to reveal the interface that will be fulfilled (see Listing 10–1).

Listing 10–1. *Testing the Addition of Two Money Values*

```
[TestMethod]
public void TestMoneyAddition()
{
    Money value1 = new Money(10M);
    Money value2 = new Money(5M);
    Money result = value1 + value2;

    Assert.AreEqual(new Money(15M), result);
}
```

This test will not only fail at this point, it will not compile at all. There is no `Money` type, no constructor accepting a decimal, and no binary `operator+` defined. Let's go ahead and implement the minimum that is required to have this test compile (see Listing 10–2).

Listing 10–2. *The Minimum Money Implementation to Compile the First Test*

```
public struct Money
{
    #region Constructors

    public Money(decimal amount)
        : this()
    {
        Amount = amount
    }

    #endregion

    #region Properties

    public decimal Amount
    {
        get;
        private set;
    }

    #endregion

    #region Methods

    public static Money operator +(Money lhs, Money rhs)
    {
        return new Money(decimal.Zero);
    }

    #endregion
}
```

At this point, the test compiles, but it will not pass when run. This is because the expected result is a Money of value 15M and the minimal operator only returns a Money of value 0M. To make this test pass, the operator is filled in to add the two Amount properties of the Money parameters (see Listing 10–3).

Listing 10–3. Second Attempt to Fulfill the Operator + Interface

```
public static Money operator +(Money lhs, Money rhs)
{
    return new Money(lhs.Amount, rhs.Amount);
}
```

With this in place, the test unexpectedly still does not compile—what gives? The test runner error message provides a clue:

```
Assert.AreEqual failed. Expected:<MyMoney.Model.Money>. Actual:<MyMoney.Model.Money>.
```

So, it expected a Money instance and received a Money instance, but they did not match. This is because, by default, the object.Equals method tests for *referential* equality and not *value* equality. This is a value object, so we want to implement value equality so that the Amount determines whether two instances are the same (see Listing 10–4).

Listing 10–4. Overriding the Equals Method

```
public override bool Equals(object obj)
{
    if (obj == null || GetType() != obj.GetType())
    {
        return false;
    }
    Money other = (Money)obj;
    return Amount == other.Amount;
}
```

With this method in place, the test now passes as expected. Before moving on, however, there are a couple of things that need addressing. With the Equals method overridden, the GetHashCode method should also be overridden so that the Money type will play nicely in a hash table. The implementation merely delegates to the Amount's GetHashCode, but this is sufficient. Also, there is a slight issue with the interface as it stands: in the test's assertion, a new Money instance must be constructed at all times. It will be beneficial if a decimal can be used as a Money instance, implicitly (see Listing 10–5).

Listing 10–5. Implementing GetHashCode and Allowing Implicit Conversion from Decimal to Money

```
public override int GetHashCode()
{
    return Amount.GetHashCode();
}

public static implicit operator Money(decimal amount)
{
    return new Money(amount);
}
```

This type is fast becoming a value type in its own right. However, the next test will require a few more requirements to be implemented (see Listing 10–6).

Listing 10–6. Testing the Addition of Two Different Currencies

```
[TestMethod]
public void TestMoneyAddition_WithDifferentCurrencies()
{
    Money value1 = new Money(10M, new RegionInfo("en-US"));
    Money value2 = new Money(5M, new RegionInfo("en-GB"));
    Money result = value1 + value2;

    Assert.AreEqual(Money.Undefined, result);
}
```

As before, there are a couple of alterations that need to be made to the Money implementation before this code will compile. A second constructor needs to be added so that currencies can be associated with the value (see Listing 10–7). This test is comparing the addition of USD$10 and GBP£5. The problem is that, without external foreign exchange data, the result is undefined. This is a value type, and injecting an IForeignExchangeService would introduce a horrible dependency potentially requiring network access to a web service that would return time-delayed exchange rates.

This is when it makes sense to simply say no and reiterate that *you ain't gonna need it*. Is inter-currency monetary arithmetic *truly* required for this application? No, the business case would rule that the implementation costs—mainly time, which *is* money—are too high. Instead, simply rule inter-currency arithmetic *undefined* and allow only intra-currency arithmetic. If anyone tries to add Money.Undefined to any other value, the result will also be Money.Undefined.

An alternative could be to throw an exception—perhaps define a new CurrencyMismatchException—but the implementation of client code to this model would be unnecessarily burdened when a sensible default such as Money.Undefined exists. One area where an exception will be required is in comparison operators. Comparing two Money instances with a currency mismatch cannot yield a tertiary value to signal *undefined*: Boolean values are solely true or false. In these cases, a CurrencyMismatchException will be thrown.

Listing 10–7. Adding Currency Support to the Money Type

```
public Money(decimal amount)
    : this(amount, RegionInfo.CurrentRegion)
{

}

public Money(decimal amount, RegionInfo regionInfo)
    : this()
{
    _regionInfo = regionInfo;
    Amount = amount;
}

public string CurrencyName
{
    get
    {
        return _regionInfo.CurrencyEnglishName;
    }
}

public string CurrencySymbol
```

```
{
    get
    {
        return _regionInfo.CurrencySymbol;
    }
}
```

```
public static readonly Money Undefined = new Money(-1, null);
```

```
private RegionInfo _regionInfo;
```

Now the test compiles, but the operator+ does not return Money.Undefined on a currency mismatch. Let's rectify that with the code in Listing 10–8.

Listing 10–8. *Adding Support for Multiple Currencies*

```
public static Money operator +(Money lhs, Money rhs)
{
    Money result = Money.Undefined;
    if (lhs._regionInfo == rhs._regionInfo)
    {
        result = new Money(lhs.Amount + rhs.Amount);
    }
    return result;
}
```

```
public override bool Equals(object obj)
{
    if (obj == null || GetType() != obj.GetType())
    {
        return false;
    }
    Money other = (Money)obj;
    return _regionInfo == other._regionInfo && Amount == other.Amount;
}
```

```
public override int GetHashCode()
{
    return Amount.GetHashCode() ^ _regionInfo.GetHashCode();
}
```

The hashcode returned by each instance is now the result of the bitwise exclusive OR operation between the decimal Amount's hashcode and the RegionInfo's hashcode. The Equals method returns false if the currencies do not match, whereas the addition operator returns the special instance of Money.Undefined.

Now that this test passes, the rest of the Money type can be implemented, using the same test-implement-refactor cycle for each method required. One of the comparison method's tests and implementation are shown in Listing 10–9.

Listing 10–9. *Testing the Greater Than Comparison Operator with a Currency Mismatch*

```
[TestMethod]
[ExpectedException(typeof(CurrencyMismatchException))]
public void TestMoneyGreaterThan_WithDifferentCurrencies()
{
```

```
    Money value1 = new Money(10M, new RegionInfo("en-US"));
    Money value2 = new Money(5M, new RegionInfo("en-GB"));

    bool result = value1 > value2;
}
...
public static bool operator >(Money lhs, Money rhs)
{
    if(lhs._regionInfo != rhs._regionInfo)
        throw new CurrencyMismatchException();
    return lhs.Amount > rhs.Amount;
}
```

After the Money type is fully implemented, there are 18 passing tests available to verify the success of any further refactoring efforts and to alert developers if a breaking change is introduced.

Account

Accounts follow the Composite pattern [GoF], which allows a hierarchical structure to form where collections and leafs are represented by different types that are unified by a common interface. That interface, IAccount, is shown in Listing 10–10.

Listing 10–10. The IAccount Interface

```
public interface IAccount
{
    #region Properties

    string Name
    {
        get;
    }

    Money Balance
    {
        get;
    }

    #endregion
}
```

The CompositeAccount is the easier of the two implementations to tackle, starting with the AddAccount and RemoveAccount tests. The first AddAccount test will result in a minimal implementation of the CompositeAccount class in order to force a successful compilation and a failing test, shown in Listing 10–11.

Listing 10–11. The AddAccount and RemoveAccount Unit Tests

```
[TestMethod]
public void TestAddAccount()
{
    CompositeAccount ac1 = new CompositeAccount();
    CompositeAccount ac2 = new CompositeAccount();
```

```
        ac1.AddAccount(ac2);

        Assert.AreEqual(1, ac1.Children.Count);
        Assert.AreEqual(ac2, ac1.Children.FirstOrDefault());
    }
    ...
    public class CompositeAccount : IAccount
    {
        #region IAccount Implementation

        public string Name
        {
            get { throw new NotImplementedException(); }
        }

        public Money Balance
        {
            get { throw new NotImplementedException(); }
        }

        public IEnumerable<IAccount> ChildAccounts
        {
            get { return null; }
        }

        #endregion

        #region Methods

        public void AddAccount(IAccount account)
        {

        }

        #endregion
    }
```

The test fails because a NullReferenceException is thrown, and it is easy to see where. The
ChildAccounts property should return some sort of enumerable collection of IAccount instances, and the
AddAccount method should add the supplied IAccount instance to this collection. The RemoveAccount
tests and implement can then be trivially written. Listing 10–12 displays the code necessary to make the
AddAccount unit test pass.

Listing 10–12. Making the AddAccount Unit Test Pass

```
public CompositeAccount()
{
    _childAccounts = new List<IAccount>();
}
...
public IEnumerable<IAccount> ChildAccounts
{
    get { return _childAccounts; }
```

```
}
...
public void AddAccount(IAccount account)
{
    _childAccounts.Add(account);
}
...
private ICollection<IAccount> _childAccounts;
```

There are a couple of further preconditions that should be fulfilled at the same time:

- An account cannot be added to the hierarchy more than once.

- Accounts with the same name cannot share the same parent—to avoid confusion.

- The hierarchy cannot be cyclical: any account added cannot contain the new parent as a descendant.

To avoid confusion during development, these requirements will be handled one at a time and have their own tests in place to verify the code (see Listing 10–13).

Listing 10–13. *Tests to Ensure that Accounts Appear in the Hierarchy Only Once, and the Code to Make them Pass*

```
[TestMethod]
[ExpectedException(typeof(InvalidOperationException))]
public void TestAccountOnlyAppearsOnceInHierarchy()
{
    CompositeAccount ac1 = new CompositeAccount();
    CompositeAccount ac2 = new CompositeAccount();
    CompositeAccount ac3 = new CompositeAccount();

    ac1.AddAccount(ac3);
    ac2.AddAccount(ac3);
}
...
public IAccount Parent
{
    get;
    set;
}

public void AddAccount(IAccount account)
{
    if (account.Parent != null)
    {
        throw new InvalidOperationException("Cannot add an account that has a parent↵
 without removing it first");
    }
    _childAccounts.Add(account);
    account.Parent = this;
}
```

Note that, after this change, the IAccount interface also contains the Parent property as part of the contract that must be fulfilled (see Listing 10–14).

Listing 10–14. Tests to Ensure that Accounts Cannot Contain Two Children with the Same Name, and the Code to Make them Pass

```
[TestMethod]
[ExpectedException(typeof(InvalidOperationException))]
public void TestAccountsWithSameNameCannotShareParent()
{
    CompositeAccount ac1 = new CompositeAccount("AC1");
    CompositeAccount ac2 = new CompositeAccount("ABC");
    CompositeAccount ac3 = new CompositeAccount("ABC");

    ac1.AddAccount(ac2);
    ac1.AddAccount(ac3);
}

[TestMethod]
public void TestAccountsWithSameNameCanExistInHierarchy()
{
    CompositeAccount ac1 = new CompositeAccount("AC1");
    CompositeAccount ac2 = new CompositeAccount("ABC");
    CompositeAccount ac3 = new CompositeAccount("AC3");
    CompositeAccount ac4 = new CompositeAccount("ABC");

    ac1.AddAccount(ac2);
    ac2.AddAccount(ac3);
    ac3.AddAccount(ac4);
}
...
public CompositeAccount(string name)
{
    Name = name;
    _childAccounts = new List<IAccount>();
}

public void AddAccount(IAccount account)
{
    if (account.Parent != null)
    {
        throw new InvalidOperationException("Cannot add an account that has a parent↵
without removing it first");
    }
    if (_childAccounts.Count(child => child.Name == account.Name) > 0)
    {
        throw new InvalidOperationException("Cannot add an account that has the same name↵
as an existing sibling");
    }
    _childAccounts.Add(account);
    account.Parent = this;
}
```

At this point, there is no default constructor for a CompositeAccount; they all must be given names (see Listing 10–15).

Listing 10–15. Tests to Ensure that a Hierarchy Cannot Be Cyclic, and the Code to Make them Pass

```
[TestMethod]
[ExpectedException(typeof(InvalidOperationException))]
public void TestAccountsCannotBeDirectlyCyclical()
{
    CompositeAccount ac1 = new CompositeAccount("AC1");
    CompositeAccount ac2 = new CompositeAccount("AC2");

    ac1.AddAccount(ac2);
    ac2.AddAccount(ac1);
}

[TestMethod]
[ExpectedException(typeof(InvalidOperationException))]
public void TestAccountsCannotBeIndirectlyCyclical()
{
    CompositeAccount ac1 = new CompositeAccount("AC1");
    CompositeAccount ac2 = new CompositeAccount("AC2");
    CompositeAccount ac3 = new CompositeAccount("AC3");

    ac1.AddAccount(ac2);
    ac2.AddAccount(ac3);
    ac3.AddAccount(ac1);
}
...
public void AddAccount(IAccount account)
{
    if (account.Parent != null)
    {
        throw new InvalidOperationException("Cannot add an account that has a parent⏎
 without removing it first");
    }
    if (_childAccounts.Count(child => child.Name == account.Name) > 0)
    {
        throw new InvalidOperationException("Cannot add an account that has the same name⏎
 as an existing sibling");
    }
    if (IsAncestor(account))
    {
        throw new InvalidOperationException("Cannot create a cyclical account hierarchy");
    }
    _childAccounts.Add(account);
    account.Parent = this;
}
...
protected virtual bool IsAncestor(IAccount possibleAncestor)
{
    bool isAncestor = false;
    IAccount ancestor = this;
    while (ancestor != null)
    {
        if (possibleAncestor == ancestor)
```

```
        {
            isAncestor = true;
            break;
        }
        ancestor = ancestor.Parent;
    }
    return isAncestor;
}
```

The `IsAncestor` method is declared as protected virtual so that any future `CompositeAccount` subclasses can use it or provide their own implementation. It traverses the `Account` hierarchy upward through all parents, ensuring that the `IAccount` instance that is being added to the collection is not an ancestor.

The final tests will be for the `Balance` property, which merely delegates through to the child accounts and provides a summation of all their respective `Balances`. Clearly, without a `LeafAccount` implementation, this will never yield any value other than zero, so a very quick implementation of the `LeafAccount.Balance` property is in order, as shown in Listing 10–16.

Listing 10–16. Tests and Minimal Implementation for the LeafAccount.Balance Property

```
[TestMethod]
public void TestDefaulAccountBalanceIsZero()
{
    LeafAccount account = new LeafAccount();

    Assert.AreEqual(account.Balance, Money.Zero);
}
...
public class LeafAccount : IAccount
{
    #region IAccount Implementation

    public string Name
    {
        get { throw new NotImplementedException(); }
    }

    public Money Balance
    {
        get
        {
            return Money.Zero;
        }
    }

    public IAccount Parent
    {
        get
        {
            throw new NotImplementedException();
        }
        set
        {
            throw new NotImplementedException();
```

```
        }
    }

    #endregion
}
```

This is the minimum that is required in order to return to the CompositeAccount and implement its Balance property. The two properties can then be tested and implemented in parallel until both are complete. The LeafAccount introduces the final class that comprises the model: the Entry. The only part of the Entry worth unit testing manually is the CalculateNewBalance method (see Listing 10–17), whose behavior is dependent on the EntryType property.

Listing 10–17. *Testing the CalculateNewBalance Method*

```
[TestMethod]
public void TestCalculateNewBalanceWithDeposit()
{
    Entry entry = new Entry(EntryType.Deposit, 10M);

    Money oldBalance = 5M;
    Money newBalance = entry.CalculateNewBalance(oldBalance);

    Assert.IsTrue(newBalance > oldBalance);
    Assert.AreEqual(newBalance, new Money(15M));
}

[TestMethod]
public void TestCalculateNewBalanceWithWithdrawal()
{
    Entry entry = new Entry(EntryType.Withdrawal, 5M);

    Money oldBalance = 10M;
    Money newBalance = entry.CalculateNewBalance(oldBalance);

    Assert.IsTrue(newBalance < oldBalance);
    Assert.AreEqual(newBalance, new Money(5m));
}
...
public class Entry
{
    public Entry(EntryType entryType, Money amount)
    {
        EntryType = entryType;
        Amount = amount;
    }

    public EntryType EntryType
    {
        get;
        private set;
    }

    public Money Amount
    {
```

```
        get;
        private set;
    }

    public Money CalculateNewBalance(Money oldBalance)
    {
        Money newBalance = Money.Undefined;
        switch (EntryType)
        {
            case EntryType.Deposit:
                newBalance = oldBalance + Amount;
                break;
            case EntryType.Withdrawal:
                newBalance = oldBalance - Amount;
                break;
        }
        return newBalance;
    }
}
```

The code in Listing 10–18 allows for the completion of the LeafAcccount.Balance property and, subsequently, the completion of the CompositeAccount.Balance property.

Listing 10–18. Implementing the LeafAccount.Balance Property

```
[TestMethod]
public void TestAccountBalanceAllDeposits()
{
    LeafAccount account = new LeafAccount();

    account.AddEntry(new Entry(EntryType.Deposit, 15.05M));
    account.AddEntry(new Entry(EntryType.Deposit, 67.32M));
    account.AddEntry(new Entry(EntryType.Deposit, 11.10M));
    account.AddEntry(new Entry(EntryType.Deposit, 112.35M));

    Assert.AreEqual(account.Entries.Count(), 4);
    Assert.AreEqual(account.Balance, 205.82M);
}
...
public Money Balance
{
    get
    {
        Money balance = Money.Zero;
        foreach(Entry entry in Entries)
        {
            balance = entry.CalculateNewBalance(balance);
        }
    }
    return balance;
}
```

Before moving on to implementing to ViewModel, there may be a small refactor available here. The Entry's behavior in the CalculateNewBalance is dependent on the EntryType enumeration. There is a possibility that two different Entry subclasses could be implemented—DepositEntry and

`WithdrawalEntry`—that use polymorphism to encapsulate that variant behavior, as the illustration in Figure 10–3 shows.

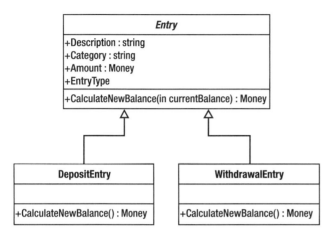

Figure 10–3. *The Possible Entry Refactor*

However, the current implementation works and the refactor would burden client code to instantiate the correct subclass depending on whether a deposit or withdrawal is being represented. If there was the possibility of further subclasses with more variations, this implementation would be far preferable to the current enumeration switch statement. That is because each additional subclass could be created independent of the `LeafAccount` code, which would remain entirely ignorant of the concrete type that it is delegating to. This would be an example of the Strategy pattern [GoF], but it is overkill for the situation at hand: there are only deposits and withdrawals in accounts, and this is unlikely to change anytime soon. It is important to know when to draw the line and give in to the temptation to over engineer a solution.

One refactoring that *is* worth doing is to unify all of the top-level accounts that the user might have so that they are easy to access and not floating about independently. There is an implicit `User` class that can be used to contain all of these accounts, and it might prove useful later on. In fact, just in case multiple `Users` are supported later in the lifecycle of the application, the class should probably be called `Person` instead, and that is what the diagram in Figure 10–4 is named.

Person
+Accounts : IAccount
+AddAccount(in account : IAccount) +RemoveAccount(in account : IAccount)

Figure 10–4. *The Person class diagram*

This will also provide a handy root object that will be referenced by the ViewModel and serialized in application support.

ViewModel and Tests

Having written a minimalistic model that fulfills some of the basic requirements that the application has set out, the next stage is to write the ViewModel that will expose model functionality in the view.

MainWindowViewModel

The main window wireframe shown in Figure 10–1 will be backed by the MainWindowViewModel class. This class will provide properties and commands that the view can bind to.

Testing Behavior

The first property to be implemented is the user's net worth, which is a very simple Money property. The value is merely delegated to the current Person instance that is using the software. The Person.NetWorth property has already been tested, and writing the same test again for the ViewModel code would be redundant and a waste of valuable time. Instead, the *behavior* of the ViewModel is tested, rather than the result.

Testing behavior is extremely useful in this sort of scenario where there is a need to ensure that the ViewModel is delegating to the model and not reimplementing the model code. This is achieved by using mock objects, as discussed in Chapter 7.

A mocking framework could be used, but, as this is a simple example, the mock will be implemented manually. In order to do this, the Person class needs to be changed so that the NetWorth property is declared virtual so that it implements an interface that requires the NetWorth property. The reason for this is because the mocking object will injected into the MainWindowViewModel as a dependency. In this case, the NetWorth property will be factored out into an IPerson interface and the MockPerson shown in Listing 10–19 will implement this.

Listing 10–19. The MockPerson Class

```
public class MockPerson : IPerson
{
    public MockPerson(IPerson realPerson)
    {
        _realPerson = realPerson;
    }

    public bool NetWorthWasRequested
    {
        get;
        private set;
    }

    public Money NetWorth
    {
        get
        {
            NetWorthWasRequested = true;
            return _realPerson.NetWorth;
        }
    }

    private IPerson _realPerson;
}
```

This mock is an example of the Decorator pattern [GoF], inasmuch as it *is* an IPerson and it also *has* an IPerson. It delegates the NetWorth property to the wrapped IPerson instance, but it also sets the NetWorthWasRequested flag to true to indicate that the value of this property has been requested. The unit test that will verify the behavior of the viewModel class is shown in Listing 10–20.

Listing 10–20. Testing the ViewModel Class's Behavior

```
[TestMethod]
public void ItShouldDelegateToThePersonForTheNetWorth()
{
    MockPerson person = new MockPerson(new Person());
    MainWindowViewModel viewModel = new MainWindowViewModel(person);

    Money netWorth = viewModel.NetWorth;

    Assert.IsTrue(person.NetWorthWasRequested);
}
```

The intent of this test is extremely simple, although it amalgamates a number of concepts. The MockPerson is injected into the MainWindowViewModel's constructor, and its NetWorth property is retrieved. The MockPerson implementation of the IPerson interface detects whether or not the viewModel class delegated correctly and did not try to implement the requisite functionality manually. The MainWindowViewModel class, shown in Listing 10–21, can now be implemented so that it fulfills this test.

Listing 10–21. The Initial MainWindowViewModel Implementation

```
public class MainWindowViewModel
{
    public MainWindowViewModel()
    {
        _person = new Person();
    }

    internal MainWindowViewModel(IPerson person)
    {
        _person = person;
    }

    public Money NetWorth
    {
        get
        {
            return _person.NetWorth;
        }
    }

    private IPerson _person;

}
```

This really is as simple as it gets, which is exactly the point of unit tests: write a failing test and implement the least amount of code to make the test pass, then rinse and repeat. The only point of note here is that there are two constructors. The public constructor automatically sets the _person field to a newly constructed Person object, and the internal constructor accepts the IPerson instance as a

parameter. The test assembly can then be allowed to see the internal constructor with the
InternalsVisibleTo attribute applied to the ViewModel assembly.

■ **Note** An inversion of control / dependency injection container would handle this for you, allowing the test
assembly to configure a MockPerson instance and a production client to configure a Person instance. For the
purpose of example, however, this would be overkill.

Hiding All Model Contents

The MainWindowViewModel class is not yet ready for consumption by the view because it exposes the Money
type, which is purely a model concept. The view needs only to display the Money type in the generally
recognized form that the Money's associated CultureInfo dictates. Thus, the Money should be wrapped in
a MoneyViewModel class that will be bound by Silverlight or WPF Label controls. Wherever the ViewModel
needs to expose a Money object it will instead wrap the value in a ViewModel before allowing the view to
see it.

Listing 10–22 shows the unit tests for the DisplayAmount property. There are four tests corresponding
to the combination of GB and US cultures with positive and negative amounts.

Listing 10–22. The MoneyViewModel Unit Tests

```
[TestClass]
public class MoneyViewModelTest
{
    [TestMethod]
    public void TestSimpleGBPAmount()
    {
        Money money = new Money(123.45M, new RegionInfo("en-GB"));
        MoneyViewModel moneyViewModel = new MoneyViewModel(money);

        Assert.AreEqual("£123.45", moneyViewModel.DisplayValue);
    }

    [TestMethod]
    public void TestSimpleUSDAmount()
    {
        Money money = new Money(123.45M, new RegionInfo("en-US"));
        MoneyViewModel moneyViewModel = new MoneyViewModel(money);

        Assert.AreEqual("$123.45", moneyViewModel.DisplayValue);
    }

    [TestMethod]
    public void TestNegativeGBPAmount()
    {
        Money money = new Money(-123.45M, new RegionInfo("en-GB"));
        MoneyViewModel moneyViewModel = new MoneyViewModel(money);

        Assert.AreEqual("-£123.45", moneyViewModel.DisplayValue);
```

```
    }

    [TestMethod]
    public void TestNegativeUSDAmount()
    {
        Money money = new Money(-123.45M, new RegionInfo("en-US"));
        MoneyViewModel moneyViewModel = new MoneyViewModel(money);

        Assert.AreEqual("($123.45)", moneyViewModel.DisplayValue);
    }
}
```

Note that the culture does not only change the currency symbol, but it also dictates how negative monetary values are displayed; in Great Britain, we prefer to place a negative symbol before the currency symbol, whereas our stateside brethren opt to wrap the entire value in brackets. The code that will fulfill these tests—see Listing 10–23—is simple enough, with the Money's RegionInfo being used to construct a matching CultureInfo value that will format the value for us automatically.

Listing 10–23. The MoneyViewModel Implementation

```
public class MoneyViewModel
{
    internal MoneyViewModel(Money money)
    {
        _money = money;
    }

    public string DisplayValue
    {
        get { return _money.Amount.ToString("C", new CultureInfo(_money.RegionInfo.Name)); }
    }

    private Money _money;
}
```

Now, the MainWindowViewModel.NetWorth property can be updated to return an instance of this class, as shown in Listing 10–24.

Listing 10–24. Updating the MainWindowViewModel

```
public MoneyViewModel NetWorth
{
    get
    }
        return new MoneyViewModel(_person.NetWorth);
    }
}
```

■ **Note** This level of model hiding might seem like overengineering for this example, but it highlights an important point—the aim of MVVM is to insulate the view from changes in the model. What if, for example, the model changed so that the Money type used a CultureInfo instance directly, rather than the RegionInfo? With full separation between view and model, the view would be untouched and the ViewModel would absorb the change. If the Money type was left exposed to the view, the XAML would have to be changed to accommodate the new implementation.

The next feature to be implemented, the tree of accounts, will also suffer from a similar problem. All that the view requires is the name of the account and a list of child accounts, if applicable, as shown in Listing 10–25.

Listing 10–25. The AccountViewModel

```
public class AccountViewModel
{
    internal AccountViewModel(IAccount account)
    {
        _account = account;
    }

    public string Name
    {
        get { return _account.Name; }
    }

    public bool HasChildren
    {
        get { return _account is CompositeAccount; }
    }

    public ObservableCollection<AccountViewModel> ChildAccounts
    {
        get
        {
            if (_childAccounts == null)
            {
                _childAccounts = new ObservableCollection<AccountViewModel>();
                if (HasChildren)
                {
                    foreach (IAccount account in (_account as CompositeAccount).↵
ChildAccounts)
                    {
                        _childAccounts.Add(new AccountViewModel(account));
                    }
                }
            }
            return _childAccounts;
```

```
        }
    }

    private ObservableCollection<AccountViewModel> _childAccounts;
    private IAccount _account;
}
```

The `AccountViewModel` wraps a single account, irrespective of whether it is a `LeafAccount` or `CompositeAccount`. The view will be able to use this to display the accounts hierarchy, but first the top level accounts must be exposed by the `MainWindowViewModel`, as shown by the code in Listing 10–26.

Listing 10–26. Adding a Top Level Accounts Property to the MainWindowViewModel

```
public ObservableCollection<AccountViewModel> Accounts
{
    get
    {
        if (_accounts == null)
        {
            _accounts = new ObservableCollection<AccountViewModel>();
            foreach (IAccount account in _person.Accounts)
            {
                _accounts.Add(new AccountViewModel(account));
            }
        }
        return _accounts;
    }
}
```

In both cases, the accounts are exposed to the view using the `ObservableCollection`, which will automatically signal the user interface to refresh if a new item is added to the collection, removed from the collection, or changed within the collection. Also, the properties use lazy initialization so that the `AccountViewModel` objects are only constructed as and when they are requested.

The final feature that will be implemented in the ViewModel before moving on to the view is the list of open accounts. This is represented as tabs in the view, but the ViewModel should stay completely ignorant of how the view represents its data, as far as is possible.

A second list of accounts will be maintained that represents the accounts that the user has opened for viewing (see Listing 10–27). Similarly, the currently viewed account (the selected tab in the view) will be maintained.

Listing 10–27. Changes to the MainWindowViewModel to Accommodate Viewing Accounts

```
public ObservableCollection<AccountViewModel> OpenAccounts
{
    get { return _openAccounts; }
}

public AccountViewModel SelectedAccount
{
    get
    {
        return _selectedAccount;
    }
    set
    {
```

```
            if (_selectedAccount != value)
            {
                _selectedAccount = value;
                OnPropertyChanged("SelectedAccount");
            }
        }
    }

    public ICommand OpenAccountCommand
    {
        get
        {
            if (_openAccountCommand == null)
            {
                _openAccountCommand = new RelayCommand(account => OpenAccount(account as⏎
    AccountViewModel));
            }
            return _openAccountCommand;
        }
    }

    public ICommand CloseAccountCommand
    {
        get
        {
            if (_closeAccountCommand == null)
            {
                _closeAccountCommand = new RelayCommand(account => CloseAccount(account⏎
    as AccountViewModel));
            }
            return _closeAccountCommand;
        }
    }

    private void OpenAccount(AccountViewModel account)
    {
        _openAccounts.Add(account);
        SelectedAccount = account;
    }

    private void CloseAccount(AccountViewModel account)
    {
        _openAccounts.Remove(account);
        if (SelectedAccount == account)
        {
            SelectedAccount = _openAccounts.FirstOrDefault();
        }
    }

    private void OnPropertyChanged(string property)
    {
        if (PropertyChanged != null)
        {
            PropertyChanged(this, new PropertyChangedEventArgs(property));
```

```
    }
}
```

The `AccountViewModel` is also changed to expose the list of entries so that they can be displayed in a data grid (see Listing 10–28). Note that there are two commands included here—one that will open an account for viewing and another that will close an already open account. Also, the `INotifyPropertyChanged` interface has been implemented so that programmatically setting the `SelectedAccount` property will be reflected as expected in the view. This is used specifically when a new account is opened; not only is it added to the list of open accounts, it is automatically selected as the currently viewed account. It is precisely this sort of behavior that would be implemented in the XAML's code behind, absent MVVM.

Listing 10–28. Adding an EntryViewModel and the AccountViewModel.Entries Property

```
public class EntryViewModel
{
    internal EntryViewModel(Entry entry, Money oldBalance)
    {
        _entry = entry;
        _oldBalance = oldBalance;
    }

    public MoneyViewModel Deposit
    {
        get
        {
            Money deposit = Money.Undefined;
            if (_entry.EntryType == EntryType.Deposit)
            {
                deposit = _entry.Amount;
            }
            return new MoneyViewModel(deposit);
        }
    }

    public MoneyViewModel Withdrawal
    {
        get
        {
            Money withdrawal = Money.Undefined;
            if (_entry.EntryType == EntryType.Withdrawal)
            {
                withdrawal = _entry.Amount;
            }
            return new MoneyViewModel(withdrawal);
        }
    }

    public MoneyViewModel CurrentBalance
    {
        get
        {
            Money currentBalance = _entry.CalculateNewBalance(_oldBalance);
            return new MoneyViewModel(currentBalance);
```

```
        }
    }

    private Entry _entry;
    private Money _oldBalance;
}
...
//AccountViewModel changes
public ObservableCollection<EntryViewModel> Entries
{
    get
    {
        if (_entries == null)
        {
            _entries = new ObservableCollection<EntryViewModel>();
            if (!HasChildren)
            {
                Money runningBalance = Money.Zero;
                foreach (Entry entry in (_account as LeafAccount).Entries)
                {
                    EntryViewModel newEntry = new EntryViewModel(entry, runningBalance);
                    _entries.Add(newEntry);
                    runningBalance = entry.CalculateNewBalance(runningBalance);
                }
            }
        }
        return _entries;
    }
}
```

At this point, the view can be built around what has been developed of the ViewModel thus far before moving on to other features such as loading and saving, creating accounts and entries, and so forth.

View

For this sample application, the view will be a WPF desktop user interface, although there will be many similarities shared with a Silverlight version. The view will use data binding as far as possible to interact with the ViewModel, although there are a couple of instances where this is not possible. The starting point of the application is the App.xaml file and its code-behind class. The App.xaml file declares the Application object that will be used throughout the user interface, and its StartupUri property dictates which XAML view to display upon application startup.

The additions that have been made from the default are shown in Listing 10–29—a reference to the ViewModel assembly and the declarative instantiation of the MainWindowViewModel as an application resource, making it available throughout the view using its provided key.

Listing 10–29. The App.xaml File

```
<Application x:Class="MyMoney.View.App"
            xmlns="http://schemas.microsoft.com/winfx/2006/xaml/presentation"
            xmlns:x="http://schemas.microsoft.com/winfx/2006/xaml"
            xmlns:viewModel="clr-namespace:MyMoney.ViewModel;assembly=MyMoney.ViewModel"
            StartupUri="MainWindow.xaml">
```

```
    <Application.Resources>
        <viewModel:MainWindowViewModel x:Key="mainWindowViewModel" />
    </Application.Resources>
</Application>
```

By declaring the ViewModel here, the MainWindow can declaratively reference it as its DataContext, setting up the data binding without having to resort to the code behind. Listing 10–30 shows the initial MainWindow, which is likely to change as features are added. The basis for the layout is a Grid control that contains a TreeView control for the accounts list (which forms a hierarchy, so a flat ListView would not suffice), as well as a TabControl to display the list of open accounts. Finally, the bottom of the window shows the net worth of the current user, as outlined by the wireframe design.

Listing 10–30. The Initial MainWindow.xaml File

```
<Window x:Class="MyMoney.View.MainWindow"
        xmlns="http://schemas.microsoft.com/winfx/2006/xaml/presentation"
        xmlns:x="http://schemas.microsoft.com/winfx/2006/xaml"
        DataContext="{StaticResource mainWindowViewModel}"
        Title="My Money" Height="350" Width="525">
    <Grid>
        <Grid.ColumnDefinitions>
            <ColumnDefinition Width="1*" />
            <ColumnDefinition Width="5" />
            <ColumnDefinition Width="3*" />
        </Grid.ColumnDefinitions>
        <Grid.RowDefinitions>
            <RowDefinition />
            <RowDefinition Height="30" />
        </Grid.RowDefinitions>
        <TreeView Grid.Column="0" Grid.Row="0" ItemsSource="{Binding Accounts}">
        </TreeView>
        <GridSplitter Grid.Row="0" Grid.Column="1" Height="Auto" Width="Auto"↩
HorizontalAlignment="Stretch" VerticalAlignment="Stretch" />
        <TabControl Grid.Column="2" Grid.Row="0" ItemsSource="{Binding OpenAccounts}"↩
SelectedItem="{Binding SelectedAccount}">
        </TabControl>
        <ContentControl Grid.Column="0" Grid.Row="2" Grid.ColumnSpan="3" Content="{Binding↩
NetWorth}" ContentStringFormat="Net Worth: {0}" />
    </Grid>
</Window>
```

The application will run at this stage, although without any data it does not do anything interesting at all. Figure 10–5 shows the application in action and leads neatly on to the next required piece of functionality.

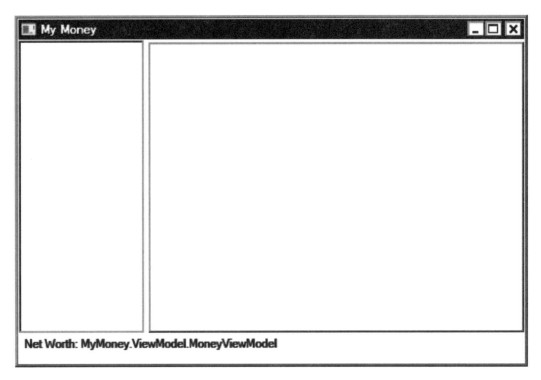

Figure 10–5. *The bare bones My Money application*

Other than the empty TreeView and TabControl, the net worth label is not displaying correctly. This is because the ContentPresenter control will use the ToString method of the class that is data bound, and, by default, the ToString method merely outputs the namespace qualified name of the class. This needs to be remedied so that, wherever a MoneyViewModel instance is encountered by the view, it outputs the correct value. For this, a DataTemplate must be added to the App.xaml so that it is globally available (see Listing 10–31).

Listing 10–31. *The DataTemplate for the MoneyViewModel*

```
<DataTemplate DataType="{x:Type viewModel:MoneyViewModel}">
    <Label Content="{Binding DisplayValue}" ContentStringFormat="{Binding↵
RelativeSource={RelativeSource TemplatedParent}, Path=ContentStringFormat}" />
</DataTemplate>
```

This DataTemplate is applied to *all* instances of MoneyViewModel that are displayed by the view. The content displayed will be a Label control that has its content set to the DisplayValue property of the MoneyViewModel. If the ContentPresenter has had a ContentStringFormat value set (such as the "Net Worth:" prefix on the main window), then this will be preserved and carried over to the generated Label control.

In order to develop the accounts list, a list of accounts is required. In order to add a new account, a dialog needs to be added that will take as input the name of the account and its opening balance, if applicable. This dialog will require a ViewModel class to bind to, shown in Listing 10–32.

Listing 10–32. The CreateAccountViewModel Code

```
public class CreateAccountViewModel
{
    internal CreateAccountViewModel(MainWindowViewModel mainWindowViewModel)
    {
        _mainWindowViewModel = mainWindowViewModel;
    }

    public string Name
    {
        get;
        set;
    }

    public string OpeningBalance
    {
        get;
        set;
    }

    public ICommand CreateAccountCommand
    {
        get
        {
            if (_createAccountCommand == null)
            {
                _createAccountCommand = new RelayCommand(param => CreateAccount(),←
 param => CanCreateAccount());
            }
            return _createAccountCommand;
        }
    }

    public void CreateAccount()
    {
        IAccount account = null;
        if(string.IsNullOrWhiteSpace(OpeningBalance))
        {
            account = new LeafAccount(Name);
        }
        else
        {
            decimal openingBalance= decimal.Parse(OpeningBalance);
            account = new LeafAccount(Name, new Money(openingBalance));
        }
        _mainWindowViewModel.AddAccount(account);
    }

    public bool CanCreateAccount()
    {
        bool hasValidName = !string.IsNullOrWhiteSpace(Name);
        decimal openingBalance;
```

```
        bool hasValidOpeningBalance = string.IsNullOrWhiteSpace(OpeningBalance) ||↵
   decimal.TryParse(OpeningBalance, out openingBalance);

        return hasValidName && hasValidOpeningBalance;
    }

    private MainWindowViewModel _mainWindowViewModel;
    private RelayCommand _createAccountCommand;
}
```

CanCreateAccount is the predicate passed to the CreateAccountCommand, which determines whether or not the account can be created. In the view, the button for creating the account will be enabled or disabled depending on whether this method returns true or false, respectively. The conditions that dictate whether or not the dialog is in a valid state to be created are:

1. the name is not null or solely consists of whitespace

2. the opening balance is blank or, if not blank, a valid decimal value

Creating the account occurs only when the user clicks the dialog's OK button, and the new account is created as a LeafAccount instance before being added to the MainWindowViewModel, which takes care of adding the account to both the current IPerson as well as wrapping it in an AccountViewModel and adding it to the list of viewable accounts.

The CreateAccountViewModel constructor requires the MainWindowViewModel to be passed in as a parameter and also declared as internal, hiding it from the view (see Listing 10–33). The MainWindowViewModel will be tasked with creating this class, passing itself in as the required parameter. WPF can then utilize the ObjectDataProvider to wrap the method that generates the necessary ViewModel class (see Listing 10–34).

Listing 10–33. The CreateAccountViewModel Method

```
public CreateAccountViewModel CreateAccountViewModel()
{
    return new CreateAccountViewModel(this);
}
```

Listing 10–34. Adding an ObjectDataProvider Declaration to the App.xaml

```
<ObjectDataProvider x:Key="createAccountViewModel" ObjectInstance="{StaticResource↵
 mainWindowViewModel}" MethodName="CreateAccountViewModel" />
```

This will allow CreateAccountDialog view, shown in Listing 10–35, to bind directly to the createAccountViewModel, generating a new ViewModel instance each time the dialog is shown.

Listing 10–35. The XAML Markup for the CreateAccountDialog

```
<Window x:Class="MyMoney.View.CreateAccountDialog"
        xmlns="http://schemas.microsoft.com/winfx/2006/xaml/presentation"
        xmlns:x="http://schemas.microsoft.com/winfx/2006/xaml"
        Title="Create Account" Height="125" Width="300"
        DataContext="{DynamicResource createAccountViewModel}">
    <DockPanel>
        <StackPanel DockPanel.Dock="Bottom" Orientation="Horizontal"↵
HorizontalAlignment="Right">
            <Button Content="OK" Width="75" Command="{Binding CreateAccountCommand}"↵
Click="CloseDialog" />
```

```
                <Button Content="Cancel" Width="75" Click="CloseDialog" />
        </StackPanel>
        <StackPanel Orientation="Vertical">
            <StackPanel Orientation="Horizontal">
                <Label Content="Account Name:" />
                <TextBox Text="{Binding Name}" Width="150" />
            </StackPanel>
            <StackPanel Orientation="Horizontal">
                <Label Content="Opening Balance:" />
                <TextBox Text="{Binding OpeningBalance}" Width="150" />
            </StackPanel>
        </StackPanel>
    </DockPanel>
</Window>
```

Before running the application, an input mechanism must be added that will show the CreateAccountDialog. A context menu added to the accounts TreeView control will suffice (see Listing 10–36), but it will need to make use of the code behind because, as mentioned in previous chapters, the display of dialogs is not something that can be easily bound. Besides, the code is so trivial that it does not matter too much.

Listing 10–36. The Add Account Menu and Code Behind

```
<TreeView Grid.Column="0" Grid.Row="0" ItemsSource="{Binding Accounts}">
            <TreeView.ContextMenu>
                <ContextMenu>
                    <MenuItem Header="Add Account..." Click="ShowAddAccountDialog" />
                </ContextMenu>
            </TreeView.ContextMenu>
        </TreeView>
...
private void ShowAddAccountDialog(object sender, RoutedEventArgs e)
{
    CreateAccountDialog createAccountDialog = new CreateAccountDialog();
    createAccountDialog.ShowDialog();
}
```

Figure 10–6 shows the next problem that is faced once the user successfully adds a new account.

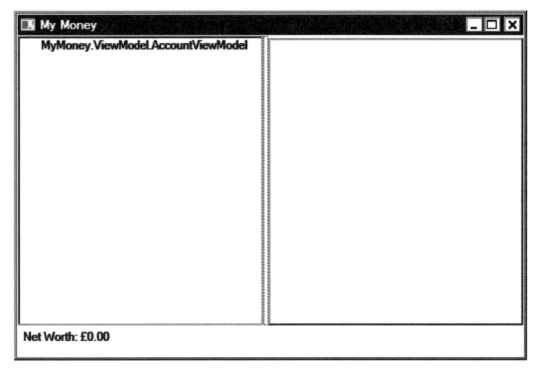

Figure 10–6. The accounts list does not correctly display the name of the account.

Just as before, with the Money value not being correctly displayed, a DataTemplate will solve this problem to show the name of the AccountViewModel wherever encountered (see Listing 10–37).

Listing 10–37. Adding a DataTemplate for AccountViewModel

```
<DataTemplate DataType="{x:Type viewModel:AccountViewModel}">
    <Label Content="{Binding Name}" />
</DataTemplate>
```

Whenever the AccountViewModel is displayed, WPF should use a Label with the Content set to the AccountViewModel's Name property, which, in turn, delegates to the wrapped model Account's Name property.

Next, whenever the user double-clicks on an account in the TreeView, it should be added to the list of open accounts and viewable in the TabControl. Sadly, TreeViewItem controls do not possess any Command properties, but, instead of delving into the code behind, the attached command behavior explained in Chapter 5 can be used.

Listing 10–38 encapsulates a number of important concepts that neatly demonstrate how powerful XAML declarations can be.

Listing 10–38. Hooking the Double-Click Event to the OpenAccountCommand

```
<TreeView. ItemContainerStyle >
    <Style
        <Setter Property="acb.AttachedCommand.Behaviors">
```

```
        <Setter.Value>
            <acb:BehaviorBinding Event="MouseDoubleClick" Command="{Binding↵
Source={StaticResource mainWindowViewModel}, Path=OpenAccountCommand}"↵
CommandParameter="{Binding}"
        </Setter.Value>
    </Style>
</TreeView. ItemContainerStyle>
```

The TreeView's ItemContainerStyle is being overridden with a new Style. The MouseDoubleClickCommand is bound to the MainWindowViewModel's OpenAccountCommand, which requires the AccountViewModel that is being shown to be sent as a parameter. This is accomplished by setting the CommandParameter property to the current DataContext; in this instance, the specific AccountViewModel as expected.

In brief, the existing display control is merely being enhanced with a double-click behavior, which just happens to be handled by a command. The result of double-clicking an account is shown in Figure 10–7, where two different accounts have been created.

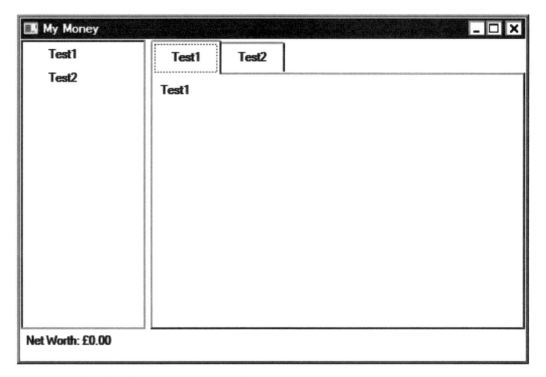

Figure 10–7. Double-clicking an account adds the account to the TabControl.

The TabControl's tabs correctly show the AccountViewModels using the DataTemplate. However, TabControls consist of two distinct parts, the tab header and the tab content. The content should be the list of entries, with the ability for the user to add new entries as required.

There are a few things that need to be considered before developing the entries view. Rather than include it directly in the MainWindowViewModel XAML, which would clutter the code, the control declaration will be factored out into its own UserControl. Also, the entries themselves will be editable, with the description, withdrawal amount, deposit amount, and date all available for the user to change. A DataGrid control will be used to display the entries, and it will be bound to the Account's Entries property, which allows new EntryViewModel instances to be added by the user. The DataGrid will handle this implicitly, but a few allowances need to be made to enforce the desired behavior. When the user creates a new entry, the data should be collated all at once and, when the user indicates he wants to save the row, a new Entry model object should be constructed and added to the Account's Entries collection so that the view and the model are constantly synchronized. Similarly, when an existing entry is edited, no changes should be reflected in the model until they are accepted by the user and, if the user cancels his changes, the Entry object should be untouched.

This implies that the process of adding and editing entries is transactional and that all changes are treated as one atomic action. Thankfully, the .NET Framework realizes this and provides the IEditableObject interface, which the DataGrid tests its items for, calling into the object at pertinent points in the process (see Listing 10–39).

Listing 10–39. The IEditableObject Interface

```
public interface IEditableObject
{
    void BeginEdit();
    void CancelEdit();
    void EndEdit();
}
```

The purpose of each method is fairly self-explanatory, but note that they provide no extra context to the implementing class. The EntryViewModel will implement this interface and, when BeginEdit is called, will make its own copies of the values that the wrapped model Entry object contains (see Listing 10–40). If CancelEdit is called, the copies are discarded and the old values reinstated, and if EndEdit is called, the copied values will supersede the original values because the user has accepted the changes that have been made.

Listing 10–40. The EntryViewModel Class

```
public class EntryViewModel : INotifyPropertyChanged, IEditableObject
{
    #region Constructors

    internal EntryViewModel(IAccount account, Entry entry)
    {
        _account = account;
        _entry = entry;
    }

    #endregion

    #region Properties

    public string Description
    {
        get
        {
            return _entry.Description;
        }
        set
        {
```

```
            if (_entry.Description != value)
            {
                _entry.Description = value;
                OnPropertyChanged("Description");
            }
        }
    }

    public MoneyViewModel Deposit
    {
        get
        {
            Money deposit = Money.Undefined;
            if (_entry.EntryType == EntryType.Deposit)
            {
                deposit = _entry.Amount;
            }
            return new MoneyViewModel(deposit);
        }
        set
        {
            if (_entry.EntryType == EntryType.Deposit)
            {
                if (_entry.Amount != value.Money)
                {
                    _entry.Amount = value.Money;
                }
            }
            else
            {
                _entry = new Entry(EntryType.Deposit, value.Money);
                OnPropertyChanged("Withdrawal");
            }
            OnPropertyChanged("Deposit");
            OnPropertyChanged("CurrentBalance");
        }
    }

    public MoneyViewModel Withdrawal
    {
        get
        {
            Money withdrawal = Money.Undefined;
            if (_entry.EntryType == EntryType.Withdrawal)
            {
                withdrawal = _entry.Amount;
            }
            return new MoneyViewModel(withdrawal);
        }
        set
        {
            if (_entry.EntryType == EntryType.Withdrawal)
            {
                if (_entry.Amount != value.Money)
```

```csharp
                {
                    _entry.Amount = value.Money;
                }
            }
            else
            {
                _entry = new Entry(EntryType.Withdrawal, value.Money);
                OnPropertyChanged("Deposit");
            }
            OnPropertyChanged("Withdrawal");
            OnPropertyChanged("CurrentBalance");
        }
    }

    public MoneyViewModel CurrentBalance
    {
        get
        {
            return new MoneyViewModel((_account as LeafAccount).BalanceAt(_entry));
        }
    }

    internal Entry Entry
    {
        get { return _entry; }
    }

    #endregion

    #region Methods

    private void Save()
    {
        (_account as LeafAccount).AddEntry(_entry);
    }

    private void OnPropertyChanged(string property)
    {
        if (PropertyChanged != null)
        {
            PropertyChanged(this, new PropertyChangedEventArgs(property));
        }
    }

    void IEditableObject.BeginEdit()
    {
        if (!_isInTransaction)
        {
            _backupEntry = _entry;
            _isInTransaction = true;
        }
    }

    void IEditableObject.CancelEdit()
```

```
{
    if (_isInTransaction)
    {
        _entry = _backupEntry;
        _isInTransaction = false;
    }
}

void IEditableObject.EndEdit()
{
    if (_isInTransaction)
    {
        _backupEntry = null;
        Save();
        _isInTransaction = false;
    }
}

#endregion

#region Fields

public event PropertyChangedEventHandler PropertyChanged;

private IAccount _account;
private Entry _entry;
private Entry _backupEntry;
private bool _isInTransaction;

#endregion
}
```

■ **Note** The `EntryViewModel` implements the `IEditableObject` explicitly. That means that the `BeginEdit`, `CancelEdit`, and `EndEdit` methods will not be available to client code *unless* they cast the `EntryViewModel` directly to the `IEditableObject` type. When implementing framework-specific interfaces such as this, explicit implementation adds extra protection to your code, disbarring clients from erroneously calling its methods.

The `EntryViewModel` will show a different value depending on whether the model `Entry` is a withdrawal or deposit. An entry can only be one type at a time so changing the withdrawal value of a deposit entry implicitly converts the entry to a withdrawal and vice versa. More intelligent changes could be handled here, such as detecting a withdrawal if a negative deposit is entered or disallowing certain entries through validation. However, these features are out of the scope of this example and are left as an exercise for the reader.

The view that uses this ViewModel is shown in Listing 10–41.

Listing 10–41. The EntriesView Control

```
<UserControl x:Class="MyMoney.View.EntriesView"
             xmlns="http://schemas.microsoft.com/winfx/2006/xaml/presentation"
             xmlns:x="http://schemas.microsoft.com/winfx/2006/xaml"
             xmlns:mc="http://schemas.openxmlformats.org/markup-compatibility/2006"
             xmlns:d="http://schemas.microsoft.com/expression/blend/2008"
             xmlns:viewModel="clr-namespace:MyMoney.ViewModel;assembly=MyMoney.ViewModel"
             mc:Ignorable="d"
             d:DesignHeight="300" d:DesignWidth="300">
    <UserControl.Resources>
        <viewModel:MoneyViewModelConverter x:Key="moneyViewModelConverter" />
    </UserControl.Resources>
    <DataGrid ItemsSource="{Binding Entries}" AutoGenerateColumns="False">
        <DataGrid.Resources>
        </DataGrid.Resources>
        <DataGrid.Columns>
            <DataGridTextColumn Width="3*" Header="Description" Binding="{Binding↵
Description}" />
            <DataGridTextColumn Width="1*" Header="Deposit" Binding="{Binding Deposit,↵
Converter={StaticResource moneyViewModelConverter}}" />
            <DataGridTextColumn Width="1*" Header="Withdrawal" Binding=↵
"{Binding Withdrawal, Converter={StaticResource moneyViewModelConverter}}" />
            <DataGridTextColumn Width="1*" Header="Balance" Binding="{Binding↵
CurrentBalance}"  IsReadOnly="True" />
        </DataGrid.Columns>
    </DataGrid>
</UserControl>
```

The DataGrid constitutes the greatest part of the control, listing the account's entries in a grid. The individual properties of the EntryViewModel are subsequently bound to column values within the grid. However, this will still not work properly as yet. Despite no warnings being given, because the EntryViewModel class has no public default constructor, the DataGrid cannot automatically construct a valid instance for use as a new row, so adding new rows is disabled.

To remedy this, a public default constructor could be added, but this would omit a vital component of the class—the IAccount instance that forms the parent of the wrapped Entry. Without the IAccount, saving the row would have no effect on the model because the entry would not belong in any Entries collection.

A better solution would be to dive in to the code behind and add a very simple one-liner that sets the EntriesView's DataContext (which is the currently viewed AccountViewModel) to the newly created EntryViewModel's AccountViewModel property. The DataGrid allows the new row to be initialized with the InitializingNewItem event (see Listing 10–42).

Listing 10–42. Hooking in to the InitializingNewItem to Customize the New Row

```
private void DataGrid_InitializingNewItem(object sender, InitializingNewItemEventArgs e)
{
    (e.NewItem as EntryViewModel).AccountViewModel = DataContext as AccountViewModel;
}
```

The EntryViewModel must be amended to allow the AccountViewModel to be set, but it is safe to prevent the value from being read. The value provided is then used to find the underlying IAccount model interface, so that the EntryViewModel can then be used.

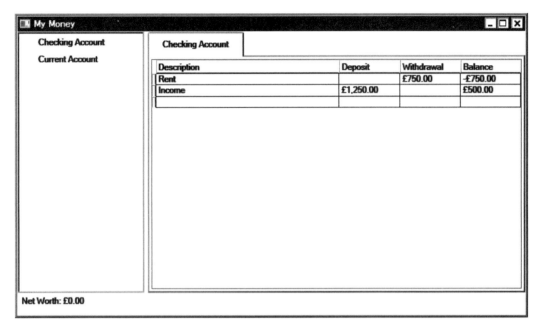

Figure 10–8. Adding entries to the account

This sample is almost finished by this point, with just a couple of small features left to be implemented. Although adding a new entry correctly calculates the current balance value, editing a previously existing entry will only calculate the balance of that specific row. The balance of any row is entirely dependent on the previous row's balance, so changing any row should concomitantly update the value of subsequent rows, as shown in Figure 10–8.

Summary

This chapter has amalgamated a lot of the concepts introduced throughout this book. The sample application is by no means a complete and sellable software product, but it hints toward the typical iterative development cycle most prevalent in today's agile environments.

You may wish to take the sample application code further and add extra features to it that have not been implemented. Such an endeavor can prove to be an invaluable learning experience. For example, this application would be unsellable without the addition of loading and saving code. This could be done using serialization to local disk storage, as described in Chapter 9, or to an online database using a data access layer, as explained in Chapter 8.

Throughout this book the emphasis has been on adding business value via software, and this underpins the use of any model/view separation framework. When WPF or Silverlight is the target user interface technology, the Model-View-ViewModel architecture is certainly worth investing in if the requirements are robust, well-organized, and unit tested code.

Index

■ ■ ■

You Need the Companion eBook

Your purchase of this book entitles you to buy the companion PDF-version eBook for only $10. Take the weightless companion with you anywhere.

We believe this Apress title will prove so indispensable that you'll want to carry it with you everywhere, which is why we are offering the companion eBook (in PDF format) for $10 to customers who purchase this book now. Convenient and fully searchable, the PDF version of any content-rich, page-heavy Apress book makes a valuable addition to your programming library. You can easily find and copy code—or perform examples by quickly toggling between instructions and the application. Even simultaneously tackling a donut, diet soda, and complex code becomes simplified with hands-free eBooks!

Once you purchase your book, getting the $10 companion eBook is simple:

❶ Visit **www.apress.com/promo/tendollars/**.

❷ Complete a basic registration form to receive a randomly generated question about this title.

❸ Answer the question correctly in 60 seconds, and you will receive a promotional code to redeem for the $10.00 eBook.

THE EXPERT'S VOICE™

233 Spring Street, New York, NY 10013

Offer valid through 6/11.